D1596756

General Ethics

General Ethics

AGNES HELLER

Basil Blackwell

Copyright © Agnes Heller, represented by EULAMA, Rome, 1988

First published 1988

Basil Blackwell Ltd
108 Cowley Road, Oxford, OX4 1JF, UK

Basil Blackwell Inc.
432 Park Avenue South, Suite 1503
New York, NY 10016, USA

British Library Cataloguing in Publication Data

Heller, Agnes
General ethics.
1. Ethics
I. Title
170   BJ1012

ISBN 0–631–15888–X

Library of Congress Cataloging in Publication Data

Heller, Agnes.
General ethics.
Bibliography: p.
Includes index.
1. Ethics. I. Title.
BJ1012.H45 1988   170   87–20880

ISBN 0–631–15888–X

Typeset in 10½ on 12pt Sabon
by Columns of Reading
Printed in Great Britain by
T.J. Press Ltd, Padstow, Cornwall

Contents

Introduction: the Three Aspects of a Theory of Morals

Moral philosophy has always involved three aspects.[1] The first can be termed *interpretative*, the second *normative*, and the third *educational/self-educational* or *therapeutic*. The interpretative aspect attempts to answer the question of what comprises morals, the normative aspect attempts to answer the question of what people should do, and the educational or therapeutic aspect attempts to answer, on the one hand, the question of how the innate propensities of people can be moulded to enable them to live up to moral expectations, and, on the other hand, the question of how a way of life conforming with the standards of goodness can be secured against the threat of misery and unhappiness. Traditional moral philosophies usually dealt with all three aspects together, or at least in *direct* conjunction with one another. Sometimes, as with Aristotle, all three were given equal attention, whereas in other cases one or another aspect was emphasized. With Stoicism, the third aspect was uppermost. With the sceptical moralists, the interpretative aspect of ethics was overemphasized, whilst the social game of moral hypocrisy was mockingly scourged.[2] In the seventeenth century, a deductivist–reductionist procedure gained momentum. What was conceived of as 'innate' in human nature was no longer treated in the form of *paideia* alone. Ever since moral principles lost their 'taken-for-granted' character (as a social a priori or as divine commandments) it has not sufficed simply to concentrate on the 'how' of their observance. The principles themselves had to be grounded. Human beings, with their supposedly 'natural' endowments, seemed to constitute appropriate foundations for such a grounding procedure. Thus moral principles, norms and virtues were deduced by the virtuosi of the process of deduction from certain constituents of so-called 'human nature'. This was the path to inferring *Ought* from *Is*, a procedure which may legitimately arouse suspicion. Indeed, it is difficult to see how moral values or norms can be deduced from the qualities of repulsion and attraction or from the statement that all human beings try to seek pleasure and avoid pain. For *what* repels us and *what* attracts us, *what* brings us pleasure and *what* causes us pain, are things at least co-determined by the *pre-existing* system of social norms and rules (including moral norms and rules).

Anthropological reductionism (the naturalistic fallacy) had already indicated that the ties between the three aspects of moral philosophy were eroding, and would eventually crumble. The naturalistic fallacy is not the cause, but the consequence, of the problematization of the *Is–Ought* relationship. The traditional method of deduction (in the manner of 'These are God's command-ments – you should act accordingly' or 'This is the supreme good, these are the supreme virtues, these you should foster and practise') became problematic, at least for the most insightful, up-to-date and far-sighted thinkers. It is in fact the first aspect of moral philosophy which is, in a manner of speaking, 'responsible' for this erosion. But, whatever the cause, we are still confronting, or rather are confronting now more than ever, the effects of this erosion. Kant, the path-breaking moral philosopher of our modern age, put all his cards on the second aspect, on that of *Ought*. He expelled both the first and the third aspects of moral philosophy by relegating them to the competence of political–legal philosophy and anthropology respectively. In so doing he provoked the scorn of Hegel, who made the last heroic effort to reconnect what had been torn asunder by construing an *Is* which, allegedly, negated and preserved ('sublated') both *Ought* and so-called 'human nature' (under the heading of needs). However, Hegel's solution did not harmonize with *Weltlauf* and could not escape the gnawing criticism of the rats of moral nihilism. Meta-ethics, this bastard offspring of a once thriving noble human endeavour, discarded moral philosophy altogether: not only was an answer to the question 'What should we do?' no longer provided, but the very question itself was outlawed.

To repeat, the component responsible for eroding the ties binding the three aspects together is the first, the *interpretative*. Our image of so-called 'human nature' has undergone drastic change. Theories of human nature are as numerous and as mutually irreconcilable as are theories of moral norms, moral autonomy, principles, rules and the like. Although 'intersubjective constitution' and several versions of it have already replaced the theories of initial Cartesianism, images of human nature, this time of a socio-historical nature, can still play the role of the grey eminence in arbitrating in matters of moral claims, in authenticating some – or none – of them. In addition, it makes an enormous difference, when (and if) it comes to the educational–therapeutic aspect of moral philosophy, whether we understand humans as language users, as digital computers making rational choices, or as struggling egos attempting to strike a balance between innate and unconscious drives and the task of coping with reality.

What are morals? Which norms are the valid ones, or, to reverse the question, which norms are valid? Which virtues are the main ones? These questions were duly answered in all traditional moral philosophies, yet, except for some breathtakingly modern efforts of Plato, they were answered only in summary fashion. The heart of moral philosophy concerned the application of norms and principles, and was preoccupied with practical judgement, with the respective motivation for good and evil, with feelings and emotions, with the moral character, and so on. In modernity, this emphasis shifted dramatically, with significant exceptions such as German Classicism. Questions such as 'Which norms are valid?' 'How, if at all, can the validity of norms be established?', 'On what grounds do we pass moral judgement?' are the focal points of inquiry. These and similar issues may become inflated to the point where all other concerns of moral philosophy, including the most difficult and puzzling ones, are relegated to the background, or even dismissed.

However, the path broken by German Classicism, and by Goethe in particular (albeit not without antecedents), did not remain barren either. In this tradition the idea of *paideia* became highly inflated. The centrepoint of attention was the development, or self-development, of all human endowments and abilities in concert, and the creation, or self-creation, of a harmonious human character. The underlying assumption was that endowments, upon developing in harmony, will become *virtuous* abilities, and the more so the more people support one another in freely chosen communities. This is not yet a theory of human deification, although the outspoken rejection of every kind of traditionalism without an accompanying attempt at substituting new norms for the old may point in this direction.

Whilst the roots of a definite differentiation between the interpretative, normative and educational–therapeutic aspects of moral philosophy should be sought in modern life rather than in any internal developmental logic of human thought, problematizing this differentiation itself is perfectly legitimate. MacIntyre's proposition that modern moral philosophers use moral terms completely out of context may be an extremist position, but it is not without foundation. The gist of the matter is that, if one aspect of moral philosophy becomes inflated whilst the other two are neglected or rejected altogether, and theories continue to claim to cover all the major problems of morals, then such theories raise a false claim. But can the interpretative, the normative and the educational–therapeutic aspects of moral philosophy be reunited? Is the social background of the present decomposition a *sufficient* cause of this decomposition? Will the attempt at reuniting all three aspects not perforce result in a form of self-delusion? These questions must be put emphatically, and they must be put now, for, MacIntyre's gloomy predictions notwithstanding, attempts at such a reunification are being made now. Kohlberg's name can be mentioned in this context because his theory has gained some prominence of late, mainly owing to Habermas's sympathetic reading of it. With Kohlberg, *Is* and *Ought* are united within a theory of moral evolution. By virtue of this simple device, the first and the second aspects of moral philosophy merge. Moreover, Kohlberg seemingly deduces philogenetic evolution from ontogenetic evolution on the basis of the observation of the moral development of children. Thus the third aspect is neatly fitted into the whole. However, Kohlberg's naturalistic solution clearly suffers from philosophical primitivism. This is why Fischkin proposed his *tertium datur* between Kohlberg's naturalism and ethical subjectivism. Yet in Fischkin's moral theory all three aspects, so comfortably unified by Kohlberg, are again, if in a relative way, torn apart.[3]

One could still go to Habermas to make a case for the attempt at reunifying the three aspects of moral philosophy. Since it is true that we raise the claim to rightness in every evaluative utterance, then the speech-act theory, and the theory of rational communication in general, succeed in bridging the gap between *Is* and *Ought* without committing a naturalist fallacy. However, the third aspect of moral philosophy is conspicuously absent from Habermas's theory. The theory of generalizable interests or generalizable needs is an extremely weak method of reintegrating actors into the moral universe. Habermas's deep suspicion of *poiesis* of all kinds, a category he relegates to the domain of 'instrumental' or 'functional' rationality, makes him fairly insensitive to the problems of moral *paideia* in general, and to the immense problem of the application of moral norms in particular. Habermas would be the last to deny that he belongs to that group of philosophers who have indeed inflated the issue of *establishing* norms as against the issue of their application to real life situations. Habermas's often-repeated statement that justice alone has remained the matter of moral philosophy, and his other statement that modern ethics must remain *reconstructive*, bear full witness to his awareness of the limitations of his own attempts, as well as to the fact that he does not even pretend to address all the relevant issues of moral philosophy in his theory.

Up to this point I have dealt with two tendencies of modern moral philosophies. The first tendency involves selecting one or another aspect of traditional moral philosophy, inflating it upon either the pretence of having raised all moral problems or by consciously refraining from raising and answering all of them, either with self-confidence or with resignation. The second involves the attempt at reuniting all three aspects in one coherent theory. Yet there is a third trend as well: reflecting on certain issues in their fixed and concrete situations without attempting to interrelate the results of such a detached reflection within the framework of a coherent and internally consistent moral theory. The first tendency or option can yield good philosophy, especially if it is free from self-deception. However, the inevitable limitation of this option lies in the fact that either answers to such questions as 'What should I do?' and 'How should I live?' cannot be provided at all, or, if they are provided, they invariably appear at such a level of formalism and abstraction as to be tantamount to preventing the average person from obtaining any relevant or meaningful understanding. The second option, as briefly demonstrated in relation to Kohlberg's case, is not philosophically viable. The third option proves philosophically fruitful for the elucidation of concretely situated moral choices as *problems*, raises the level of consciousness, supports the process of deliberation, and helps to develop moral sensitivity. All three aspects of moral philosophy are imbued with the spirit of reflective inquiry in this attempt, irrespective of whether it is the moral responsibility of parents, the ethical implications of artificial insemination, the arms race, AIDS, or the issues of human rights that is being discussed. Without trying to belittle the immense potential of this approach, it must be said that it falls short of being or becoming a moral philosophy proper. The fluctuation between everyday wisdom and philosophical inquiry, this very essence of the enterprise, cannot substitute for moral philosophy. Moreover, good and consistent moral philosophies can provide a solid background for this kind of elucidation and edification provided that, on their part, they take everyday moral wisdom seriously.

Is there a fourth possibility? Can we make a case for a modern moral philosophy that would encompass the interpretative, the normative and the educational–therapeutic aspects of traditional moral philosophies without inflating one aspect to the detriment of the others and without unifying all three aspects in a single theoretical proposal? In what follows, I endeavour to do precisely that.

I call this research programme as a whole *A Theory of Morals*. A theory of morals is a philosophical enterprise, but not fully so. The theory addresses the problem of morals *three times*, each time from the viewpoint of one of the three different aspects of moral philosophy. I term the first part (coinciding with the present volume) *General Ethics*, the second part *Moral Philosophy* and the third part *A Theory of Conduct*. The first part will be characterized by the *interpretative approach* (including genealogy or 'reconstruction'), the second by the *normative approach*, and the third by the *approach of paideia*. This division does not imply the exclusion of the problem of *Ought* and that of the *paideia* from the first part, the exclusion of the reconstructive approach and that of *paideia* from the second part, and the exclusion of the reconstructive, as well as the strictly normative, approach from the third part. It is, then, primarily the approach, rather than the subject matter, that is being divided. True enough, the approach determines the *emphasis*. In the first part the interpretative problems will be emphasized, in the second part the normative claims, in the third part issues of *paideia* and therapy. Also, the first part will be chiefly concerned with meta-ethical, sociological and historical problems, the second part will elaborate on historically situated transcendental existential moral philosophy, and the third part will concern problems of personality. The crucial part of the triad is *Moral Philosophy*, for it is with the voice of the particular moral philosophy elaborated there that all three stories are told. Yet it is *General Ethics* and *A Theory of Conduct* which will vouch for the veracity of *Moral Philosophy*. *General Ethics* organizes the experiences and ideas which have left their imprint on the memory of histories; it will narrate significant stories while relying on an intersubjective recollection of the past and the present. For its part, *A Theory of Conduct* will be anchored in the everyday experiences of contemporaneity.

To repeat, general ethics, moral philosophy and the theory of conduct are three aspects of the same project. A project can be referred to as *one and the same* if, and only if, *one and the same* decisive question is raised and answered throughout the entire inquiry. The three parts of the programme can be justified as three aspects of the whole if, and only if, this decisive question cannot be answered except by all three parts coming together and acting in conjunction. There is indeed *one* decisive question I raise and try to answer throughout the whole inquiry. A complete answer to this question can only be provided by the three parts together and in concert. The fundamental question addressed is this: *'Good persons exist – how are they possible?'*[4] This question will be answered in the first part from *the position of theoretical reason* (that of the participant observer), in the second part from the *position of practical reason* (that of the participant member of the contemporary world), and in the third part from the *position of the human person as a whole* (that of the individual who seeks the good life). This distinction sheds new light on what has already been emphasized concerning the primacy of moral philosophy as against general ethics on the one hand and a theory of conduct on the other. The reconstruction is performed and the narrative is told by and for the participant member of our modern contemporary world from the position of such a participant member, while the 'whole human person' addressed by the theory of conduct is simultaneously the participant member of the modern social condition. However, three distinct approaches require three distinct forms of discourse. In *General Ethics* the discourse is in the main *theoretical*, in moral philosophy it is *practical discourse proper*, and in the theory of conduct it can be called *elucidation* in the sense in which the term has been used by Castoriadis.

The question 'Good persons exist – how are they possible?' is, and has always been, the fundamental question of moral philosophy, whether or not the question itself was always spelt out. Without the presupposition that there are at least a few 'good persons', the venture of moral philosophy makes no sense whatsoever. Whether one believes that norms are sacred and authorized by divine legislation, or that they represent mere convenience or convention, norms and values cannot be considered *valid* unless there is someone to validate them, just as they cannot be considered *moral* unless they are observed by at least a few people who regard them as moral and *therefore* observe them. In short, there can be no moral philosophy without the (at least tacit) presupposition that the statement 'Good persons exist' is true. Even cynics presuppose this much. Cynics may contend that good people are weaklings or stupid or ignorant, or that they do not contribute to social progress, and so on, yet even they would not deny the truth of the assertion 'Good persons exist'. Of course, moral philosophers can, and indeed do, pass judgement on particular interpretations of goodness, on its *real*, *apparent* or *essentially* good character. But in order to construe a moral philosophy they must assume that in fact essentially good people do indeed exist, that there are such people, if only a few of them. Also, the variations in the interpretation of goodness are surprisingly limited. In societies which to some degree share this or that cultural inheritance, there exists a *basic stock* of virtues and action types by which 'good people' are easily identified. Even positivists, who are terribly annoyed by the fallacy of deducing 'Ought sentences' from 'Is sentences', grudgingly assent to the obvious, namely that so-called 'good sentences' can be true or false.

Philosophers who want to make a case *for* and not against morals, even if they make a case against a *particular* understanding of goodness, a particular morals, address the matter of 'how good persons are possible' with utter seriousness. There are various answers to this question. With some exaggeration one might even claim the existence of as many answers as there are moral philosophies. In my view, this very question must now be raised again, but this time *in two distinct forms*. I also believe that two separate though *not unconnected* answers to this question must be provided. The first question is the old and general one, which has always been the same: 'Good persons exist – how are they possible?' The second question is situational, and thus a particular modification of the general: 'Good persons exist *now* – how are they *now* possible?'

Had only the contents of moral norms, virtues and ideas undergone a substantial change in modernity, the duplication of this question would be neither relevant nor reasonable. Indeed, the contents of moral norms, virtues and ideas have always changed – they have always been variable in kind, and still are, in contemporary traditional and modern societies alike. On the other hand, it is not particularly difficult to pinpoint certain constants in the content of values, and even virtues, within one and the same cultural tradition, or even in all cultures known to us. And our society is no exception in this respect. Thus what justifies the duplication of the question (and the answer) is not the change in content but the *change in structure*. By and large, one can distinguish *two* basic structural changes in morals. The first occurred with the very differentiation between the regulation of shame and the regulation of conscience in human conduct within certain civilizations some three thousand years ago. The second came with the simultaneous universalization, pluralization and individualization of morals in the recent past of our present. The birth of moral philosophy (and of philosophy in general) was due to the first cultural change. The question 'Good persons exist – how are they possible?' could eventually be raised because of this structural change. Good persons exist *now* – this is proof enough of their *now* being possible. But *how* are they possible *now*? To my mind, the answer to this question not only diverges from any particular previous answer but even from all these answers combined. Precisely because the structure of morals has changed in modernity, and is still in the process of changing, the answer must be consciously located in the modern world where this structural transformation has taken place: it must be located in the very world where the structure of morals is increasingly crystallized around universalization, pluralization and individualization.

It sounds odd to refer to a moral structure as particular and situational which, besides pluralization and individualization, has been crystallized around *universalization*. And yet, whereas the very features of modern morals shared by all kinds of morals are, by definition, *empirically universal*, and the very features of modern morals common to all morals where the regulation of conscience and the regulation of shame had been differentiated are *empirically general*, the universality peculiar to the modern structure is *not* empirically universal, nor is it empirically general. Empirical universality and empirical generality are *claims* carried by modern *normative* universality. Obviously, normative universality cannot be empirically generalized or universalized retrospectively. But it *can* redeem this claim *prospectively*. It *can* but will not *perforce* redeem it. To construct or reconstruct a neat moral development which has, through some kind of internal logic, been propelled towards its present 'highest stage', alias universalistic moral sophistication, is a meta-narrative of a kind which veils rather than discloses the ambiguities of the new moral structure. The incipient ambiguity or 'dialectic' of this structure opened up two diametrically opposed possibilities for its eventual unfolding. We can say quite clearly that the new moral structure can be mastered such as to open up the path towards a more sublime and less repressive moral world, but it can also turn in the direction of a moral universe which dismantles the greatest moral achievement hitherto in human histories, the achievement associated with the first structural change in morals. We cannot ascertain whether the second structural change presently evolving will embody the 'highest' possible moral development or will prepare the way for unprecedented regression. This is one of the most compelling reasons why the matter of contemporary morals must be discussed in its situatedness. The question of how good persons *now* are possible cannot be answered in general terms: the question itself demands a situational answer. Such a self-restriction might sound unworthy of the enterprise called philosophy, which prides itself on speculating *sub specie aeternitatis*. But is there any eternity beyond the horizon of our historical consciousness? This is more than a poetic question and is one that must be squarely faced. My own answer is clear: within the framework of this research programme there is no eternity beyond this horizion; or, more precisely, I address this problem *as if* there were no 'eternity' beyond the horizon of our historical consciousness.

The first part of *A Theory of Morals*, *General Ethics*, addresses the fundamental question generally: 'Good persons exist, how are they possible at all?' The problem that will be examined is this: '*What kind* of *Is* generates *Ought*?', or, rather, 'What kind of *Is* is *Ought*?' As mentioned, practical reason, with all its implications, will be the subject matter of theoretical reasoning. One can never be a total outsider if moral issues or structures are being discussed, even when these are issues or structures of a bygone period. This stands to reason, for there are certain empirically universal moral propensities as well as moral contents and forms that we share with members of such pre-modern moral structures. Moreover, our modern moral universe is one particular structure among the three to be understood, interpreted and reconstructed by general ethics, if only from the viewpoint of its *generality* and not from that of its specific features and propensities. It should be noted that the questions of what we should do and how we should live will not be directly raised within the framework of this first part. That is why I term this venture 'general ethics'. General ethics is a kind of moral theory rather than moral philosophy proper, because it heavily relies on the body of knowledge provided by social sciences. Outstanding sociologists have contributed at least as much to the problem area of general ethics as have thinkers remaining within the boundaries of post-classical philosophy. Naturally, I have Durkheim and Weber in mind here, as well as the tradition they founded. The major differences between Durkheim and Weber in theory construction and theoretical outlook notwithstanding, both gave prominence to the interpretative and observational standpoint, and both were aware that such a position is *not* the attitude of moral philosophy and that it does not replace the latter. Weber and Durkheim raised two questions in one, namely (1) 'What are morals in general, and what do people do if, and when, they act morally in general?', and (2) 'What kind of historical changes occurred at particular historical junctures, and in regard to what propensities do certain moral worlds differ from others?' This contrast was brought into relief in their works either by theoretical juxtapositions or by narratives, and thanks to their efforts the practice of demonstrating this contrast gained prominence.

Whether or not it is thus *termed*, general ethics has opened up new areas of theoretical inquiry since Weber's and Durkheim's time. Subtle structural changes of which we were completely ignorant have been discovered, evidence of the moral attitudes of our ancestors has been uncovered, and surprising new light has been shed on our own present via the narratives about the genesis of that present. It will suffice merely to mention Elias, Foucault, Aries and Luhmann to indicate how much has happened in this field. However, within the project of a theory of morals the interpretative–observational aspect must be kept to the level of *generality*. General ethics is a philosophical language game which must combine meta-ethical, normative, reconstructive and genealogical discourses and combine them into one coherent approach.

General ethics must commence with the discussion of the *general 'human condition'*, of which morals is one of the most decisive aspects. Yet the problem of the 'human condition' will re-emerge in both moral philosophy and the theory of conduct. Since, as mentioned, I shall offer a *situational* answer to the question 'What should we do?', moral philosophy must reflect upon the *particular human condition we now share*. One cannot raise and answer the question 'What should we do?' or 'How should we act?' except as a participant member of a particular human condition we all share. Moreover, in order to raise and answer this crucial question we must determine what this particular human condition is all about. What 'now is' must thus be treated as the *condition*, the situation, but not as the sufficient condition, for determining the answer to the question 'What should we do?' Finally, the problem of the 'human condition' must be faced for the third time at the beginning of *A Theory of Conduct*. The human condition must be treated there as the dialectical unity of the general human condition and the particular human condition of the present age. The 'backing' of the first part is historical and sociological in nature, that of the third part psychological and aesthetic in nature. Yet, the *topic* of the first part is *not* history or sociology, nor is the *topic* of the third part psychology or aesthetics. The theory of conduct, having gained only relative independence in modernity, is an *aspect* of moral philosophy to the same extent as is general ethics. Yet, in contrast to general ethics, the theory of conduct must be addressed solely from the perspective of the participant member of the contemporary world, just like moral philosophy. But, whereas in moral philosophy we only presuppose, at least at the start, that both those being addressed and those doing the addressing share the same world, in a theory of conduct we already presuppose that, over and above the same shared world, these parties also share the commitment to Good. Thus the end result of moral philosophy is the starting point of a theory of conduct. How can individuals live up to the *Ought* they are committed to whilst deriving as much enjoyment from life as is humanly possible? – this is the particular question which can only be answered in educational/self-educational, therapeutic and self-therapeutic terms. It is my view that in this respect we can draw inspiration from the philosophical traditions of Stoicism and Epicureanism. Of course, neither Stoicism nor Epicureanism can provide the denizens of the modern world with a theory of interpretation of the modern world or with norms of good action. Yet they can provide us with guidelines for conducting a good life, perhaps even more than ever before. If the modern structure of morals could indeed be viewed in the light of a one-track progressive development which has achieved its inherent goal in precisely that modern structure, were we to believe that the promises of the simultaneous universalization, individuation and pluralization of morals have already been generally redeemed, *then* the Stoic and the Epicurean morals would indeed be fully outdated. Since, however, I do not share the simplistic optimism of moral evolutionism, even though I believe that moral progress is one distinct possibility incipient in the modern moral structure on which we should stake our chances, I attribute as much importance to the revitalization of the Stoic and Epicurean traditions as to all speculations, including my own, concerning the establishment of norms. Women and men, denizens of our world, living and fearing, desiring and suffering, we are the carriers and vessels of moral norms, moral discourse and moral obligations; we are, therefore, the protagonists of moral philosophy. Without our commitment, norms are mere shadows.

1

The Human Condition

All those who ponder moral problems are attempting to find out why certain people are vicious and wicked, whereas others are reasonably good, or even virtuous; and, further, why both the good and the wicked people are considerably outnumbered by those who are neither good nor wicked, but who sometimes do the proper thing and sometimes the improper thing. This simple and banal observation makes people wonder about 'human nature', the knowledge of which might provide an explanation. Meaningful world-views, always available, offer the basic conceptual clues of an understanding of this kind. For example, it suffices to know that 'men' are born with unruly passions, that they are conceived in sin, or that the instinct of self-preservation drives them to pursue their own interests above everything else. This and similar all-encompassing explanations make us understand that even people who know what is good fall short of practising it. Philosophies, as a rule, elevate the simplest everyday questions to a level of high sophistication. This has been happening in this context as well. Whether morals 'derive' from 'nature' or contradict it is a problem no moral philosophy can circumvent. If we probe behind the surface of the complicated methodological devices of modern philosophies, the same 'naïve' questions keep surfacing. And this stands to reason, for the question 'How are good persons possible?' cannot even be addressed, let alone answered, without having first developed a theory of 'human nature', whatever this compound termed 'human nature' means.

As far as the direct relationship between the so-called 'human nature' and ethics is concerned, all four *logical* possibilities have been exhausted several times, each time in a different orchestration. The first solution is that human nature is bad (evil) and *hinders* people in becoming good (virtuous): in other words, we are good *despite* our nature. The second solution holds that human nature is good and thus *furthers* people in becoming good and virtuous, so we are then good *in accordance* with our nature. Yet here something other than nature must be held responsible for all evils; 'society', 'civilization' and even norms (including moral norms) compete for the title of the malefactor. According to the third solution, human nature is *morally indifferent*, raw material able to become both good and evil. But here again something other than nature must be held responsible for a good outcome as well as an evil one. Laws, habits, knowledge and ignorance are the respective agents of the ambivalent product in this version. In the fourth solution there are good as well as evil propensities in human nature; some natural endowments *further* and others *hinder* our becoming good and virtuous. The catalogue of logical possibilities is indicative, despite its obvious emptiness: it indicates that the purely rationalistic *explanation* of morals is clearly outnumbered. Only the advocates of the Socratic tenet, in terms of which those who know the good will do the good (wickedness being ignorance), can be termed rationalist. Still, the rationalist *project* of the improvement of morals is not out-numbered: with the exception of the first solution, all at least allow for a rationalist interpretation of the project.

The problem of 'human nature' is primordially *ontological*: relating ethics to 'human nature' presupposes the *knowledge* of that nature. The naïve ontology of the everyday attitude has to be replaced in philosophies by reflectively construed ontology (meta-physics). In naïve everyday ontology the *referent* of the compound 'human nature' is as obvious as it needs to be for *everyday* explanatory purposes (for example, in employing the notion as an extenuating circumstance, as in 'He could not do any better', such is 'human nature'). In philosophy, though, the referent should be clarified, and usually is. Yet even a beginner in philosophy is aware that the *referent* of the compound category 'human nature' is *not the same* in different philosophical systems. The extension of the category varies because certain phenomena viewed as part of 'human nature' by some theories are excluded by others. But there is more to it than this. The diverging interpretation of certain constituents of 'human nature' is in itself tantamount to a shift in the referent, even if the extension of the category remains constant. If one mentions 'human nature' within the framework of Aristo-telian, Spinozian, Kantian, Hegelian or Marxian philosophy, one simply *does not mean* the same thing in each case. Does *reason* belong to 'nature' or not? Does 'nature' encompass every *innate* human propensity and nothing else, or only *some particular innate* propensities and nothing else, or *both certain innate and certain acquired* propensities? Do philosophers also have in mind organs such as the lungs when they describe human nature *qua* 'everything innate'? Or do they have in mind only those innate propensities which supposedly 'motivate' human beings? What kind of *acquired* propensities belong to 'human nature'? (Aristotle said, for example, that something common to *all* cities *is* human nature.) Is 'human nature' common to all people or are there different kinds of people 'by nature'? Is there a particular 'male nature' and a particular 'female nature'? Do slaves and free men share the same 'nature'? Do different races share the same 'nature', and do they share it completely or only partially? Is 'human nature' part of 'nature', or is it to be understood as a juxtaposition to 'nature'? Is 'human nature' a microcosm which mirrors the macrocosm of 'Nature'? Is 'human nature' something internal in contrast to 'external' Nature? Is culture equivalent to 'human nature', or is it 'the other', the opposite of 'human nature'? To make matters even more complicated in relation to this issue, the referent may shift, or alter in extension, within the same philosophy.

In each and every particular philosophy the shift in referent is intrinsically interwoven with the theoretical project as a whole. For example, how would one answer such questions as these: Is 'human nature' constant or is it open to change through time? *How and to what extent* is 'human nature' open to change? *What instances*, happenings and interventions can change 'human nature' – 'progressive development', 'invention', 'contract', 'culture', 'breeding', 'reason'? Can all of these change 'human nature'? Some of them? Or perhaps none at all? Are certain elements in 'human nature' static, whereas others are open to change, and so dynamic or variable? And is it the static or the variable elements that are more crucial from the viewpoint of moral philosophy?

Or this: Is 'man' by nature gregarious or 'individualist'; altruist or egoist; sympathetic or aggressive?

Or these: Is 'human nature' an *indivisible whole*? Does it *'consist' of two* parts, such as 'soul and body' or 'mind and body'? Or does it *'consist'* of *three* parts, such as 'mind–body–soul', 'cognition–emotion–volition', or 'Id, Ego, and Superego'? If 'man' 'consists' of two, or eventually three, parts, *which* part, if any, is responsible for evil and *which* part is more open to good? Is 'body' the source of evil in the world, or is it rather the inquisitiveness of mind? In a more picturesque formulation, do unconscious instincts drive us towards the forbidden, or is it the 'devil' who puts evil ideas into our heads?

Or these: Which is the crucial, the essential component of 'human nature' – sociability, cogito, work, language, communication? What is 'our' relation to 'our' nature – repression, self-development, selective control, acceptance, rejection, *laissez faire*? What *should* 'our' relation to 'our' nature be?

Or these: What is our relationship to the 'nature' of another person? Is communication and interaction with other humans communication between and/or an interaction of distinct 'human natures', or *am I* the *only* human person to whom I relate as to 'human nature', as to 'internal nature' in a manner of speaking, whereas others are part and parcel of an 'external nature'? How can I relate to others as to 'internal nature' if *their* internal world is external to me? How does my attitude toward external human nature differ from my attitude to my own 'internal nature'?

How does society fit into this picture? If one juxtaposes 'society' to 'nature', one should explain *how* we came to live in society rather than in the 'state of nature', and, simultaneously, one should *reintegrate* the 'natural part' of 'man' into Nature in general. But what kind of Nature are we dealing with here? With a Nature imbued with spirit, this object of sublime contemplation? With a Nature conceived of as a well-constructed machine? Or with a Nature society must control and conquer, a nature equipped with an inexhaustible arsenal of materials for the means of production, the passive target of instrumentalization? Alternatively, one could design a model, say a model comprising three circles. One circle, the middle one, represents society, whereas a circle on the right stands for 'internal nature' and a circle on the left for 'external nature'. The circle representing society cuts across the other two and makes it apparent that a part of both natures has been socialized, whereas the other parts have not been socialized, or not yet to the same degree. This is clearly a historicist model which is connected with the idea of 'progress': the larger the circle termed 'society', the further we have progressed. If, alternatively, one conceives of 'human nature' as social by definition, and human individuals as mere subunits of the system termed 'society', we are left with a two-circle model, one circle representing society, the other 'external nature'. A model such as this can be combined with the idea of progression, regression and eternal repetition alike, all circling around the notion of 'homoeostasis'.

At this point I shall stop this ironic examination of 'human nature'. It has become clear that the very notion 'human nature' is polymorphic, vague, and overloaded with secondary connotations. 'Human nature' is a metaphor which can stand in the main for *three* theoretical proposals, each different in kind. In terms of the first proposal, human nature is a subsystem of the system 'Nature'; in terms of the second, a subsystem of the system 'Society'; and, in terms of the third, a combination of these two major systems. Since I reject completely the first two suggestions and regard the third as being inextricably tied up with a one-sided evolutionist theory, I prefer to eliminate the notion of 'human nature' altogether and replace it with a concept I term the *human condition*. But my substitution of 'human condition' for 'human nature' does not result from the above-mentioned considerations alone. Although this term is not less metaphoric, it has its own traditions, of a different colour. No great sophistication is needed to discover that 'human condition' can be associated with the age-old notion of 'human destiny'. Whereas the notion of 'human nature' elicits images of mere passivity ('living according to nature') or, alternatively, images of warfare (conquest, bringing under control or, as Marx put it, 'pushing back nature's borderlines'), the concept of 'human destiny' elicits images of 'being destined to something' or, alternatively, 'living up to our destiny'.

I commenced this chapter with the observation that we usually start raising questions about 'human nature' when we intend to ascertain why certain people are vicious whilst others are reasonably good, and why both wicked and good people are considerably outnumbered by those who are neither good nor wicked but who sometimes act properly and sometimes improperly. I immediately added that philosophers reshaped the question using a great deal of sophistication. No aspects or components of 'human nature' were left unexplored by these philosophers, and 'human nature' became a subject of inquiry in its own right. In the process of searching for these constituents and attempting to establish their relevance, the original focus of the inquiry was more often than not obscured to such a degree that the *explicandum* ceased to be the moral behaviour of 'man'. Naturally, the notion 'human condition' is not immune from such a fate either. Marx's ontology of 'generic essence' or Heidegger's ontology of *Dasein* (both being interpretations of the 'human condition' and not of 'human nature') are cases in point. To make my position clear, I wish to interpret the notion 'human condition' such as to make it suitable for providing an ontological background for the raising and the answering of the question 'How are good persons possible?' Hannah Arendt has already made a strong case for such an interpretation. I am thoroughly indebted to her, even if I formulate the basic question differently and so expect that I shall produce different answers. I am convinced that, if we keep in mind the fundamental *explicandum* throughout our investigation, the category 'human condition' will prove to be a far better and more reliable metaphor than that of 'human nature'.

Human life on Earth is the outcome of self-domestication. Crossing the threshold dividing the 'human' from the 'animal' has, according to archaeologists, taken several million years. 'Several million years' is not *human time* because we cannot relate to such time: it can be measured, but not *imagined*. Human time is historical time. During this period of self-domestication, *social regulation* was substituted for *instinct regulation*. After this substitution ended, 'human condition' began, or, to put it another way, social regulation *is* human condition in its abstract indeterminacy because it defined both the potential of and the limits to 'human condition' – that is, the potential of and limits to *itself*. Since social regulation is self-created (humans are self-domesticated), all particular social regulations can be changed and replaced by others. Social regulations can undergo thorough structural transformations. Nevertheless, since 'human condition', in its abstract indeterminacy, is tantamount to social regulation, to shed all such regulation is to go beyond the limits of that condition.

We shall never come to know the social life of the prehistorical *homo sapiens*. Consequently, what follows is not based on any empirical evidence but is intended to be the *explication* of the definition of the 'human condition'.

Humans were never *beasts* or *savages* giving vent to their 'barbarian instincts'. They were humans precisely in the sense that their actions and interactions were no longer controlled by instincts.[1] History has nothing to do with the so-called process of 'humanization' of our 'nature'. We cannot be *more* humanized than by *being human*.[2] The assumption that the supposed 'borderlines of *internal* nature' have been gradually pushed back 'by civilization' is but an empty analogy shaped upon the process of 'pushing back the limits of *external* nature'. The idea underlying the analogy is that increased *control* of 'nature' is accompanied by an *increased* control over so-called 'human nature'. When people today discover that actions forbidden in our society are permitted in certain others, mainly in tribal groups, they attribute this phenomenon to a lack of social control and equate it with a low level of humanization. However, this sort of observation more often than not disregards the equally significant fact that certain actions permitted in our civilization are very much under control in one or another tribal society. Hence it is retrospective assessment, and not the observation of facts, which creates the semblance of a unilinear and progressive 'humanization'. By this I do not intend to deny that enormous human potentials were indeed developed in the course of the histories of various civilizations. I only reject the description of this development as 'pushing back the borders of internal *nature*' or as 'a socialization of human nature'.

The newborn infant is *not* a 'piece of nature'. The general genetic endowment of the infant is a product of self-domestication: we *are born* human infants because social regulation has already been substituted for instinct regulation. The human infant is *programmed* for a 'life-in-society'; she or he is endowed with the *readiness* to speak, to work, to act (and not only to behave), with the readiness to cope with social regulations. Not the brain alone, but the entire organism is so programmed. Nor is the newborn infant a 'piece of society'. It can develop into a complete human being *in* society but it does not produce or reproduce society *by the simple fact* of being born a human infant. The infant does not 'mature' into a social being unless it is brought up *in* and *by* society. Thus the newborn child is neither 'nature' nor 'society', but an independent system in its own right.

We are human because we are born with 'human programmes' and because we are brought up in and by, and in the company of and in interaction with, humans. We learn to be a member of a given society primarily by coming to know and practise the norms and rules of that society. Social regulations develop, as well as pattern, our thinking, action and behaviour. Of course, we not only learn *about* social regulations, but also learn *within the framework* and *under the guidance* of these regulations. 'Knowing *what*' and 'knowing *how*', as embedded in language, customs and artefacts, and as mediated by speech, action and interaction, provides the horizon of our personal experiences. Thus everything we can refer to as *a posteriori* (personal experience) is the result of 'dovetailing' of two *a prioris*: that of the *genetic a priori* and that of the *social a priori* (both are 'given' prior to experience). However, a complete unity of the two a prioris does not always occur. In terms of my hypothesis, the more complex the society the more such a complete unity will be the exception rather than the rule. The more the horizon of personal life experience broadens, the more potentials of the genetic a priori can surface, and the more multifarious the potentials become the less the *sum total* of these potentials fit completely into any strict and concrete regulation. It is precisely the problematization of this incomplete 'dovetailing' of the two a prioris that gives rise to speculation about 'human nature'.

Every human is an example of the *general* genetic a priori. But every human is also unique; every infant is born with an idiosyncratic, *individual*, genetic a priori; there are no two persons completely alike, not even identical twins. Equally, there are no two societies completely alike, not even amongst small bands of hunter–gatherers.

Each person is thrown into a particular society by the accident of birth. The *conception* of a particular personal a priori via an individual's progenitors is in itself an accident. It is also an accident that this person is thrown into this or that particular social a priori. There is nothing in the genetic make-up of an embryo that would predestine its 'being thrown' into any *particular* social a priori; it is only predestined to be thrown into a social a priori. Destiny as *accident* is thus twofold. Transforming this accident into determination and self-determination is precisely what 'growing up in a particular world' is all about. I term this 'dovetailing' of the two a prioris 'historicity'.

To repeat, nothing is 'written' or coded into the general genetic a priori which would predestine anyone for one particular social a priori, because every newborn child is fit for human life in *any* social a priori. The general genetic a priori is constant, whereas social a prioris are different and subject to change. On the other hand, while nothing is 'written' or coded into the personal genetic a priori which would predestine anyone for one particular social a priori, not all personal genetic a prioris fit equally, or equally well, into a particular social a priori. If a hundred infants are born into the same social a priori, it is obvious that some will find it more difficult, and others will find it easier, to fit into the *same* social a priori. Social and genetic a prioris can be dovetailed to a greater or lesser extent, and sometimes they do not fit together at all. One must conclude that there are a great number of potentials in the genetic a priori of every person which remain barren within the framework of every social a priori, but more so in one than in another. One can equally surmise that potentials are developed in every particular society, and yet these potentials can be strong in one personal genetic a priori and weak, or even absent, in another. *The 'human condition' can thus be concretized as the determination and self-determination of historicity under the condition of a historical hiatus.* This hiatus is historical in two respects:

1　the general genetic a priori is a constant, but the social a priori is practically *infinite* in its variations, and is changing; and

2   the personal genetic a priori is idiosyncratic, but almost *infinite* variations of personal genetic a prioris can be comprised and 'integrated' by the *same* social a priori.

To make my position clear, even if the two a prioris are *completely* 'dovetailed', a human being will never be a subsystem of society, for the simple reason that there are two parties to this 'dovetailing'. Society can be described, albeit not defined, as the patterned relationship of humans to one another, to the sources of their subsistence and to the creations of their imagination. The patterns are the social regulations substituted for instinct regulation, the very rules-and-norms that ensure repetition, constancy, the economy of 'energy intake and output', regularity; in short, the homeostasis of every human group, and therefore of the human species. A complete 'dovetailing' of the two a prioris has three aspects:

1   the full internalization of all regulations;
2   the ability to observe these regulations 'as if' they were instincts; and
3   the absence of choice between regulations or any aspects thereof.

Whether or not all three conditions have ever actually been met in respect of every adult member of a human community is of limited interest here. What is crucial is the fact that a complete 'dovetailing' of the two a prioris does not generally occur, at least not in respect of every adult member of a community in any society we *know of*. Even the slightest discrepancy results in a kind of tension, and, the greater the discrepancy, the more this tension is experienced. The tension I have in mind is not the tension *between* the genetic a priori and the social a priori, as is the case before and during the bridging of the hiatus, but rather the tension *within historicity*. Although the latter is due to the incomplete 'dovetailing' of the genetic and social a priori, the very tension within historicity is not that between the so-called 'natural' (the genetic a priori) and the 'social' (the social a priori). This is so for the very reason that certain elements of the genetic a priori have been completely fitted into the social a priori in the already terminated process of socialization. Moreover, this tension itself can be explained, dealt with, even mobilized, by the meaningful world-view(s) of the society (community) in question (myths, both local and universal, artistic practices, philosophy, science and the like). Thus the thematization of tension is inherent in the social a priori. A greater than average tension of historicity can result in a 'subjective deficit' as well as a 'subjective surplus'. The latter is the constant source of the creation of cultural surplus, and can be absorbed by the meaningful world-views just as it can contribute to the change (modification) of social life patterns, if other conditions are met.

There is no Self, nor is there society, without 'fitting together' the two a prioris. Yet such a complete dovetailing would be a very rare occurrence. A perfectly dovetailed Self is *one-dimensional*, and a society in which all Selves are perfectly dovetailed would be unable to change (and would be characterized by the absence of meaningful legitimizing world-views). Historicity is imbued with tension. The quantity, the quality and the character of this tension vary, yet it is always present. *The 'human condition' can thus be further concretized as 'living in tension'*. We are destined to live with this tension. We can attempt, in vain, to rid ourselves of it. We can also try to make the best of it.

I have *described* the 'human condition' in three consecutive steps:

1   as social regulation substituted for instinct regulation;
2   as the determination and self-determination of historicity under the condition of a historical hiatus; and
3   as historicity *qua* 'living in tension'.

Of course, one could enumerate certain concrete elements of the 'human condition': humans must work to subsist, humans are language users, humans kill members of their own species, and so forth. Yet, whatever humans do, whether they work, talk or kill, whether they make love or war, whether they write poems or turn to God in prayer, they never do so in accordance with an innate pattern, but in accordance with or in relation to norms, rules and regulations. Whatever they do, they must bridge the hiatus and they must learn how to bridge it, in order to become a person. And, whatever they do, they live in tension.

As mentioned, the quality, quantity and character of the tension of historicity constitute a variable. Let me now add that it is both a historical and a personal variable. The historical factor must be heavily emphasized, but it cannot be dealt with in any detail within the narrow framework I have set here. It stands to reason that, the more complex a society becomes, the stronger this tension can become, yet for various reasons it does not necessarily become stronger. Among these reasons are the differentiation of the system of elementary norms and rules, and the differentiation of meaningful world-views which explain and channel the existential tension and make use of it. In addition, the internal tension can be externalized in different ways and in different modes; self-awareness can be transformed into self-consciousness; the same ideas and world-views as increase the tension by making it conscious, can at the same time decrease this tension by *verbalizing* it. I shall return to these problems shortly.

The existential tension does not make its appearance in a constant state of mind or body, but rather in a *pendulum-like* movement with a smaller or larger amplitude. If I set my own Self swinging on a larger amplitude, this action is accompanied by a heightened degree of emotivity, and sometimes, though not always, also by a heightened degree of cognitive awareness. Yet it is still the case that, whilst one swing unites, another separates. Examples of this are: binding ourselves to others/separating ourselves from others; identifying ourselves with others/distinguishing ourselves from others; seeking security/reasserting personal freedom; longing for dependence/longing for independence; transcending ourselves in a trance, mystical contemplation, love, immersion in Beauty/defending ourselves against the loss of the Self; dissolving into communities/ seeking solitude; sharing 'public opinion'/trusting only our own eyes. These and so many other feelings and cravings are but the forms of our ongoing attempts to cope with existential tension. I have chosen to illustrate this with pairs of attitudes which are *per se* value-indifferent, as moral issues proper cannot yet be dealt with.

General theories of 'human nature' chart a *map* of the Self, presupposing that each and every Self is correctly represented by the same map. Admittedly, one or another part of this 'map' can be 'larger' or 'smaller', 'stronger' or 'weaker', in respect of different people, but all are presumed to have the same map 'inside' – this much is taken for granted. There were times when people knew they consisted of a body and an immortal soul. These days we throw out the old map as useless and replace it with several new maps, all claiming to be the 'correct' one. Some of these maps gloomily contend that there is a territory within each Self which remains *terra incognita* and no traveller engaging in soul research will ever locate it. Others cheerfully assert that this particular 'territory' does not exist except in our fancy, so all maps should go into the rubbish bin. Yet most of us are still busy drawing new maps. All such maps provide us with *regulative theoretical ideas* (in the Kantian meaning of the term), by which to organize and reorganize internal experience, as well as our experiences of others. If there is only *one* theoretical idea of the Self provided by the dominant meaningful world-view, every person will understand his or her Self under the guidance of that idea. The internal experiences of some people will fit in comfortably with this theory, those of other people with varying degrees of difficulty. Yet, if there exist *competing* theories offering different theoretical ideas for the organization and reorganization of our internal experiences and of our experiences of others, as is the case today, people can choose that which provides the best understanding of their *own* experiences. If someone asks the question of whether our Self 'consists' of Id–Ego–Superego or 'I and Me', or if someone argues, as Wittgenstein did, that our Self does not belong to the world but is rather the *limit* to the world, I would say 'Out of these take your pick. Choose that which organizes your own self-experience best', because one of the theories will no doubt make you understand *your* internal world better than the rest. If you wish to explain other selves by relying on introspection and, in addition, on the observation of *certain* other selves, then you must commit yourself to *one particular* explanation. The fact that not *everybody* recognizes his or her own experiences or experiences of others in one single theory of the Self, but that many people recognize some of their experiences in one theory and some in another, and also recognize their experience of one person they know in one particular theory, and their experience of another person they know in another theory, is for me evidence enough to conclude that *the internal differentiation of the Self is itself a variable*, and, moreover, not only a historical, but also a 'personal', variable. At first glance, this conclusion seems unjustified. It could be said that the *facts* of the 'internal world' are the same, but are only interpreted in different ways within different theories, and so become facts of those theories. Yet theories of the Self are not like theories of the natural sciences, and not even like social theories, but are similar to philosophical theories; in fact, *they are* philosophical theories. Philosophies can always be verified, never falsified, though we can abandon philosophies if they provide no answer to the meaning of life, if they do not raise our historicity to the level of historical consciousness where historicity can recognize itself in that consciousness. Life experience, prestructured in everyday life and thinking, is co-constitutive of the choice of philosophies, not only so far as one's viewpoint, 'regard' or evaluation, but also so far as 'ipseity', is concerned. Two people with sharply diverging life experiences will not recognize their historicity in the *same* philosophy. Different self-experiences are rooted in different life experiences, and *vice versa*.[3] And one could still contend that, since there are ideal-typical life experiences in every particular world, so there must be an ideal-typical self-experience as well. I do not deny the existence of ideal-typical, or perhaps dominant, self-differentiations in every particular social a priori (including our own world); I only assert that not all of us carry the same map 'inside'. Thus my answer to the question of whether the Self 'consists' of the trichotomy of Ego–Superego–Id is that some Selves do, others do not.

So what can in fact be stated about the 'Self' that has a claim to general truth? Firstly, Selves are the only bodies that are connected to all other bodies by meaning. *Body as Self* feeds on meaning. The Self is created by other Selves, which for their part are bodies connected to all other bodies by meaning, and the same Self creates other Selves, which are equally destined to be connected to these other Selves by meaning.[4] The Self also comprises long-term memory, both conscious and unconscious (total loss of memory is tantamount to total loss of Self). Memory is not simply equivalent to the coding of information. It involves encoding the *relation* of the entire body to all previous items of information to any particular subsequent item of information; in other words, memory constitutes *involvement in rendering meaning*. Memory also involves forgetting, and thus the decoding of the relation to long-term information, and so memory also constitutes *involvement in rendering meaninglessness*. *Conscious experiencing* is guided by the medium of language. Accordingly, conscious experience can only be subjective ('mine') if it is first *shared* (language being shared meaning). I can only know of *my* headache if I know that *there are headaches* which others also have, though they do not have *my* headache. The more meaning I share with others, the richer and more complex is the meaning I render to the unshared experience.

I *understand* (identify, cognize, comprehend) my internal perceptions with the *same conceptual tools* I use to understand (observe, identify, comprehend) others, although the two perceptions are *different in kind*. Let us take, for example, affects such as fear, shame, disgust, gaiety, sadness, anger. These are all innate feelings, and are accompanied – unless they are deliberately suppressed – by equally innate facial expressions. Yet I do not see *my* own face, only the faces of others, and I do not see that *I* am blushing; I only see that others are blushing. On the other hand, I *feel* that I am ashamed whereas I *do not feel* that others are ashamed, or, if I do, the feeling is secondary (reflective), not primary; it is not an affect but an orientative feeling. However, I *know* that *others*, when blushing, feel like me when I feel ashamed and blush. The concept 'being ashamed' is adequate in both cases, and the conceptual tool of understanding is the same. This simple example can illuminate more complex situations. I can know myself better than others know me because I have *privileged access* to my own feelings, ideas, thoughts, conscious desires, plans, suspicions, and I can disclose these things or keep them to myself as I wish. Yet it is also true that others can know me better than I know myself, because they *see* me *relate* to them, and it is *in human relations that meaning is disclosed*. But there is more to it than this. The attitude of all Selves is ontologically particularistic. Selves are the *navels* of the world for themselves. All relations to other humans and to the world in general are as to so many umbilical cords: the Self is tied to the world by all these cords. If a community is more or less homogeneous, and the distinction between I-consciousness and We-consciousness is slight, then the community is perceived as *the navel of the world* or almost so. However, what is historically contingent and changing in the case of communities, is ontologically ultimate for the Self. It is not possible to conceive either of a Self which steps outside itself completely, and thus ceases to be the navel of the world, or of a Self which severs these umbilical cords and ceases to be the bundle of those cords. This is not even the case with the mentally ill, unless these people permanently lose their Self. To see oneself *completely* with the eyes of others is humanly impossible, and so is complete solipsism. This is an additional reason for knowing ourselves better than knowing others, as well as for others being able to know us better than we know ourselves.

To repeat, the Self is the only body connected to all other bodies by meaning. The bundle of umbilical cords is the bundle of meaning. Actions performed carry meaning, and this statement is but the reformulation of the basic statement concerning the 'human condition' that social regulation has been substituted for instinct regulation. The non-observance of social regulations also carries meaning. If deliberate, it carries meaning for both the Self and the other Selves. If unintentional, it *may* carry meaning for both the Self and the other Selves, or for either the Self or the other Selves.

Social regulations, which always include the primary objectivations of ordinary language, customs, and the patterns for using man-made objects, are not the sum total of Selves. They are the social system. Selves are not subsystems of the social system but are the fountainheads, as well as the products, of this system. The more heterogeneous the regulations, the greater the range of options for rendering meaning; the greater the range of options for rendering meaning, the more numerous the differentiations of shared meanings; the more numerous the differentiations of shared meanings, the greater the variety within the bundle of umbilical cords binding the Self to a particular world; and, the greater the variety in the bundle of umbilical cords, the more *individualized* Selves may become. Yet, as discussed, there can be cords in the bundle of single Selves which cannot be connected – or at least comfortably connected – to the meaning offered by standing regulations. Selves can also seek for meaning which has not yet been 'provided', thus creating a cultural surplus.

Self is always *self-awareness*. This follows from everything said hitherto. Still, Self is not always *self-consciousness*. Self-consciousness is not tantamount to our long-term memory as defined above. Nor is it tantamount to privileged access to internal occurrences (the perception of the Self by the Self). It concerns *a specific use of the privileged access*. Self-consciousness is, moreover, not tantamount to *self-reflection in general*. Self-awareness cannot exist without some sort of self-reflection. Finding out whether I am really hungry or really angry is self-reflective, but has nothing to do with self-consciousness; it is not the kind of self-reflection we normally attribute to self-consciousness. Not even the *evaluation* of certain internal occurrences necessarily goes with self-consciousness. Whether I am 'a little' thirsty or 'very' thirsty is a matter of evaluation. I can *evaluate* certain impulses negatively (as bad) *because* they are unpleasant, even if they are only unpleasant *because* we are forbidden to carry them out. None the less, self-consciousness presupposes a specific kind of self-reflection, *the combination of empirical and transcendental self-reflection*, which I shall term *double-quality* (self-) reflection. The *standpoint* of a self-reflection of this kind is always an idea, an abstraction, be it a theoretical idea, an abstract norm, the idea of supreme beings, the idea of moral good and evil, or even the idea of the Self. (I shall elaborate upon this problem later.) Our Self becomes an *object of scrutiny* in the process of double-quality self-reflection. We want to discover who we are, what we are, 'what is inside'. It is under this scrutiny that *the Self becomes individually differentiated*. The differentiated complex Self is not 'there' at the outset, nor is this double-quality self-reflection *a means to fathom* the 'depths of the soul': in fact it *creates* these depths. How and to what degree our Self becomes differentiated and 'deepened' depends on the theoretical or practical idea on which the double-quality reflection rests. If we do not stop searching, the Self becomes a *bottomless* mine or a terrifying abyss (and whether it becomes mine or abyss again depends on the regulative idea). And, even if we stop searching, as we always do when being guided by *practical ideas*, we return to self-scrutiny upon withdrawing from acting (or from a particular crucial act). But we should not forget the distinction between the perception of one's own Self and one's own perception of other Selves, or of the perception of one *by* other Selves. Double-quality self-reflection can accompany double-quality reflection *upon* and *by* others. Given a proper balance between double-quality reflection and double-quality self-reflection, with both being guided by practical and theoretical ideas, and given that practical reflection gains the upper hand either way (the search stops to allow action), our inner world will be construed as 'deep' not only by us, but also by others. However, if I become too reflective and continuously scrutinize my 'soul', rendering it a bottomless world, the only one worthy of being scrutinized, I shall perceive my self as a bottomless mine or abyss, while others will perceive it as flat and hollow. A narcissistic Self is hollow; the Nought is at the bottom of such a Self. This can be formulated as an objective statement; that is, *irrespective of the regard.* For the hypertrophy of self-reflection leads to the loss of the double quality of that self-reflection: *it loses its transcendental dimension.* The transcendental moment of self-reflection is due to the *standpoint* of the particular reflection, which is also non-empirical (an idea, an abstract norm, and so on). But self-searching as a goal in itself loses grasp of the transcendental standpoint of reflection. The idea *of* searching the Self is not an idea *for* reflecting *upon* the Self. Self-searching thus ceases to be an act of *self-consciousness.*

The knowledge of rules (regulations) *per se* does not yield self-consciousness; nor does knowledge of the 'rules of the game'. Being seen by others and *vice versa*, and seeing others who see you, involves self-awareness, but not yet self-consciousness (at least, not in the sense in which I have defined it). The temporary self-alienation which occurs when the Self places itself in the position of another Self and views his or her character or action from the standpoint of this other Self is not the beginning, or the decisive pattern, of self-consciousness. Temporary self-alienation *per se* does not yield double-quality reflection, because the transcendental element is missing. The attempt to judge our Selves from the viewpoint of a particular Other, or to live up to the expectation of particular Others, becomes an act of self-consciousness (self-reflection) if and only if *the attempt itself* has already been preceded by, and has resulted from, the act of double-quality reflection.

The double-quality reflection, and in particular the *transcendental* aspect of self-reflection, is traditionally expressed by a powerful image. It seemed obvious that we can reflect upon ourselves from the standpoint of a *non-empirical entity*, an abstraction, an idea, because we too carry an abstraction, an idea *inside*: a particular substance to do with thinking or evaluating. The Self, the 'real' Self or the 'supreme' Self, dwells, so it seemed, in its vessel: the body. The body is contingent to the substance, and the immortal soul can move from one body into another without changing its substance. Or, to quote a more modern version of the story: I am because I carry *mens animus sive intellectus*. This traditional image has been strongly challenged of late, although sometimes the baby has been thrown out with the bath water. In such instances, although *mens animus* has disappeared, so has the whole inner life of the Self, and eventually also the Self as the *navel* of the Self's own world.

A little earlier I described the Self as comprising long-term memory of *experience*, conscious or unconscious. I added that conscious experiencing, as well as the encoding of that experience, is guided by language. And yet, although language (conceptualization) guides the process of experiencing, the latter is not purely or completely conceptual, and neither is experience. Experiences are so hetero-geneous and all-encompassing that even their main forms elude enumeration. These main forms can be images, interpretations, ideas, voices, scents, passions, deliberations, intents, moods, streams of events, problems and their solutions, flashes of insight, puzzles, stories of natural or supernatural beings 'who live on, under or above Earth', shocks, fears, joys, elations and humiliations – one could obviously go on and on. Experience as sedimented experienc-ing carries the meaning which relates our body to other bodies of meaning. It orients, selects and motivates as a kind of internal regulatory system. Experience is the *internal* regulation (orientation) for actions (in the broadest sense of the word – acting, understand-ing, judging, communicating, evading, evaluating, loving and the like). To repeat, personal experience and experiencing are engulfed in and redeemed by shared experience, but personal experience is not a subcase or an item of shared experience. It is not the 'internalization' of shared experience, though it presupposes such internalization. The movement of the pendulum discussed earlier on, the alternation between *isolation* and *blindedness, self-reassertion* and *self-abandon*, and the like, is the alternation between sustaining *my* experience, *my* meaning, *my* orientation, *my* selection, *my* self-regulation, and the *oblivion of those experiences in the shared*: the shared meaning, the shared orientation, the shared selection, the shared regulation, and eventually the total oblivion of long-term memory as sedimented and accentuated experience (Nirvana, death). In every society there is a certain amount, a certain kind, of 'alternation tolerance'. Remaining within the limits of this tolerance is what is generally termed 'normality'. And, if normality is the case, mutual recognition can also be the case. The Self grants recognition to the shared meaning, recognition to the shared world, whilst claiming recognition for itself. The term 'recognition', as used by Hegel, is a subcase, albeit a decisive one, of recognition in general. The mother already recognizes the Self of her child while smiling at this child, and the child recognizes the world of Others in smiling back to the mother. The reciprocity of smiling is shared experience, although the experience of the mother (which is conscious) and the experience of the infant (which is preconscious) are different not only in degree but also in kind. If Others help us to bridge the hiatus, we are already recognized as members of this particular world. Mutual recognition takes different forms and shapes. It can be selective to a greater or lesser degree. It can be general (due to one's membership of a particular world) or personal (recognition by people who hold us dear) or special (personal recognition granted to specific achievements, merits and excellence). It can also occur in the reverse manner, as recognition of my world in general, personal recognition of those I hold dear, and selective recognition of certain aspects of my particular world (which involves non-recognition of other aspects). But, whatever forms and shapes this recognition takes, both kinds of recognition presuppose 'normality'. Yet, if the degree of alternation exceeds the limit defined as 'normal', both forms of recognition can break down. On the other hand, it can also happen that the person in question will contribute to the cultural surplus and thus embody the promise of another world.

If the two aspects of recognition are in complete balance, *then life has meaning*. If there is a 'recognition deficit' on one or both sides, and the deficit can be thematized and problematized, life can be *rendered meaning*. But if such a deficit cannot be thematized and problematized, life cannot be given meaning. Meanings are present because meanings are everywhere when there is speech, action and work. Meanings (but *not* 'Meaning') are present even in a situation of total subjection and submission. Meanings without a 'meaning to life' are precisely what *suffering* is all about. Animals can be 'in pain'. *But suffering is a human privilege.* To attribute virtue to suffering is a tribute paid to the human condition.

2

Sittlichkeit: the Norms and Rules of Proper Conduct

Wittgenstein stated, 'Ethics must be a condition of the world, like logic.' The sentence is ambiguous. It can be read as saying that it is necessary to assume that ethics is a condition of the world to the same extent as logic, but an equally possible reading is that ethics must be the condition of the world in the same way as logic. The latter interpretation brings us into the vicinity of the Kantian idea that there exists a universal law of morals which necessitates our action, just as the universal laws of logic necessitate our thinking, and that this universal moral law can be discovered, just as the universal laws of logic have been, and are being, discovered. Good action accords with the moral law in the same way as good thinking accords with the laws of logic. However, the first interpretation above yields a simple *empirical statement*: that a world without ethics does not exist, just as a world without logic does not exist. This is the statement to which I subscribe.

Ethics is the condition of the world. Chemical substances or organisms can exist without ethics, but there is no *world* without ethics. 'World' is not the sum total of lifeless and living things but the *meaning* of all those things, and meanings are constituted by humans because humans are the only bodies tied to *all other bodies* – including non-human bodies – by meaning. Yet meaning is provided by norms and rules. Systems of belief, knowledge 'at hand' and cosmic knowledge are embedded in and mediated by the same norms and rules as regulate proper conduct. Only in very recent histories have the norms of true knowledge of the world and the norms and rules of proper conduct in the world been *relatively* uncoupled. We 'have' a world because we are norm-and-rule-regulated and not instinct-regulated. It is 'all right' to observe rules and 'all wrong' to infringe them. 'All right' means 'good'; 'all wrong' means 'bad'. The very fact that social regulation has been substituted for instinct regulation implies that there *is* good and bad. Since there is no *world* without norms and rules, and the very existence of norms and rules is tantamount to the distinction between good (observance) and bad (infringement), *the distinction between good and bad (ethics) is the condition of the world.*

I have termed the distinction between good and bad the *primary* category of value orientation. The primary category of value orientation is a *human universal*, both empirically and logically. Since we do not have empirical knowledge about *all* human societies hitherto, but only about those that have left traces we can read, I have made a case for universality on ontological grounds. It is impossible to imagine human life *without* the primary category of value orientation. It is impossible to imagine a *world* without people *who can dwell upon and imagine a world.* One dwells upon a world of good and bad. It is impossible to dwell upon any other.

Let me now proceed quasi-empirically – that is, by constructing ideal types supported by empirical evidence. The norms and rules of the primary sphere of objectivation are heterogeneous. The primary sphere of objectivation, which I term the 'sphere of objectivation-in-itself', consists of the rules of ordinary language, the rules and norms of conduct, and the rules of using objects, in particular man-made objects. Although these three elements are interwoven, their rules do not completely coalesce. For example, hunting according to the rules of hunting presupposes the use of ordinary language, but the rules of ordinary language are not those of hunting, and *vice versa*. In addition, the different actions performed according to their own rules and norms do not necessarily interact in a *systematic* manner with one another, and, the more complex the society, the less they do so. One can do one thing without doing all the other things. *But there are always certain things everyone must do.*

The distinction between norms and rules is of great significance. For the moment I shall disregard the more complex problems and discuss this distinction in relation to *application* alone. The application of rules does not allow room for manoeuvring, or, if it does, the amount of room will be very small.[1] If, in case X, you do Y, then, every time that X is the case, you cannot think about doing Z rather than Y without infringing the relevant rule. Crossing an intersection if the light is amber is a matter of judgement, but, if it is red and you say to yourself 'This is not important' and cross, you have infringed a traffic rule. Ceremonies, either religious or 'social', are by definition 'rule-like'. Of course, even rule-conforming behaviour permits a great variety of action patterns. For example, we can compose all sorts of different sentences, but none of them should infringe the rules of grammar. However, norm application differs from rule application in several respects. Norms are prescriptions which one neither *completely* fulfils nor *completely* infringes but which one lives up to in varying degrees. However, there is a *critical limit* to norm application, and once this is exceeded the norm has been infringed completely. All virtue norms have this character, as have the norms of 'civility'. (Aristotle, in his theory of *mesotes*, discussed virtue norms in exactly this way.) The norm or rule character of regulation does not perforce depend on the specificity of an action pattern, although it *might* depend on it. At any rate, norm application offers greater personal space for deliberation, judgement, choice and the like than does rule application.

Both norms and rules can be imperative as well as optative. A norm or rule is imperative if it prescribes that every member of a social cluster *must do this* or *must forgo* doing this, to be this particular way and so avoid being another particular way. Imperative norms and rules are *unconditional*. The observance of such norms and rules has nothing to do with the 'if–then' formula, for they are not like instructions for use. There are two kinds of imperative norms and rules. There are those the infringement of which is *self-punishing*, such as the rules of grammar, and there are those the infringement of which *calls for punishment*, such as the Ten Commandments. These commandments comprise both rule-like and norm-like statements. The following is a perfect case of an *imperative rule*: 'Remember to keep holy the sabbath day. Six days you may labour and do all your work, but the seventh day is the sabbath of the Lord your God. No work may be done on this day either by you, or your son or daughter, or your male or female slave, or your beast, or by the alien who lives with you.' This is a rule because it prescribes *completely* what you should do and should not do and *how* you should do it. It is similar to the traffic rule above in that you cannot ponder whether or not this sabbath is an 'important sabbath'. 'Honour your father and your mother' is an *imperative norm*. This commandment does not specify *how* you should honour them, so you can ponder whether or not this or that particular act infringes the commandment. Accordingly, you can honour your father and mother to a greater degree or to a lesser degree. (Though again there is a *critical limit* which when exceeded means that you have violated the commandment.) 'You shall not kill' is also an imperative *norm* and should be properly read as saying 'you shall not commit *murder*', yet it does not prescribe behaviour (as with the commandment 'Honour your father and your mother'), but rather *forbids* an action. Even so, this commandment does not specify which forms of 'taking human life' *are* cases of murder. Consequently, one can reflect upon whether this or that form of 'taking human life' is indeed murder (whether or not it is forbidden).

Both norms and rules can be optative. Optative norms and rules do not prescribe what *everyone* should do or should forgo doing, but rather *how* one should act (what one should do) *if* one has chosen to do this or that. Not following such a norm or rule can be automatically self-punishing, but, if it is not, then rule infringement must, under certain circumstances, be punished. To quote the Bible again: 'When a man uncovers or digs a cistern and does not cover it again, should an ox or ass fall into it, the owner of the cistern must make good by restoring the value of the animal to its owner; the dead animal, however, he may keep.' To cover the cistern is a rule, but there exist norms of an optative nature (such as the norms of friendship enumerated by Aristotle). The infringement of *commandment* is *always punished*, but the infringement of *certain* commandments is more severely punished than the infringement of others. In the case of norms, the 'greater or lesser degree' of infringement might be 'put right' with a greater or lesser level of punishment. The infringement of *optative* rules and norms is normally, though not always, punished if a specific result occurs. Here, punishment is *normally*, though not always, less severe than in the case of the infringement of commandments (imperative restitution).

Norms and rules can thus be very complex and highly differentiated. But to observe *any* norm or rule is proper (good, right) and to infringe any norm or rule is improper (bad, wrong), irrespective of whether the infringement is self-punishing or calls for punishment, whether the punishment is severe or light, or whether it is a rule or a norm which has been infringed. The differentiation of the world of norms and rules goes hand in hand with the *differentiation of the categories of value orientation*. The primary category of value orientation is to be differentiated in *secondary* categories of value orientation such as holy/profane, Good/Evil, right/wrong, true/false, useful/harmful, correct/incorrect, beautiful/ugly, pleasant/unpleasant. The holy, the Good, the right, the true, the useful, the correct, the beautiful, the pleasant are all *good*, whereas their opposites are all 'bad'. There is, however, a *hierarchy* embracing all norms and rules. The norms and rules the observance of which is described in terms of the 'holy' or 'Good' carry the greatest weight, and infringement of them (described in terms of the 'profane' or 'Evil') involves the greatest punishment (the death penalty, or perhaps being cast out, which may amount to the same thing). Since being holy is tantamount to being Good in every society where this holiness occupies a distinguished position within the hierarchy of norms and rules, a *general* statement can be made about it: that the secondary category of value orientation Good/Evil is at the top of this hierarchy. If it comes to a conflict between the various norms and rules, then 'Good comes first'. To put this the other way round, the norms carrying the greatest weight in society are those the observance of which is called 'Good' and the infringement of which is called 'Bad' ('Evil'). These are the *unconditional* moral norms and rules (commandments), whether or not they are formulated as commandments. Sometimes certain conditional norms and rules are referred to by the category of value orientation Good/Evil, sometimes by the category of value orientation right/wrong. (This can be so even if there is no *categorical* distinction; the same noun can be used in two different ways.) If the latter holds, this indicates that the infringement of norms and rules carries a lighter penalty (it is less severely punished or not punished at all). For example, if a person does not obey the rules governing the gathering of plants, he or she may not be punished at all, but, if the taboo plant is eaten, the person concerned must die.

It would be difficult for us to see the association between the term 'good person' and someone who abides by *all* norms and rules without distinction. But, if we take into consideration the differentiation of the secondary categories of value orientation, the picture will become more familiar. Putting other and more complex issues aside, one can understand why people who give preference, in all their actions, to the secondary category of value orientation Good/Evil (holy/profane) over other secondary categories of value orientation are regarded as good. Everyone who has the *competence* to distinguish between the different categories of value orientation can be termed a *rational actor*, but not all rational actors can be termed good. Competence in doing something is not tantamount to doing that thing. If a person employs competence in abiding by the in-built hierarchy of rules and norms, then he or she is considered to be 'all right' by the carriers of those norms – that is, by the community of which he or she is a member. Otherwise this person will be corrected or rejected.

It has already been emphasized that there is no necessary *systemic* interplay among the various kinds of actions performed in a social milieu with a certain complexity. The emergence of the secondary categories of value orientation already indicates a fair amount of differentiation. All human *action patterns* (although not all single actions) make sense, all of them embody and carry meaning. But the *hierarchy* of norms and rules can carry meaning only if a *particular kind of meaning is rendered precisely to this hierarchy*. And, indeed, such meaning is rendered to any particular hierarchy of norms and rules by a *meaningful world-view* (such as myth). A meaningful world-view justifies and legitimizes the hierarchy of norms and rules as the good, the proper, the sacred *order of things*. I term this aspect of the meaningful world-view *historical consciousness*. It is historical consciousness in that it justifies and legitimizes the given hierarchy as *the* order of things by the *genesis* of that order. The genesis is not only embodied in but also *repeated* in the given order. The constitution of the world is at first tantamount to the constitution and mediation of a *particular* world. The world of such and such norms and rules, the world of such and such images, representations and types of knowledge, is *the* world. 'A' world is 'the world'.

The meaningful world-view renders meaning to all human action patterns, to all norms and rules, and to their hierarchy. However, the meaningful world-view is *not* tantamount to the sum total of regulations which every person born into a particular world must appropriate. Being 'fitted into' the regulations of a social environment does not require, and sometimes does not even permit, the appropriation of the meaningful world-view *in toto*. One need know, and, sometimes, is permitted to know, only so much as is necessary for abiding by the normative hierarchy of the pre-given order, which must be taken for granted. In addition to the sphere of objectivation that I have termed the 'sphere of objectivation-in-itself', there is *another sphere*, a higher, a more subtle, a sacred sphere, which I term the 'sphere of objectivation-for-itself'. This latter sphere has norms and rules of its own. To practise these norms and rules is more often than not a privilege granted only under specific conditions and only to a few. One must be 'initiated' into this sphere; one must learn its language. This second and higher sphere is characterized by a *homogeneous medium*. The function of this sphere is to provide the sphere of objectivation-in-itself with meaning. Yet this function does not exhaust the operations of this sphere. It can and does absorb the subjective surplus created by those who cannot be fitted into the world of the sphere of objectivation-in-itself. In addition it can store *cultural surplus* and *cognitive surplus* – in other words, action patterns and forms of knowledge which are not used and implemented in the given world. Without presupposing an accumulation of cultural and cognitive surplus, the first drastic change in the *structure* of morals cannot be explained. Yet, for the time being, let us abstract from the change in the structure of morals and concentrate on examining certain moral contents and forms.

The distinction between rules, on the one hand, and norms, on the other, can be implicit or explicit. The *content* of a norm is usually specified, interpreted and concretized in one rule or in several rules, particularly if the norm is a commandment. *In principle* a norm is open to interpretation, but *in fact* it is not open to interpretation, because people are confronted not only with this norm but also with its 'proper' interpretation. 'You shall not kill', the commandment reads, but in the books of Exodus and Leviticus meticulously elaborated rules are provided for the observance of the commandment, rules of both an *imperative* and an *optative* nature. You come to know *what forms* of 'taking a life' constitute murder and what forms do not; you come to know under what circumstances you should avoid acting in this or that way in order to live up to the commandment. The same holds true of *virtue* norms. People are confronted not only with such norms as 'be courageous', 'be temperate' or 'be charitable', but also with concrete instructions for *how* to be this or that, *what* they must do in *particular* circumstances in order to conform to these virtues. Imperative and optative rules, and the interpretations of commandments, virtues and all other norms of goodness and rightness *embody* the *moral customs* of a given world that I shall term, following Hegel, *Sittlichkeit*. *Sittlichkeit* is the identity of identity and non-identity because the distinction between norms (virtue norms and commandments), on the one hand, and their concretization–specification, on the other, is *implicit* in the ongoing social practices, and can eventually be made explicit. I account for this 'dialectic' by the tension between *abstract norms* and *concrete norms*. I mean by 'concrete norms' the specification, concretization, rule-like interpretation of abstract norms, be they commandments, virtue norms or optional norms. I mean by 'abstract norms' the norms proper (the 'idea' of norms); that is, commandments, virtue terms and optional prescriptions open to interpretation as far as their meaning, and thus their application, is concerned (what, when, how, towards whom, and so on). *Sittlichkeit* (moral customs) involves both concrete and abstract norms, although usually it is the concrete norms that preponderate. To challenge all or even most concrete interpretations of abstract norms cannot be customary, but challenging a number of them does not go so far as to upset a particular kind of *Sittlichkeit*.

In stratified societies, moral customs too are subjected to stratification. Like Luhmann, I mean by 'stratified societies' all those societies in which people perform a certain set of actions and fulfil certain functions *because* they have been born into a particular social stratum. (By contrast, we can term modern society 'functional' because people become members of specific social strata *because* they perform a specific function.) Moral customs are subjected to stratification in so far as *different sets* of moral customs are assigned to different strata. In a stratified society the 'accident of birth' is twofold. The newborn is 'thrown' by the accident of birth not only into a specific world but also into a specific stratum of this world. She or he must 'fit into' the requirements of a 'sphere of objectivation-in-itself' which is *particularistic* in a double sense – particularistic in relation to other 'worlds' and particularistic *within* his or her world – *without having a chance* to move by *his or her own choice* into another particularistic world. Alongside the division of *Sittlichkeit* in accordance with social strata there is a strict division of *Sittlichkeit* between the sexes in all stratified societies. To be born a female marks a person to an even greater extent than to be born a slave. A slave may eventually be freed and so alter his or her stratum and moral customs. A female can never be freed from gender identity, and therefore, in most societies hitherto, from being subjected to a master. Apart from personal chances and the lack thereof that life offers to a woman, the moral customs are not only different in kind for a woman, but also different in degree of sublimity. The highest, the noblest, the most sublime moral customs are the customs of the *male members of the highest social stratum*. The moral customs allocated to lower social strata, and hence to women and to slaves, were considered *inferior and base*. Indeed, there has existed and still exist a great variety of stratified societies, and apart from the prevailing general pattern they have sometimes had little in common. How this general pattern operates depends mostly on the meaningful world-view of a particular society. But even in ancient Jewish culture, where masters were obliged by divine law to liberate their slaves after six years of servitude, and where the commandments were equally binding for all, God, or his mouthpiece, addressed *free males* only. Free males had the task, and thus the burden, of implementing divine orders; in other words they had to *order* their *dependants* (wives, children, servants, slaves) to observe the commandments. The free male obeyed these divine orders directly, whereas his dependants obeyed through the master's will. And in the cities of Greece, the Roman Republic, and the caste system of India, this stratification of *mores* was even more rigid and unequivocal.

The stratification of *mores* into 'sublime' and 'base' (according to the division of labour) *is* domination. It *expresses* domination as well as being the *tool* of domination. As far as the latter is concerned, domination is legitimized and justified as the domination of the *noble* over the *base*. It goes without saying that legitimation and justification did not constitute a blatant lie or crude falsification, but rather the reversal of the cause–effect relationship. (This can be clearly seen in Aristotle's *Politics*.) It is not absurd to assert that the freest of humans in a particular world *can* also be, though they are not necessarily, the *most morally noble*. The less dependent one is, the nobler one *can* become. But it is not baseness that creates dependence; it is rather dependence that *might* create, but does not necessarily create, baseness.

The association of the *mores* of the highest classes with 'sublimity' or 'nobility', and those of the lower classes with 'rudeness', is the *general perception* of the division of *Sittlichkeit* in all stratified societies, an unforgettable example of which is the moral hierarchy in Shakespeare's dramas. And yet 'sublimity' and 'nobility' are not always identified with *moral goodness*. I shall return to this later.[2]

The stratification of *mores* in accordance with both a social and a gender-related division of *Sittlichkeit* is the stratification of *concrete norms*. If the tension between abstract and concrete norms is only implicit (and never explicit), then all norms are *clusteral*. By this I mean that norms and rules constitute *human clusters*, one set of norms and rules one particular cluster, another a different cluster. The members of a particular cluster are bound to subject themselves to the norms and rules of *their* cluster. If a person belongs to cluster B, his or her actions will be judged by a member of cluster A according to the standards of cluster B, and *not* by the standards of the person judging (the standards of cluster A), and *vice versa*. There will be no *common yardstick* with which to compare and evaluate the actions of members of *different clusters*. In other words, A and B will be completely *unequal* as moral agents. If there were only *one* general norm, it would be possible to compare *all* social agents (irrespective of the cluster they belonged to), and every person would be *morally equal* from the standpoint of that general norm. But no such general norm exists. If all norms are clusteral, the relationship of members of different clusters to one another is a relationship of *asymmetric reciprocity*.

Whether or not there is a social division of *mores*, and irrespective of the *content* (the substance) of concrete norms, the *method* of coping with clusteral norms is always constant. If certain norms and rules constitute a social cluster, these norms and rules must be applied to all members of that cluster consistently and continuously.

I have termed this form the *formal concept of justice*, which is at the same time the *maxim of justice*. The latter phrase means that all kinds of justice can be brought under this formula. The kind of justice we deal with under the condition that all norms are concrete as well as clusteral is *static* justice. It is static in that we cannot raise the question of whether the norms and rules themselves are just: they are taken for granted. If social *mores* are stratified, then the golden rule of justice only applies within each social cluster; it does not apply to relations between actors of different clusters. This provides sufficient ground to say that, *since ethics is the condition of the world, so is justice.* Each and every time a particular set of ethical customs is denounced as immoral, a form of justice is denounced as injustice.

Although the division of concrete norms along the lines of social and gender stratification is the rule rather than the exception in human histories, the *complete absence* of transclusteral virtues or norms is the exception rather than the rule. By *transclusteral* virtues I mean certain qualities of character or of an action pattern which are *generally approved* by all members of society, who *internalize* this approval irrespective of social status. In the absence of transclusteral (abstract) norms, such virtues – exceptional beauty, exceptional bodily strength, great cunning, being 'possessed', being a seer, and the like – are different from the type of virtue we now associate with the adjective 'moral'. An elementary and instinctive utilitarianism is involved here. It contributes to the prestige of the whole community (people, city) to take pride in people with these attributes. In addition, advantages can be gained because of these larger-than-life qualities. Such people are treated with awe and are often elevated to the highest social rank, or even beyond, to the rank of divinity. What you do not understand you must hold in honour and regard with fear. Transclusteral virtues may be considered as being 'beyond justice', and for two reasons: first, because such larger-than-life virtues are *incomparable*, or at least seem to be; and, secondly, because the embodiments of such virtues *are not supposed to be just* (they can, like tyrants, follow their own whims and fancies).

Transclusteral norms must be observed by *all* members of a given social world irrespective of social status and gender. These norms are not particularistic but *general*. Abstract norms are *general norms*. However, certain abstract norms are duly concretized as customary norms along the lines of social and gender stratification. But *not all* general–abstract norms are particularized in this way. Some of the Ten Commandments were particularized and concretized; others were not. If a *general* commandment takes the form of a general and imperative rule, then particularization along the lines of a social and gender-related division of labour is ethically un-called for and logically impossible. All members of the tribes of Israel had to believe in Yahweh, and no Israelite was allowed to honour any other divinity. This was an equally absolute imperative for men and women, masters and servants, rich and poor. Thus the general imperative *equalized* all Israelites: they were good or wicked as judged by the yardstick of the *same* general–imperative rule. This and similar transclusteral norms and rules put certain *transclusteral virtues* at the apex of moral life. As transclusteral norms and rules and transclusteral virtues become established, the less will the 'sublimity' and 'nobility' of the highest social cluster be regarded as the *sine qua non* of supreme *moral goodness*. Since transcultural norms can be observed by members of all clusters, and since members of all clusters (and both genders) can equally excel in transcultural virtues, members of the lower clusters, even of the lowest cluster, *can be morally 'better'*, can be superior, to the members of the highest cluster, just as *women can be morally superior to men*. In the catalogue of *saints*, both servants and princesses manifest the same standards of supererogatory virtue.

It must be noted that *general* (abstract) norms and rules are *not universal*, or, to formulate this more cautiously, not all such norms are formulated with the intent of universalization, and not all of them can be universalized. All norms can be called general (and in this sense transclusteral) if they command allegiance irrespective of any social and gender-related stratification. Although transclusteral in one decisive respect, general norms are still *clusteral* in another respect: they constitute the cluster of a specific *culture*. This cluster can be coextensive with one particular people, but can also be an 'ideal' cluster encompassing several peoples. The greater the claim of general norms to constitute an *ideal* cluster, the more a claim to the universality of such norms can be raised (whether rightly or wrongly). *The claim to universality is tantamount to the claim that the general norm is valid not only transclusterally but also transculturally.* Whereas general (abstract, transclusteral) norms are both *substantive and formal*, attempts to formulate transcultural (universal) norms have ended in *extreme formalism*.

The diversity of ethical customs is not a modern discovery. Tribes with totally different normative patterns have lived in close proximity without influencing each other in any way whatsoever. People know that the 'outgroup' promotes a different kind of behaviour from the 'ingroup'. Except in times of deep crisis, the perception of differences is neatly inserted into the image of the cosmic order. The outsiders are regarded as non-human, or only partly human, as inferior, barbaric and the like. Absolute 'ethnocentrism' is the usual reaction to the perception of diversity. Only when abstract and concrete norms have already been differentiated, and our own system of concrete norms is no longer *completely* taken for granted (the first condition can be met without the second being met), can absolute ethnocentrism give way to *relative* ethnocentrism. Then, and only then, can the *mores* of any outgroup become the object of theoretical scrutiny. Then, and only then, can elements of the moral patterns of 'others' be *positively evaluated*, and perhaps even *more* positively evaluated than the parallel elements in our own culture. (*Germania* by Tacitus is an unforgettable testimony to this trend.) Most importantly, then, and only then, can the matter be raised of the *common features* between these two sets of morals. This is how we embark on the long journey of discovering features of *empirical universality*.

To claim universality for our general norms, and to discover empirical universality amidst moral diversity, are *not identical* procedures. It is unnecessary to make sweeping generalizations to reveal the presence of an *opposition* between the two, though this opposition does not apply to modernity. The first attempts at ethical–cultural relativism were coeval with the *loss* of trust in the validity of decisive *general norms* rather than with any penchant for universalizing them (for example, this was the case with the second generation of Sophists). However, in Western modernity both these tendencies gained momentum simultaneously, and occasionally in concert. The terms 'in concert' and 'simultaneously' cover two different propositions. The second proposition asserts that *the same historical consciousness*, or, to use Castoriadis's term, the same 'imaginary institution', enhances normative universalism *and* the search for the common features inherent in all hitherto known human societies, diverse as they may be, without asserting that whoever explores human universals will stand for the universalization of certain norms as well. To say that 'morals of all kinds are the tools of oppression' is to make a generalized statement concerning the *single major common* feature of all ethical customs without laying *any* claim to the universalization of *any* norm. Rather, the opposite is true. To say that 'morals of all kinds repress innate human instincts' is also to make a generalized statement concerning the *single major feature common to all ethical customs*. This statement does not involve any claim to the universalization of any norm, but it *does not exclude* in principle that such a claim can, or even should, be raised. Similarly, if someone claims that every hitherto known moral places a premium on weakness, servility and submission, it is very unlikely that this person will simultaneously raise a claim to the universality of a general norm, although even this possibility is not *completely* excluded. The second proposition (that both tendencies appear in concert) is true in every example of norm universalization, for if we claim universality for a general norm this claim *must be backed* with at least one fact of empirical universality (such as goodwill in Kant). Aside from these two extremes, even tentative and not strictly systematic philosophical claims to universality go hand in hand with a search for certain empirical universals. The question 'Is there anything common to all ethical worlds?' is replaced by the question 'Is there anything common to all ethical worlds which *we* can, with our universal claims, rely upon?' But the claim to universality can also elicit another kind of inquiry. We can ask such questions as 'Can we detect a development in ethics?', 'Is there ethical progression?', 'If there is, what are the criteria of moral progress?' Ethical diversity will thus be historicized and simultaneously organized in a *hierarchy*. This form of questioning raises further problems which can be formulated in further questions, such as 'What has progressively developed in ethics: the substantive element, the form, or the structure?' Yet there is one qualification to be made here, and an important one: if ethics has developed, then there must be something constant in *all* ethics, for, if there were no such constant, we could not apply the same noun (or the same category), such as 'ethics' or 'morals', to a phenomenon that had been there, is there now, or should be there. Nor can the quest for empirical universals be circumvented by evolutionist moral theories, of whatever provenance, without running the risk of talking nonsense.

It is generally accepted that the *structure* of morals is not an empirical universal. I have put my view that there have been two structural changes in morals, the second one still in the making. Consequently, when looking for moral universals, we look for constant substances (substrata, contents), constant forms, and constant combinations of substance and form.

Ethics is the condition of the world (of all worlds). Our condition is the human condition because social regulation has been substituted for instinct regulation. No human life is possible without observing certain rules and norms. No human life is possible without the distinction between good and bad. No human life is possible without the consistent *and* constant application of norms

and rules to members of the same cluster: in other words, no such
life is possible without formal justice. These are *universals of the
first order*. First-order universals are *purely formal* because the very
existence of regulations, the very existence of the primary categories
of value orientation (good/bad), the very existence of static justice,
does not indicate the presence or absence of any concrete ethical
substance (*what* is the rule, *what* is good, *what* is just).

The gist of the matter, however, is that we cannot think of
universals of the first order without thinking in the same breath of
concrete people who live up to the norms and rules of a human
community, without presupposing that the proposition 'Good
persons exist' is true, that it is *always* true, and that it is
empirically–universally true. The proposition 'Good persons exist'
does not refer to a *form* of ethics, nor does it refer to a content
(*substance*) of morals or to any kind of combination of form and
substance. It refers to the *bearers* of morals. As I have already
indicated, there are different types of good persons. But these types
do not vary in the same way and to the same extent as do the
substances or *second-order forms* of ethics. Rather, the types of
goodness vary with the *structure* of morals. Because there has so far
been only one structural change in morals, with the second still in
the making, we do not face great difficulties in *recognizing* good
persons (or the goodness of persons) in *old stories* even if the
substance of the norms these people observed differs considerably
from that of the norms we observe. More precisely, we feel
immediate empathy with good persons of the second type (after the
first structural change in morals occurred), whereas it may be
difficult for us to feel empathy with good persons of the first type
(before the first structural change of ethics occurred), though we can
feel empathy with the latter after a certain kind of hermeneutical
reflection.

So far we have arrived at two kinds of universals of the first
order: on the one hand, the purely formal, inherent in the human
condition in general, and, on the other, the bearers of the ethical, the
good persons themselves. If we now turn from the universals of the
first order to the universals of the second order, we run the risk of
being caught up in the huge task of sorting out the basics from an
enormous amount of historical and ethnological material. My
programme here of outlining a *general* ethics does not allow me to
undertake such an excursion. It will have to suffice to indicate the
direction of explanation.

The empirical universality of an ethical *substance* (*content*) can be
asserted if the *same concrete norm* is valid in every society. Since we

do not have knowledge of 'every society', it suffices to pinpoint the presence of the same concrete norms in all known *types* of society or, alternatively, to infer the necessary presence of that norm from the universals of the first order. In Weber's view, 'solidarity with our brethren' is one of a number of universal empirical substantive norms of this kind. Weber inferred this from the study of religion, though he could have inferred it from universals of the first order as well. The prohibition of parricide can also be pinpointed as an example of an empirically universal concrete normation.

An ethical *form* can be termed empirically universal if in every society we can *understand* the *relation* between *norm-related* action (observance or infringement) and reaction (reward and punishment) whilst bringing all cases, whatever their content, under the same scheme. Such purely formal empirical universals can also be inferred from the empirical universals of the first order. If, as I have argued, static justice is a first-order universal, we can infer that the so-called 'golden rule of justice' is also an empirical universal, if not between, then at least within, social clusters. The scheme of the 'golden rule' both in its positive and negative formulations ('I should do unto you what I expect you to do unto me', or 'I should not do unto you what I do not wish/expect you to do unto me'), is a merely formal empirical universal. This is so because all kinds of concrete and even abstract norms can provide the content (substance) of that form. The norm that 'Wrongdoers must be punished in proportion to their wrongdoing' is also a merely formal empirical universal of this kind. Different acts can count as wrongdoings and different forms of punishment can be considered as proportionate.

Merely substantive and merely formal universals are *absolute* empirical universals.

The richest hunting ground for empirical ethical universals is the realm of 'mixed' universals: the wide range of *abstract norms and virtues*. Abstract norms and virtue norms embody the *unity* of substance and form. There is a *common* substance in each of these forms because they all order or prohibit a certain *kind* of action. The prohibition 'You should not steal' cannot be understood as a mere form, because only certain kinds and not all kinds of action can be brought under this form. If someone gives false testimony, you cannot say, 'You should not steal', whereas you can punish this person in proportion to such wrongdoing to the same degree as in respect of stealing, murder, blasphemy and so on. Yet the substance of abstract norms (and virtue norms) is also a *form*, because what *counts* as stealing, murder, perjury and so on varies (historically, culturally, and according to membership of a social cluster or gender). The expectation that *one should be courageous* is undoubtedly an empirically universal virtue norm. However, what 'being courageous' means, how one lives up to this virtue norm, and particularly the question of *who* should be courageous, are all matters left undecided. *The norm is constant, yet the interpretation of the norm is variable.*

The same holds true, if not in the same fashion, for *abstract values* such as happiness, freedom and equality. Even such values as '*my* family', '*my* community', '*my* city', '*my* religion' are abstract. What happiness is, what freedom is, what equality means, *who* should be happy and *how*, *who* should be each other's equals and *how*, are all matters of interpretation. X belongs to a different family from Y, and to a different community from Z, and so on. Different concrete norms can be valid within city A and city B, religion A and religion B, but these and other kinds of *integration* are equally values, and sometimes even the supreme values, for the members of these integrations.

This striking similarity between abstract norms and virtue norms, on the one hand, and abstract values, on the other, is far from being accidental, since *all* abstract norms and virtue norms are *related* to abstract values (just as all concrete norms are implicit in concrete values).[3] A stuntman is not courageous in the sense that his actions are evidence of a 'virtue', because a stunt is not related to a shared value. The modern claim to the *universalization* of norms accompanies, or rather follows from, the universalization of certain values (in Kant's case, that of the value of *freedom* and of the integration value of 'humankind').

Mixed universals (abstract norms and virtue norms, on the one hand; abstract values, on the other) can be termed *relative empirical universals* or *absolute historical universals*. One must presuppose (on both ontological and empirical grounds) that there are or were human societies where abstract norms, abstract virtue norms and abstract values did not appear, and that such societies are indeed possible. One must equally presuppose that, even after abstract norms, virtue norms and values did appear, they did not regulate moral practices within all the clusters of any given society. I have termed these *historical* universals not because human history or ethics began with them, but because the emergence of *decisive aspects of morals* cannot be considered without them. And I have termed them *absolute* historical universals because they are empirically universal in every society where the *first decisive structural change in morals* has already occurred. I shall now address this matter.

Morals can be described as *the single person's practical relation-ship to the norms and rules of proper conduct*. This is not the definition of morals, for social–human universals cannot be properly defined, but rather a generalized sentence which will be specified in due course. Presupposing the presence of certain secondary cate-gories of value orientation (in particular, those of Good/Evil and holy/profane), the phrase 'practical relationship to the norms and rules of proper conduct' also denotes the existence of a practical relationship to the hierarchy of norms and rules ('Good comes first').

Let us first assume that abstract and concrete norms have not yet been differentiated, and that all values are concrete. If this is so, then the practical relationship of the single person to the norms and rules of proper conduct does not in fact differ from the practical relationship of every other single person to these norms and rules, even if their actions differ. One person may observe all the rules, another person may observe most of them and infringe some of them, and a third person may infringe only a few of the rules and yet do so to a very serious degree, and so on and so forth, yet in none of these cases does the *relation* to the norms become individualized. It is impossible to infringe any concrete norm and rule with good intent (moral reason). It is impossible to surpass the moral standard. It is also impossible to pit one kind of good action against another, to give preference to rules by choice.

Let us now assume that the distinction between abstract and concrete norms has already appeared. Abstract virtue terms, abstract values, and eventually certain abstract imperatives (commandments) are concretized, but they can also guide action via their 'pure', abstract quality. If this is the case, the relationship of the single person to the norms and rules of conduct can be *individualized*. One person can relate to these norms in one way, another in another way. At the very least, the application of norms in different situations can be performed under the authority of the individual. Moreover, the individual can choose to observe certain abstract norms to a more extensive degree than is expected, demanded or prescribed. Finally, the individual has some liberty in *reinterpreting* abstract norms and rejecting hitherto valid concrete norms as invalid from the standpoint of the abstract norms so reinterpreted. The individual can utter re-evaluative statements such as 'It is not this which is good, but that which is good', and raise the claim that this statement is true. The option to apply reason in the realm of morals and to comply with the results of moral deliberation is opened up for individuals, and consequently for collective actors. One form of

good action can be contrasted to another; a choice between two
moral options can be made. The immediate identity of theoretical
and practical reason ('Good consists of what everyone knows to be
good: I know what everyone knows to be good; I know what good
is; I act accordingly') becomes disrupted. Theoretical and practical
reason are differentiated and thus mediated, and *practical reason
proper* emerges in this process. Against the background of the
theoretical tradition of contrasting reason to emotion, it must be
noted that the emergence of practical reason proper accompanies a
heightened emotionality concerning moral matters. Unique moral
feelings and emotions of all shades develop, among them the most
decisive moral emotion, occupying a position among the absolute
historical universals: that of *conscience.*

The first structural change in morals, and its outcome, the second
structure of morals, can be described – again, described, not defined
– as follows: *Sittlichkeit* encompasses concrete norms and customs,
on the one hand, and abstract norms, virtue norms and abstract
values, on the other, intertwined, and charged with tension. The
identity of the identity and non-identity of concrete and abstract
norms, of concrete and abstract values, of ritualized behaviour and
virtue norms, is manifested and *made conscious via the differentiation of the individual relation to the norms and rules of proper
conduct.* This individual relationship to *Sittlichkeit* I term *morality.*
The terms *Sittlichkeit* and 'morality' are used in a similar sense by
Hegel. In a thoroughly Hegelian spirit I could say that morals
consists of two components: the objective (*Sittlichkeit*) and the
subjective (morality). Yet I do not identify the standpoint of
morality with the attitude of Ought, least of all with the attitude of
pure Ought, just as I do not identify *Sittlichkeit* with the standpoint
of Is. Abstract norms and values are themselves embedded in
Sittlichkeit. The individual who reinterprets such norms does not
necessarily reject *Sittlichkeit* in full. The kind of morality Hegel had
in mind is a subcase of morality – namely, the romantic–modern
type.

Morals, after the first structural change, can be described as the
individual relationship to *Sittlichkeit* where 'individual relationship'
stands for morality and *Sittlichkeit* stands for the identity of identity
and non-identity of concrete/abstract norms, and concrete/abstract
values (abstract norms and values encompass universal norms and
values as well).

The emergence of the second structure of morals does not go hand
in hand with the generalization of that structure. It is not just
employing a sweeping generalization to assert that following this

structural change of morals most people behave as if it had never taken place (sometimes through no fault of their own). But this is of minor importance from the standpoint of general ethics. What is of great importance is the fact that we could not speak about morals, we could not philosophize about ethical issues at all, had this change not occurred. By only saying this much, we perform an evaluation, yet an evaluation which is purely objective because it does not pertain to one or another moral discourse or moral philosophy, *but to all of them*. This purely objective evaluative statement reads as follows: the first structural change in morals is progressive, and unambiguously and incontrovertibly so. This was, or is, the only contradiction-free moral progression amidst the frequent changes in ethical substances and forms. If a person cannot subscribe to this statement, she or he resigns altogether from discussing morals.

3

From Voluntary Action to Moral Autonomy

Every action is *voluntary*. If doing something does not have the quality of being voluntary, then 'doing' is not action. A reflex movement is not an action, nor is blushing or trembling. Being raped does not constitute an action, although one does something whilst being raped. Or, to refer to Aristotle's example, if someone grasps your hand and kills someone with it, he has performed the act, not you. Also, the voluntary character of action does not depend on motivation. If you *know* that *you* are *doing something*, then you are acting, irrespective of whether you act under the influence of a passion or after calm deliberation, whether you aim at a particular goal or whether the action is a goal in itself, whether you achieve the goal you had in mind or achieve something you did not intend. Since you perform and act, your 'doing something' is voluntary.[1] What does it mean that I know I am doing something? It means that I *know that* I am doing something, that I know that *I am the one* who does something, that I know that I *do* something, as well as that I know the *something* (if only vaguely and inadequately) I am doing. Everyone who has raised a child knows that the first step towards inculcating moral conscience is to make clear the difference between 'I did it' and 'I did not do it.' Assessing motivations, the knowledge of circumstances and consequences in moral terms, *presupposes* the abstract form of taking responsibility. *The question of how far and to what extent an act can be imputed and eventually fully ascribed to an actor as a moral actor is an altogether different matter.* Where there is action, there is responsibility; where there is no action, there is no responsibility. The quality and the degree of responsibility depend not on the voluntary character of the act but on numerous factors. The problems of *moral choice* and *autonomy* (including moral autonomy) should not be confused with the issue of voluntary action. Moral choice is not simply a 'higher degree' of voluntary action, and moral autonomy is not an extreme version of voluntary action, as all three terms refer to issues different in kind. For, if the voluntary character of the act has anything to do with *moral* choice or *moral* autonomy, people could not have been either punished or rewarded prior to the emergence of morality, but of course they were. The longstanding tradition of thematizing all aspects of morality under the general heading 'freedom *versus* determination', and under the particular heading 'freedom of the will *versus* determination of the will', obscured rather than illuminated the complexity of the issues involved.

To attribute an act to an actor ('He did it!') means that this person must *answer for it*, irrespective of motivation. The *right* answer to a question about a voluntary act is, as we know, 'I did it.' When God asked, 'Where is your brother Abel?', Cain's answer, 'Am I the keeper of my brother?', was the *wrong* answer. And this is so despite the fact that in this case we are aware of the motivation (envy). Cain was required to answer for his action, not to state his motivation (God did not ask, 'Why did you murder your brother?').

Imagine a community in which all norms are concrete, a community without either abstract norms or abstract values. A person is 'all right', is good, if he or she acts according to regulations, and observes the 'pre-given' hierarchy of norms and rules. The only alternative is deviance. Even in a case such as this there must be a distinction between an involuntary act and voluntary action, at least in relation to *infringing* norms and values. Involuntary infringement is not deviance, and there is nothing to answer for if this happens. Anthropologists provide us with information about communities which fit into this ideal type, for people must answer for their actions irrespective of motivation. It still occurs in certain traditional societies that any member of a tight-knit community (or family) can answer for actions committed by *another* member of the same community (or family). This is another indication of the absolute irrelevance of whether a motivation is of a deliberated or a passionate nature.

Regarding the *voluntary* character of an act, the question of 'freedom' is not to be raised. To consider whether the actor *could have acted otherwise* is *irrelevant*. If a person observes the rules, the question is senseless; if this person infringes the rules, it is irrelevant. Put bluntly, to consider why people do things which are taken for granted by everyone, themselves included, and whether one is free to do something else, is nonsensical. (It contradicts 'taken-for-grantedness'.) On such grounds we might even consider whether we are free to jump along the street instead of walking along it, or whether we are free to stop greeting one another. Such examples indicate that, if a kind of action is taken for granted by everyone, ourselves included, we reflect upon the 'freedom' of acting differently as little as do so-called 'primitive' peoples. Yet there is no doubt as to the fact that *we* are the ones who do these things (who walk, greet others and the like). The problem of 'freedom or determination' can only be raised after the emergence of *morality*. There must be something beyond the *concrete* norms and their concrete hierarchy to *rely upon*. There must be something which is *not* taken completely for granted. There must be something *open to choice* and so something to deliberate upon, a choice of *moral relevance*. Of course, humans always choose between *alternatives* as far as applying regulations goes. Yet such alternatives are not *moral* in character. If I decide *not to greet* X, I must have a reason for doing so, and this reason must be rooted in *something other* than the custom of greeting.

If the problem of the *freedom* or *determination* of my action can only be raised from the perspective of morality, this holds all the more for the problem of autonomy. The emergence of morality is concomitant with an increasing *differentiation of the Self*, albeit not with the same form of differentiation in all cultures and in all Selves. How and to what extent the Self becomes differentiated depends on the extent and the quality of the type of self-reflection I have termed *double-quality self-reflection*. Here I take a step further. Empirical self-reflection is an empirical human universal. Without self-reflection of this kind I could not possibly tell voluntary from involuntary action. I compare my experience of myself as an actor with my experience of other actors who abide by concrete norms. Thus I can tell whether I have done the right thing or the wrong thing. With double-quality reflection (the unity of empirical and transcendental reflection), I reflect upon myself not only from the standpoint of concrete norms given as *experience* but also from the standpoint of abstract norms, abstract virtue norms and abstract values – that is, from the standpoint of *ideas*. Ideas as such are *not* experienced: we do not experience 'courage' or 'dignity' *as such*. What we experience is the people who live up to these norms and the people who do not. Furthermore, the differentiated Self is not completely open to experience either. We differentiate our Self by ordering experiences into theoretical ideas such as 'reason', 'will' and 'inclination'. We *experience* concrete emotions, we experience our cognitive processes, we experience our purposes, but we *do not* experience 'reason', 'will' or 'inclination'. If we differentiate ourselves from the perspective of certain *practical ideas* via *theoretical ideas*, our self-reflection will be characterized by an admixture of a posteriori and a priori elements. The *Self* as *morality* is both *subjected to and created by* this double-quality reflection and self-reflection.

This is not to say that after the emergence of morality the distinction between voluntary and involuntary action is relegated to the background. This distinction remains of primary importance. What does happen is that voluntary action itself is 'subdivided', for it is attributed not to the Self as such but to one or another aspect of the already differentiated Self. Questions such as these can be asked: 'Was the action willed or not?' (action is related here to the idea of 'will'); 'Was the consequence of the action the purpose of the action or not?' (action is related here to the content of 'will'); 'Did we or did we not know what we were doing?' (action is related to the truth content of knowledge, to 'theoretical reason'); 'Did some passion carry us away?' (action is related to the idea of 'inclination', 'passions', 'unconscious' and the like). If the action was not willed, if the consequence of the action was unintended, if we did not know what we were doing, if we were at odds with a passion that carried us away, then we shall be sorry for what we have done, we shall wish to undo it, we shall suggest reparation, 'make up for it', atone for it, or ask for forgiveness or even for punishment. However, all this is applicable if and only if the act was *voluntary* (an action). I may also be very remorseful over an involuntary act, but to allow myself to feel incapacitating pangs of conscience as a result of an involuntary act, and as a consequence offer reparation or ask for punishment, would be to indulge in sheer moral hysteria. The importance of distinguishing between voluntary and involuntary acts can be demonstrated in either simple or complex cases. If someone jumps in front of your car, running him over is obviously an involuntary act (not an action). If you ignore a traffic light and then run over someone, this is an action and by definition voluntary. Whether you have done this on purpose, through negligence, because of intoxication or for any other reason, does not change the simple fact that you were the author of the act, you performed it. My intention here is to indicate in advance that to judge an action as *almost* involuntary (but never completely so) is always irrelevant from the perspective of a *single choice*. Yet it is not completely irrelevant from the perspective of *autonomy*. I turn now to these matters.

Although the problem of free choice (as *liberum arbitrium*)[2] *versus* the determination of choice, and the problem of autonomy *versus* heteronomy, are intrinsically related, given that 'freedom *versus* determination' is the cornerstone in both, their *referents* are different in kind. The referent of *liberum arbitrium* is action; the referent of autonomy is character. There is no contradiction involved in the assertion that a *completely* autonomous moral person has no choice whatsoever. Philosophers can disagree about what autonomy is and if and how it can be achieved, but they all basically agree, from Aristotle through Spinoza to Kierkegaard, that the actions of a fully autonomous human being, if there can be such a person, are absolutely determined, namely by the autonomous Self.

Theories of 'freedom' and 'determination' are simultaneously *practical* and *meta-ethical*. They are meta-ethical in that they supply an answer to an *ontological* problem without including or excluding the validation or devalidation of any single moral norm, virtue or value. They are practical in that they are themselves *open to choice to the same extent* as single moral norms. Dominating meaningful world-views sometimes *canonize* an ontological theory, and if this happens an adverse choice will be highly unlikely. However, a similar situation obtains where certain moral norms are canonized by a meaningful world-view. The canonization of *any* ontological (meta-ethical) theory indicates by itself the *presence* of morality, the presence of the *problem* of the freedom or determination of choice, and this is precisely why the ontology too is a matter of choice, though it can be asserted that one was determined to choose between the ontology of freedom and that of determination, or that the ontology of freedom was chosen because of the determination to choose such. If the dominating meaningful world-view does not canonize an ontology (which is the case now), the directly practical relevance of the aforementioned meta-theories lies at hand. The choice of a theory of this kind not only provides a framework for ordering life experiences, but also a framework for interpreting duties, obligations, responsibilities, for affirming motivations for certain actions or, conversely, motivations for inaction. It deserves to be mentioned that both the theory of 'freedom of choice' and that of 'determination of choice' can, for their part, mobilize life experience, particularly if the theory is about *moral* choice. Sometimes we *feel* that we choose freely, that we can do either this or that. We feel that the future is *open* and that good and evil *hinge upon a particular decision*, and on it alone. Sometimes we *feel* that whatever we do we are like a puppet on a string, and that it is an alien power, good or bad, that pulls the string. We feel that our decision is only an apparent one and not a real one, for nothing depends on us. We feel that fate governs the world, our world as well as the world of others. In fact we can experience both these feelings, and we can even vacillate between them.

To this point, I have left open the problem of which of the two ontologies yields the *better* and the *truer* theory. This issue can be more easily approached the other way round. I therefore contend that the theory of total determination is *theoretically false* and *morally wrong*. This contention can be supported by both logical inference and empirical observation.

Apel introduced a very ingenious refutation of the theory of determination to demonstrate that it involves a serious logical fallacy. According to Apel, were we completely determined by our psychology or our society in making a choice, ethical or otherwise, we could not possibly raise validity claims or truth claims. However, if we could not so do, we could not claim either that absolute determinism is true.

I would proceed on ground that is more empirical than this. To exemplify the dilemma of freedom *versus* determination, I prefer to thematize what could be called *longue durée* in human life: the *continuum* rather than the isolated moment. Thus I shall address the question of whether people can *change* themselves within a given limit. If we conclude that people can change themselves (within this limit) then we must also assume that such a change is the result of single, chronological, albeit interrelated, voluntary actions. If we assume only this much, we have not yet made a case *for* the acceptance of the theory of *liberum arbitrium* but we have certainly made a *case against* the theory of total determination.

Now, we do practically assume that people can indeed change their moral make-up to some degree, for otherwise speech acts such as advising, passing judgement and encouraging would simply be exercises in self-righteousness and vanity. Everyday language users take it for granted (and we need no greater certitude) that all such speech acts make sense, so we can assert with Wittgenstein that 'changing ourselves' constitutes a series of voluntary actions. We equally know that speech acts such as these do not by themselves *determine* any change, for the listener can reject as well as accept our advice. As we only have indirect evidence of the internal goings-on of another Self, and since introspection is not a reliable basis on which to make sweeping generalizations, it would be best to illustrate our assumption by examining the external occurrences of other selves; that is, by examining the *visible body*. Let us say that we are talking to an obese man; in advising him to do something

about his obesity we assume that he is *able* to do so, that his looks
are not the result of fate but depend, in part, on him as well. Goethe
rightly said that over the age of thirty one is *responsible* for one's
own face. This obviously does not mean that one is responsible for
the colour of one's eyes or the shape of one's face, but it does mean
that one determines whether one displays an attentive, a friendly, an
intelligent face, or conversely, a dull, a rude, a cruel face. Since the
Self is a whole, that which is true about a change in your external
constitution is also true about a change in your moral constitution.
If you have gorged yourself with self-interest, self-complacency or
indifference, if you are obese with envy, vanity or resentment, you
can still look to the good advice of a 'moral diet' and take exercises
in empathy, sympathy, rational conduct and the like. In other
words, one's 'moral constitution' too can change, given time. It is
also obvious that changing moral habits is *not equally* easy for each
'morally obese' person, that some will not change even if they accept
the advice, and, finally, that some will not accept the advice at all.
The latter stance is, by the way, proof, rather than disproof, of the
controversial 'free choice' theory, to which I now turn.

The issue I raise here is that of 'free choice', not that of 'freedom
of the Will'. The idea of Will is a metaphysical construct. We will
different things but we do not have a Will. This fact alone would
not prevent me from using the category of Will, for no philosophy
can help but operate with certain metaphysical constructs. Rather, I
reject the metaphysical construct of 'Will' on holistic grounds. I do
this because I believe, as already argued, that the Self, albeit
differentiated, does not consist of distinct *faculties*, one faculty being
the source of one kind of action, another that of another kind of
action. To quote Hegel, the Self is not a soul-bag. I aver that the
different *attitudes* of the Self should not be ascribed to separate
faculties, because all faculties (empirical in nature) are mobilized in
all attitudes, albeit in different proportions, combinations and so on.

The 'free choice' theory is believed to be the ontological
cornerstone of morality. Indeed, if people could not choose between
Good and Bad (Evil), morality would only exist as a false semblance
(*Schein*). The choice between Good and Bad (Evil) is realized or
comes about in concrete, single choices. Before I embark on a
certain action, I must first determine whether this action is good,
bad or indifferent from a moral viewpoint. If I see this action as bad
from a moral viewpoint but good from another viewpoint (it
furthers my self-interest, it is pleasant, and so on), I can either
embark upon it or forgo embarking upon it. This is a *matter of
choice*. I *can* decide either for or against. The same holds true if I am

confronted with alternative patterns of possible actions. Before I embark on one of them I must first determine which of these possible actions is morally superior, though I can still embark on an action of a less positive, even of a negative, moral nature. Freedom of choice, then, means that I *can* choose action A or action B.

Still, it is a commonplace that options open to choice are always restricted, and restricted for certain people more than for others. It is also a commonplace that access to sublime moral reasoning has always been a privilege, and that to a certain degree it still is. However, whether the scope of choice is wide or narrow, we must assume the existence of some scope in every possible case because the choice is created by our *attitude* towards the situation. We *open up* an avenue to choice in so far as we regard our situation as a *moral situation*. To put this more cautiously, we construe a new alternative for choice in so far as we regard our situation as a moral situation. An isolated action choice can be pictured graphically: two paths are open before me and I turn left or right (or stay put). That such situations exist is beyond doubt. Yet other situations do not lend themselves to graphic representation. For example, a particular path, once I become aware of it, can shine in the light of absolute certitude like Jacob's ladder. Such a choice of the absolute differs from the choice between two paths. I do not ruminate whether I should turn right or left. Instead, the idea carries me away. I can take my chance, I can make my bet and engage myself; I can put my entire personality in the balance. This attitude can be described as the resolve to carry out a series of actions. It can be argued that the great variety of choice patterns makes no difference; that the gist of the matter is that everyone could have chosen a different course from the one actually chosen. But how can we know this? And why is it important in *moral consideration and judgement* that every single decision could have taken a different and even opposite course?

Let us approach this issue from another angle. Once an action is undertaken it cannot be undone. One can in retrospect repent a decision for moral reasons; one can be sorry about an action after having come to grief. Yet, even if you cry out in despair, 'I should not have done that! I should have known better than that!', the act itself will not be undone, although it might eventually be counterbalanced by a new choice (new action). If the original action choice was similar to the graphic representation of *liberum arbitrium*, then in retrospect it will appear as a *mere accident*. Mere accident is more closely affiliated with the concepts of 'fate' and 'necessity' than with that of freedom. If, however, we have taken a *calculated* risk and engaged ourselves, if the path selected has shone in the light of absolute certitude, then in retrospect the action will *not* appear as a mere accident. It could be argued that all single actions imply an element of chance, are partly of the nature of an accident. This is a generalized ontological statement and I for one do not know if it is true or false. Yet, even if it were true, the answers to the questions 'An accident to *what degree?*' and '*What kind* of accident?' are implied in one or the other action choice, and have been left open.

'Free choice' theory is a kind of *ontological pointillisme*. It centres our freedom upon *single choices*. It equalizes all our single choices as if they had an identical structure and an identical weight. It equalizes all situations imposed upon us and opened up by us. It assumes that we constantly choose and that we invariably start choosing from square one. Every minute is conceived as the absolute present, every decision as the absolute accident. To my mind this is all erroneous.

For one obvious reason, it is worth giving further attention to this matter. Contemporary 'rational choice' theory is but a streamlined version of *liberum arbitrium*. It advises us that there are firm and incontestable principles for rational choice in *all* situations. To act according to these principles is tantamount to choosing rationally. Although 'rational choice' theory forgoes direct 'ontologization', it is guilty of ontological *pointillisme*. It pins our freedom on *single* events rationally chosen. It equalizes all our single choices as if they had an identical structure or an identical weight. It disregards the possibility that a situation can be opened up by us.[3] Rational choice is described as a choice of means to achieve certain ends. Both our goals and the value hierarchy of our goals are treated as constants (not open to rational choice). Yet the fact is that every time we 'take a chance' (a calculated risk), every time we are carried away by some kind of 'certainty' (to mention only two of the many possible ways), we *choose goals* or *choose a new value hierarchy*. Thus the 'rational choice' situation is the very situation which can be graphically presented by the juncture of paths A, B and C, plus the person standing at this juncture and deciding which path to take. In this theory, only one item is added to the picture: we can calculate which path is rational. Yet this addition is not a plus but rather a minus compared to the traditional *liberum arbitrium* theory, at least where the choice of *moral content* is concerned. Consider the following situation: a person is vilified in the presence of a number of people and in her absence and I choose to defend her, although this is against my well-considered interest. Can this choice be described in the following terms: I have two goals; one stands higher than the other; I choose the means to realize this (second) goal? Such a presentation would be laughable, and rightly so. If I am asked whether I have done a particular thing and I answer in the affirmative (I tell the truth and take the consequences), what is my goal, what are the best means to achieve it? It can of course be argued that my *end* was to become honest, and this is why I chose the best means to this end. But what if *I am honest*? What if I tell the truth *because I am honest*? In this case it is clear that honesty is not the goal but the *ground* of my telling the truth. If one operates with the *pointillisme* of separate choices, one cannot assume that the *character* of the person *grounds* the choice. Furthermore, the 'rational choice' theory insists that, if we do not know how our goal(s) can best be achieved, we must postpone action. One could answer to this that sometimes you must postpone action, sometimes you must not. Here too a decision, a choice, is involved; whether you must or must not act. If your friend is in mortal danger and you are unsure of the best means to save his life, you must not postpone action, you must take a chance (otherwise your friend will die). If, however, you are unsure about advising your friend on a matter which might contribute to his happiness or unhappiness, you can decide to postpone or to take action – here is the choice.

Further, the 'rational choice' theory insists that if two goals are equal (in value and desirability) I should decide upon the one which is most easily achieved. Certain Stoic philosophers argued the reverse: that it is better, and thus morally more rational, to choose the goal more difficult to achieve. Both of these are sweeping generalizations. If equally valuable goals (or values which are not goals) are already *given*, it is not *morally irrational* to choose the 'difficult path', precisely *because* it is difficult, because it is the *greater challenge*. It depends not only upon the *particular situation* whether this or that path is more rational from a moral viewpoint, but also upon the *character of the actors*. The character of the actor is *part* of the situation in which the choice is made, and what is more rational for one person may well be less so for another person. For example, if you have a lot of doubt about your will power, it is clearly more rational for you to choose the goal that is easier to attain (if both goals are equally valuable and desirable), whereas, if you have great self-confidence, the opposite will most likely be true.

To sum up, one can reject the theory of determination without having fully to defend the 'free choice' theory. Although we must presume that in most cases people could have acted differently from either the way in which they in fact decided to act or the way in which they acted without having first made a reasoned decision, we cannot presume that this is so in all cases. *The idea of moral freedom* can be considered, defended and verified (indirectly) without denying the *determination of certain choices.* Put more emphatically, *only if we can think that certain moral choices are completely determined can we think of the idea of moral freedom without contradiction.* The idea of moral freedom is the idea of *moral autonomy.* As I have pointed out, *if a completely autonomous moral being existed, all of this person's relevant actions would be completely self-determined.* A fully autonomous moral being could not have any moral choice at all. Philosophers who have made a case for full moral autonomy have theorized it in very different ways: 'moral autonomy' *à la* Spinoza and 'moral autonomy' *à la* Kant have very little in common theoretically. Yet I repeat that, despite theoretical differences, all of them agree on one point: complete and full moral autonomy *is* the determination of all acts by freedom.

In what follows I am going to make a case for *relative autonomy.* Human autonomy cannot but be relative. Human autonomy *should* be relative. But autonomy it is and should be. Within the framework of a general ethics the emphasis must be put on the quasi-empirical element of the theory of *moral autonomy.*

'Autonomy' is the ontological term for personal freedom. *Absolute autonomy* means that the person is *fully free* qua *person.* Relative autonomy means that a person *qua* person is free to a certain degree, but not fully so.[4] *Absolute heteronomy* means that the person *qua* person is fully determined by factors external to him/herself. *Relative heteronomy* means that the person *qua* person is subjected to certain constraints or authorities external to him/herself. *Relative heteronomy presupposes relative autonomy and* vice versa, *whereas absolute autonomy excludes both absolute and relative heteronomy. Absolute autonomy* means that the person is a *fully free moral agent.* This means that every morally relevant act of this person stems from his or her character alone; that these acts are totally determined by his or her freedom; that whatever this person does cannot be other than the good and right thing; that his or her pure conscience or pure practical reason is the sole guide. An absolutely autonomous moral person cannot act according to any norm or rule the validity (the goodness) of which this person has not first verified according to the criteria of intrinsic goodness laid down in his or her conscience. No constraint can induce this person to infringe any norm or rule which his or her conscience has concluded is good, and thus valid. *Absolute moral heteronomy* means that the person *qua* person is a complete puppet in every morally relevant action. There are two types of strings with this puppet: the strings of the concrete norms and rules of the environment, which are taken for granted by this person, and the strings of 'personal interest', desires and passions. *Relative moral heteronomy* means that the person *qua* person can be subject to situational constraints of a nature such that acts of moral relevance must be carried out that this person would not be willing to carry out if these constraints did not exist. *Relative moral autonomy presupposes relative moral heteronomy*, and *vice versa*, whereas absolute moral autonomy excludes both absolute and relative moral heteronomy. One can *theoretically* conceive of a person who has absolute autonomy *and* absolute moral autonomy (as Spinoza did). Likewise, one can theoretically conceive of the simultaneity of absolute moral autonomy and relative heteronomy. Yet, in order to construct such a model, one must divide the person into two (into 'personality', on the one hand, and 'person', on the other) as Kant did. But absolute moral autonomy and absolute heteronomy cannot even be imagined as being together. ('Legality' was not *absolutely* heteronomous in Kant, only relatively so. Otherwise his doctrine of law and his political philosophy would have been sheer nonsense.) Relative moral autonomy and absolute heteronomy cannot be imagined as being together either. *Yet relative moral autonomy and relative heteronomy presuppose one another.*

The above distinctions have not been made for the sake of a pedantic exercise. When I stated that relative moral autonomy goes not only with relative moral heteronomy but also with relative heteronomy/relative autonomy, I did *not* equate autonomy and moral autonomy or heteronomy and moral heteronomy. As much as moral autonomy and autonomy, and moral heteronomy and heteronomy, are interlocked, the referent of the respective terms is different in kind. 'Autonomy' refers to all possible actions, whereas 'moral autonomy' refers only to actions of moral provenance or moral content. The importance of this distinction becomes clear in every instance of *specification*. The notion 'relative' covers a large number of possibilities, ranging from 'almost absolute' moral autonomy to 'almost absolute' moral heteronomy, from 'almost absolute' autonomy to 'almost zero' autonomy. If we look at this continuum from 'more' to 'less', it at once becomes obvious why I have spent so much time on a seemingly insignificant differentiation. A given degree of moral autonomy can go together with a quite different degree of autonomy, and *vice versa*. A tyrant can be *almost* completely autonomous yet have very little moral autonomy, whereas a slave may have very little autonomy and yet be highly morally autonomous. I shall return to this problem shortly.

I stated that one can *think* absolute autonomy as well as absolute moral autonomy. Yet we cannot imagine *actors* as being 'absolutely' autonomous or morally autonomous. *Amor dei intellectualis* is an attitude of *sheer contemplation*; the absolute autonomy of the Kantian *homo noumenon* rests on the *choice of universal maxims for action* (a speculative, mental process). It is not extended to action itself. Yet if a person has achieved autonomy only through the attitude of contemplation, she or he has not achieved autonomy of that kind as a person. For the person always switches from action to contemplation and back to action again. If 'autonomy' is the ontological term for personal freedom, and if the person is constituted both in action and in contemplation, autonomy, and, similarly, moral autonomy, cannot be other than relative.

From here onwards I shall restrict the discussion to the problem of *moral autonomy*, and I shall refer to autonomy/heteronomy in forms different from that of just moral, from the viewpoint of moral autonomy alone. And, since it is understood that the moral autonomy of a person is relative, I shall no longer append the adjective 'relative' to the compound noun 'moral autonomy'. Further, as I have suggested, the term 'relative' can stand for 'almost absolute' and 'almost zero' autonomy alike. Yet, if the counterfactual ideal of moral autonomy is absolute moral autonomy, we must reserve the term 'moral autonomy' for that form of relative autonomy which comes closest to the counterfactual ideal of moral autonomy. I term this kind of moral autonomy *maximum moral autonomy*. Maximum moral autonomy is still relative moral autonomy, yet it is the *maximum* possible degree of moral autonomy. Finally, it is assumed that 'maximum moral autonomy' does not presuppose specific endowments, not even specific moral endowments. Consequently, the term 'moral autonomy' stands for maximum relative moral autonomy.

If morality exists, a certain degree of autonomy also exists. Morality has been viewed here as the individual component of the practical relationship of the single person to the norms and rules of proper conduct. A person does not obey every prevailing concrete norm, but is also guided by abstract norms, values and ideas, and observes those concrete norms reconfirmed as valid by his or her conscience. Yet it should be constantly remembered that we are discussing here a *practical relationship* to the norms of proper conduct. Morality cannot be 'located' in the mind of the actor (the monological model), nor can it be 'located' in the process of rational communication or discourse concerning the validity of norms (the dialogical model). Still, there is no morality without the component of 'monological thinking'; that is, without the dialogue that the Self conducts with itself as a 'two in one', to use Hannah Arendt's formulation. Further, there is no morality without rational communication, because no mind generates norms on its own. One can modify and query only existing norms and rules, norms and rules other people stand for and defend, and more often than not one engages in the process of validation or devalidation together with others, via dialogue, discussion and mutual support, in an atmosphere of conflicting opinions and mutual self-clarification. Nevertheless, morality is not tantamount to value choice, normative choice or action choice. It becomes explicit, it 'comes to its notion' in actions *other than mental acts or speech acts*. Morality means 'acting out' normative commitments, and not only in this or that situation but *continuously*. Morality has no other 'locus' but *Sittlichkeit*; it is the *attitude* individuals *take up* within the ethical life of a community. In short, morality is nothing but *moral autonomy* constituted, preserved, enlarged and maintained in every action of moral relevance. Moral autonomy is the freedom to choose the course of action which accords with the norms a person has accepted as valid. Here, 'choice' means *engagement*. One engages oneself, commits oneself, and *does* what one is committed to doing. One acts with others, for others, against others. Both the *critical* aspect of moral autonomy (devalidation, rejection of certain concrete norms of conduct) and the *positive* aspect of moral autonomy (standing up for abstract norms, ideas, and even for universal norms) are *actualized* in interaction.

If we mention 'good persons', 'good characters', 'virtuous persons', we have in mind *morally autonomous persons*. We are confident that such people will not be manipulated by circumstances, raw opinions, their own passions and inclinations. It is unnecessary to assume that all the actions and choices of such persons are, or eventually will be, completely determined by their good character. Yet we do assume that their most decisive actions and choices, though perhaps not all their morally relevant actions or choices, are and will be good, which is to say that they will be determined by their moral character. To refer to a person as a 'good person' is a speech act of *basic trust*. This speech act (judgement) would make no sense if moral autonomy did not exist.

Everyone can at times be carried away, everyone can err in certain judgements, everyone can act in a manner which in hindsight is lamented. Not even the best person is an exception in this matter. However, a morally autonomous person does not 'rationalize' errors of judgement but admits them and apologizes. And this would occur not under compulsion but in an effort to rectify actions, because this person's character determines his or her acts in this way, because goodness is intrinsic to such a person.

As mentioned, moral autonomy is to be thought of together with relative moral heteronomy and with relative heteronomy.

Relative moral heteronomy is presupposed, for the very reason that no morally autonomous person can test and check the validity of *every* norm and rule of *Sittlichkeit*. And, even if we examine a norm and claim that it can be replaced with a better one, we sometimes need to act according to intersubjectively shared norms, especially if the latter are legally binding. For example, I could make a case for mercy killing as a moral act, and yet refrain from practising this act because it is rejected by others on moral grounds and is illegal. Moreover, if we act together, for or with people whose norms are different from our own, we might even choose *relative* moral autonomy autonomously and decide to act according to *their* norms. A man may disapprove of being married in church and yet marry there, if his partner's moral conscience so demands. Yet norms and rules which not only differ from ours but contradict them in the sense that *we will that they should not be valid or we will that they should not be permitted* cannot be observed by an autonomous moral person.

Relative heteronomy refers not to normative limits to our autonomy but to *social constraints* of non-moral provenance. If we believed that social constraints determine our choices or our personality, we could not make a case for autonomy at all. Yet, even if social constraints do not determine either our choice or our personality, there still exist those 'situations' in which our character is moulded and our actions take place. Sartre illustrated this problem in his play *Les Morts sans Sépulture*. All the *dramatis personae* of this play find themselves in a situation of the gravest constraint: they can choose only between disgraceful submission to Evil and death. All of them finally choose death, yet each chooses a different form of death, *his or her own death*. True enough, this decision, the most difficult of all decisions to bear, is the easiest problem to solve on the theoretical level, because the decision to die is similar to a withdrawal into the realm of mere contemplation in so far as it is withdrawal from any subsequent action. And I could also turn here to Kant's model case, that of telling a lie in a situation of choice. Kant was right: telling a lie because the situation so dictates contradicts absolute moral autonomy. But it does not contradict maximum moral autonomy (which is always relative). 'Telling a lie' is foreign to the moral character of a good person, yet a good person can still lie if the alternative is something contrary to his or her moral character to the same or a greater extent. Of course, Kant made a case for (relative) heteronomy, for otherwise the imperative would not be *categorical*, but he dismissed the problem of situated choice, the choice under constraint, as irrelevant. Yet it is precisely under social constraints that we must act as autonomous moral beings, and as autonomous moral beings we *can* act under such constraints.

Plato's dictum is that it is better to suffer wrong than to wrong others. Obviously, such a choice only exists amidst social constraints. No person likes to suffer wrong. Suffering wrong is the state of heteronomy because in suffering wrong we are 'acted upon' by others, because others do something to us we would not choose for ourselves, because something is being done to us that does not emanate from our character. Yet, even if the choice between suffering and committing wrong is a choice amidst heteronomy, *the choice itself* can be morally autonomous, and fully so. If I choose to suffer wrong rather than commit it, I make this choice out of my moral autonomy.

The statement 'It is better to suffer wrong than to commit wrong' cannot be proved. What can be proved is only this: that there *are* people who prefer to suffer wrong than to commit wrong. These are the people we can call *morally good*. The morally good are all those men and women who in their *practical* everyday living *underwrite the truth* of the assertion that it is better to suffer wrong than to commit wrong.

I end up by defining *moral autonomy* as maximum moral autonomy. A person is morally autonomous if he or she prefers to suffer wrong than to wrong others because it is *better* for him or her to suffer wrong than to commit it. We cannot even think of moral evil as morally autonomous, as a morally evil person would perforce choose to wrong others rather than to suffer wrong. Evil can be viewed as relatively autonomous, but not as morally autonomous. The definition of moral autonomy is the definition of the good (honest) person.[5]

Thus, moral autonomy (goodness as honesty) and relative heteronomy presuppose one another. This is not said in defence of social and other constraints. Rather, the opposite is the case. Morally autonomous people are the people who challenge social constraints. They 'void' the legitimacy of social domination and power. They are the real heroes of resistance.

I cannot emphasize frequently enough that moral autonomy (the 'idea' of moral autonomy) is pre-eminently practical. Those who accept as true the assertion 'It is better to suffer wrong than to commit it', and when the chips are down prefer to commit wrong than to suffer it, are *not* morally autonomous but heteronomous. Those who accept as true the assertion 'It is better to suffer wrong than to commit it' and yet withdraw from all kinds of action into the solitude of mere contemplation, are neither morally autonomous nor morally heteronomous, for contemplative sympathy with the good, attractive as it may be, is rather adiaphoric.

4

Responsibility

The actor is always responsible. Or, to use Goethe's formulation, the actor is always guilty, and only the spectator is innocent. This premise should really be read the way Schutz put it: pure mental acts are reversible, but actions are irreversible. Before we embark on an action, while we are still in the stage of deliberation, everything can be undone. The process of action transmutes the reversible into the irreversible. Once an act has been undertaken, it is in the world, either reinforcing or conflicting with the acts of others, and we are no longer in control. Every act that stems from an action – that is, from *voluntary acting* – is a *precedent*. While performing actions, we create precedents. And we must answer for the precedents we have established. Responsibility accompanies the duty to assume responsibility. Assuming responsibility for an act stemming from my action means, first and foremost, responding to the question 'Who did it?' 'I did', or to the question 'Have you done this or that?' 'Yes I have.' Whether the action is meritorious, morally indifferent, morally controversial, wrong, criminal or wicked, the performer of the action is always responsible and, all other conditions being equal, *equally* so. However, everyday language users normally associate 'responsibility' with 'wrongdoing': they speak of being responsible in relation to reprehensible actions. And, without being correct, this one-sided use of the concept suits the purpose. Rarely are people reluctant to take responsibility for actions that both they and others consider meritorious or morally indifferent. Since a virtuous or meritorious act is not a debt-guilt (*Schuld*) which must be duly settled via some form of reparation, but rather a credit which should be honoured by *others*, the refusal to take responsibility in a matter of merit is either not a moral matter or it is a supererogatory act. Although the notion 'responsibility' has shifted towards taking on the meaning of 'responsibility for mischief', one *attributes* good acts to actors to the same degree as acts of misconduct. Attributing an act to an actor is what 'regarding someone as responsible' is all about.

Whereas all actors are by definition responsible for their actions, neither the *amount* nor the *quality* of this responsibility depends on the voluntary character of acting; rather, both depend on several other factors. The main question here is not whether the act is attributable to the actor but whether the *negative content* of the act is attributable to this person. Does this negative content issue from the character of the actor, from one of his or her character traits – that is the first question. Did this person know what the act really meant? Was the act performed under the influence of delusion or illusion? Did the person act under unusual strain, duress, or abnormal social or personal pressure? Was this norm infringed on purpose? If so, what was this purpose? How far and to what extent could this person have done better? These and similar questions are related to *autonomy, but not necessarily to moral autonomy*. If a person follows exclusively his or her self-interest and is strong-willed enough consistently to suppress moral inclinations such as pity and empathy, this actor is relatively, though *not morally*, autonomous. Thus an offence committed out of self-interest can be fully ascribed to one actor, whereas the same offence, if committed under social constraint (heteronomy of a considerable magnitude), may not fully be ascribed to another actor.

The premise that the amount and the quality of responsibility depend on the presence or absence of autonomy is a truism. But, as with every truism, it is only approximately true, because of the high level of abstraction at which it has been formulated. I shall shortly concretize this issue from different perspectives, but first of all the *types* of responsibility must be briefly examined.

In discussing *types* of responsibility I shall for the time being disregard the amount and the quality of responsibility, except for the case where *type* and *amount* coincide.

The two main types of responsibility are *retrospective* and *prospective* responsibility. In the case of retrospective responsibility the noun is always singular, whereas with prospective responsibility the noun can be plural. Hart defines the second type, 'responsibilities', as 'being in charge'.

When in chapter 3 I described the *fact* of responsibility, I only discussed *retrospective* responsibility, not because I believe in its philogenetic primacy as against prospective responsibility but because *we answer* only for something we have done (or have forgone doing when we should have done it). And *making someone* responsible is always a retrospective matter if responsibililty is used as a *moral* term. Of course, every moral term has been used to underpin and legitimize domination, and 'responsibility' is no exception. People were made responsible for being born slaves, women or hunchbacks. But in its proper (moral) use, a person can only be *made* responsible for actions or for forgoing an act.

Everyone is responsible for his or her action, so retrospective responsibility is *general*. But not everyone has prospective responsibility. This type of responsibility is *particular* in kind. If someone assumes a particular *position*, this person also assumes the 'responsibilities' accompanying this position. *Responsibilities* in plural are *obligations*.[1] One can be elected to or selected for a position, one can volunteer for a position, one can inherit a position. But whether one is elected or selected, whether one volunteers or inherits, one is invariably committed to perform all the obligations accompanying the position. If the position is institutional, obligations take the form of concrete norms and rules. If it is not institutional – for example, if a parent volunteers to take the local children on an outing – obligations are only roughly defined, yet they are still present. Although 'responsibilities' alias obligations can be matters of sheer routine, prospective responsibility can also entail a *promise* to go beyond such obligations in the event of something unexpected occurring. Prospective responsibility is 'responsibility towards and for'. The captain of a ship is 'in charge'; he is responsible for every passenger on board, and his obligations consist of both daily routines and certain *norms* which should be obeyed in extreme situations. (For example, in the event of shipwreck the captain is the last to leave the vessel.) Or, if something else unexpectedly happens, such as an epidemic breaking out, it is again the captain who should secure the well-being of all the passengers, although in doing so he may not be able to proceed 'by the book'. Here, the passengers have no 'responsibilities', though they are responsible for their actions (as well as for forgoing actions they ought to have performed). The adult passenger who leaps for the lifeboat, leaving children behind, is indeed responsible for this action, and must answer for it. However, should a crew member act likewise his responsibility will not only be greater but also be different in kind: this person has infringed not only a moral norm but also an obligation, an unconditional *promise* (such a person having not only a responsibility but also 'responsibilities').

We should not conclude from this that certain people have responsibilities, and responsibilities alone, whilst others have no prospective but only retrospective responsibility. The two main kinds of responsibility are not 'allocated' to two different groups of people. Nowadays everyone, or almost everyone, has certain responsibilities alias obligations, and normally more than one set of them. To the extent that these are sets of obligations, they all carry the same weight, and if they do not carry the same weight this does not follow from their being obligations but concerns the *consequences* of *positionally* different obligations. *The 'position of consequence'* goes with obligations the infringement of which carries the gravest *consequences*. But this is a matter to be discussed later. Where we have obligations we are in a position similar to that of the ship's crew. Where we have none, we are like the passengers. We are all both members of a particular crew (or several crews) and passengers simultaneously; thus we all have certain responsibilities (of greater or less consequence) and we all perform actions having nothing whatsoever to do with our obligations. For actions of the latter type we are only responsible retrospectively.

The distinction between the two main kinds of responsibility is so old and so much taken for granted that it has often eluded examination. When Cain answers God's question 'Where is your brother Abel?' by asking in turn, 'Am I my brother's keeper?', he disavows *prospective* responsibility. He declares that he is not his brother's keeper in so far as he disclaims responsibility for his brother's whereabouts. But in fact he was questioned about his retrospective responsibility, his responsibility for his action (in this case, fratricide), which he certainly has irrespective of obligations towards his brother. When the sons of Jacob experiment with the idea of fatricide, Reuben averts the murder by referring to their *prospective responsibilities*: the father had committed Joseph to their care. In this sense, the tyrant is a criminal who commits crimes against those in his charge.

As mentioned, retrospective responsibility is the overarching category, even if responsibility is prospective. Yet, if prospective responsibility is also the case, then *not doing what should have been done* is almost as weighty an offence as doing something that should not have been done. Of course, the gravity of the offence depends mainly on its *character*, and this, again, depends on various factors. In this respect guilt by omission cannot be more leniently treated because obligations are normally concrete: people *know* what their obligations are. Obligations are also *public knowledge*, and one cannot plead ignorance in respect of them. Neglecting such obligations, forgoing them, entails *knowing* perfectly well that something has not been done that should have been done, and it entails others knowing this too. This is why the forgoing of an obligatory act becomes a *debt* (*Schuld*) owed to one's community (the people in your charge and those who put them in your charge), so one must *answer* for it. If there is an authority *above* the person in charge, forgoing an act when one ought to have acted calls for punishment. Moreover, not acting in the way one should have acted is an offence *irrespective of consequences* (negative consequences only aggravate the situation).

With pure retrospective responsibility, however, action is always a graver matter than inaction. This is so even if you forgo acting *before the public eye*. Everyone with a sound mind knows the difference between beating a person up and standing by whilst a person is being beaten up. In the latter case you may consider your own well-being ('Look at what would happen to me if I got involved!'), unlike the policeman, who is *obliged* to interfere. No one will punish you for failing to intervene, but everyone will praise you if you do intervene. There is no merit in merely performing an obligation; yet there is merit in not forgoing action if this action is not obligatory. It often happens that only you yourself know that you have not done something you should have done, or that only a few people know it. If you notice that your friend is deeply depressed, but decide for reasons of self-interest not to talk to him about the reasons for this depression, and this friend commits suicide shortly afterwards, no one but you will know that you might have helped him but did not. You answer only to yourself. It is easy to detect here a kind of *responsibility*. The very fact that *not* forgoing an act if this act is not obligatory is considered *meritorious* indicates the presence of responsibility (responsibility for a good and eventually a supererogatory action). But, if there is responsibility for the good (meritorious, supererogatory) action, there must also be some responsibility for inaction.

The main elements of responsibility over inaction (if responsibility is merely retrospective) are therefore as follows: you *answer* first and foremost to your own conscience; you can plead *ignorance* ('I didn't know the cause of my friend's depression; I didn't notice that he was on the brink of suicide'); you can plead *self-interest* ('Had I intervened in the brawl, I should have been badly hurt'). Finally, you can plead with reference to *consequences*, and in three ways: had I interfered, the consequences would have been even worse; the consequences of my inaction were not grave; or, had I interfered, the consequences would have been just the same.

Retrospective responsibility can again be subdivided into responsibility X and responsibility A.

In all communities there are basic norms prescribing what

everyone must do or what everyone must refrain from doing. These norms I have termed 'imperatives'. Responsibility X is the responsibility related to the infringement of any of these basic norms. I term it responsibility 'X' because, if one of these norms is infringed, something has been done that no one must do or something has not been done that everyone should do. Only with *imperatives* is it the case that failing to act when one should act carries an equal weight to doing something that must not be done. The infringement of the imperative of *static justice* (if norms and rules constitute a social cluster, the same norms and rules must be applied to all members of the cluster consistently and continuously) implies *both* doing something you must not do and not doing something you should do, for in discriminating in favour of some and against others you forgo the fulfilment of norms. Every member of a community should be just. I mention static justice because in the main this is the only general imperative that in *modern times* induces us *to do* the right thing, and not only to forgo doing the wrong thing. General positive commandments carrying responsibility X beyond justice are no longer *conspicuous* (commandments such as performing our duties to God, honouring our parents as stated in the Bible, or participating in the political business of the city and in the business of war as the ancient Greeks knew it, and, as even Socrates was aware, being determined to prove that he had not neglected these duties). The general negative imperatives have in modernity taken a legal form. No one should commit murder or break into his fellow citizen's house: anyone who does so will answer for it.

Responsibility A is a far more complex matter. A person is responsible in terms of responsibility A for an action or for forgoing an action if this person *either should have performed a particular action or should have forgone a particular action* when in the given context no such obligation prevailed for anyone else. Responsibility A is therefore the case if a person is endowed with abilities that others are not endowed with or is in a situation that others are not in, where both 'abilities' and 'situation' pertain to *privileged knowledge*. Abilities based on privileged knowledge as well as situations involving privileged knowledge are concerned with imperatives to perform certain actions not everyone else must perform (alternatively, one must refrain from such actions if this knowledge is not available). If a person having privileged knowledge does not do the right thing or in fact does the wrong thing, this person invokes 'responsibility A'. If a child is drowning, those who can swim are responsible for its death if they do not attempt a rescue; those who cannot swim are not responsible. If a professional boxer does not intervene in an attack, and lets an innocent person be beaten up, his responsibility is in the form of responsibility A. If in the middle of a civil war a person learns that prisoners are being executed and that no one else knows of this, and yet this person does not act to halt this grave infringement of the just conduct of war, this inaction involves responsibility A. If someone has a heart attack on a 'plane and there is a doctor on board who does not respond to the call but remains silent, he is responsible for the harm caused, even if he is not formally in charge of the passengers. An example of responsibility A for refraining from action (where the person ought not have acted because of a lack of privileged knowledge) is the following situation: a person volunteers to guide a group of hikers who intend to climb a steep mountain. This person doesn't know the terrain at all, but only wants to show off, and owing to this inexperience an accident occurs. The guide invokes responsibility A. He did not refrain from action. Yet responsibility A has further important ramifications.

In discussing responsibility I have not yet mentioned *virtue norms*. We can fulfil virtue norms by being courageous, empathetic, caring, trustworthy, benevolent, magnanimous, liberal, helpful, sincere, tolerant, loyal and the like. And we can act contrary to virtue norms by being cowardly, egoistic, uncaring, untrustworthy, malevolent, petty, illiberal, unhelpful, rancorous, intolerant, stingy, disloyal and the like. There are a number of fundamental virtues in every complex and traditional society buttressed by meaningful worldviews other than the scientific one. Every member of a cluster should display these virtues, just as every member should avoid manifesting their opposites (vices). For example, every male adult in the city state should be courageous, or all Christians should be charitable, humble and godfearing. It is a reasonable assumption that someone who has fundamental vices has responsibility A, for *everyone* should avoid such vices. And yet it has never been required that everyone should manifest *every possible virtue* (above and beyond the fundamental or 'main' virtues). First, it was always well known that certain virtues are *positional*. As Aristotle put it in relation to the donating of money, everyone can be somewhat liberal, but not everyone can be 'magnificent' (in spending) for great public donations presuppose considerable wealth. Further, everyone can practise forgiveness, but not everyone can practice clemency, for the latter implies the holding of public office. In addition, not everyone can practise particular virtues, and this is *not* from reasons of position. Such virtues are supererogatory virtues. In modernity, where we can hardly speak of *any* consensus concerning *fundamental virtues and vices*, no virtue norm (perhaps with the exception of that exhorting courage) can be related to responsibility X. Yet, contrary to MacIntyre's claim, we still think in terms of virtue and vice, so much so that the first moral terms we learn, and the moral terms we most frequently use in everyday life, are *virtue terms* and *vice terms*.

However, even so-called 'fundamental' virtues and vices involve responsibility X only so far as, or so long as, they are identified *with their manifestation in a concrete action*. For example, not taking up the gauntlet is cowardice. Every nobleman should take up the gauntlet, and one who does not is a coward. But, as far as, or as soon as, virtues and vices are regarded rather as *conditions* or *motivations* of action, the infringement of an action norm and the infringement of a virtue norm do not completely coincide. The more deliberation must be used in relation to a prospective action, the more judgemental powers must be used in order to make the right decision. In other words, the more *idiosyncratic* an action becomes, the less will it completely embody virtue or vice. Virtues and vices will thus be regarded as 'character traits' affecting the *judgemental procedure* to a greater or lesser degree directly and the action directly or indirectly.

Virtues and vices are acquired *in action*, even if they have an affinity with the individual 'genetic a priori'. Nevertheless, not all virtues and vices are acquired *in the same kind of action*, though certain virtues acquired in one type of action can be mobilized in performing another type of action. Moreover, virtues and vices are rarely 'all-encompassing'. One can be brave on the battlefield and cowardly before the commander. One can be gentle to family members and cruel to the rest of the world. There is nothing particularly modern in a kind of functional differentiation in relation to practising virtues. Even Aristotle made reference to this. However, owing to the unprecedented differentiation of the separate spheres in modernity, a development to be discussed later, the breaking-down of virtues into sphere-specific subvirtues has gathered momentum in the last few hundred years. It has become more and more difficult to acquire overall virtues except in everyday life. Even so, that which is difficult to achieve is not completely beyond reach. We can still distinguish between responsibility for an act and responsibility for living up to a virtue norm. Consequently, responsibility for our virtues and vices becomes responsibility A almost without exception.

Responsibility for our so-called 'character traits' seems to be a subcase of autonomy, yet autonomy is an *additional* problem in this context, and a complex one. For example, if under considerable social constraint a man acquires vices, he must be considered *less* autonomous, and his responsibility for his character is to be considered a diminished responsibility, whereas under favourable social circumstances this responsibility becomes full responsibility. The same holds true in respect of a substantial genetic deficiency or the lack thereof. As we know, moral autonomy and relative heteronomy presuppose one another, yet, if heteronomy is only slightly relative, any lack of moral autonomy cannot be ascribed to someone as a personal responsibility. But, whereas the examples of general heteronomy just mentioned (heavy social constraint or substantial genetic deficiency) diminish a person's responsibility for his or her character, instances of moral heteronomy rather aggravate it. This is the case with mindless adherence to all concrete norms or commands, lack of will power, or the placing of the goals of power, wealth and pleasure above everything else.

Responsibility A (for our virtues and vices) is, however, related to responsibility X, something discussed by Kant precisely in this context in his *Doctrine of Virtue*. Kant refers to a norm; moreover, to an imperative applying to all of us whatever virtue norms we observe or fail to observe. This imperative is '*Know thyself*'. Knowing oneself is a *moral* imperative. It does not exhort that continuous self-reflection that so often degenerates into narcissism. It says, 'Know your virtues and vices!' One is, of course, responsible for one's virtues and vices, and something can be done about the latter if one can identify them. Yet the imperative 'Know thyself' has further implications. As already argued, responsibility for character and responsibility for action *do not coincide*. Yet, if a person can identify his or her vices, as well as the virtues this person does not excel in, he or she can act as if those vices did not exist. It is thus possible to neutralize, through self-knowledge, problematic character traits, or, to a degree, the incapacity to achieve excellence. And what if this person perceives that certain negative character traits too difficult to control still remain? Since certain vices (as well as certain virtues) become active in particular situations, and none of these is 'all-embracing', one can still choose *not to enter* into situations where residual vices evade control. If a person realizes that he or she is incapable of loving, this person should not accept the love of another, nor marry and have children. If a person senses a deeply ingrained cowardice in his or her character, he or she should not join an underground movement, even if in total agreement with the views of the members. If a person is aware of having an uncontrollable lust for power, he or she should avoid situations that would grant excessive power. To act in these ways is within the power of everyone.

Up to this point, the types of responsibility have been exemplified via a *synchronic model*. The standpoint of *morality* has all along been presupposed to be constitutive of responsibility, since I have repeatedly emphasized that a person rejects certain norms from the vantage point of other, mainly abstract, norms, and reinterprets certain traditional norms by attributing to them a new practical meaning or relevance. Yet in discussing responsibility, prospective or retrospective, X or A, one of the most decisive problems of the 'standpoint of morality' has not even been touched upon. What kind of responsibility does a person bear when, after having rejected a moral norm, this person sets the precedent of infringing that norm for moral reasons? This problem can only be discussed via a *diachronic* model, the model of *moral change* involving at least two parties or groups: those defending traditional norms as valid, and those devalidating them. The act which is an offence, a crime or a sin for one of these groups shines in the light of the most sublime merit in the eyes of the other group. The virtue norm of the first group is no virtue norm at all for the second group. 'Humility is not a virtue', 'Remorse is not a virtue': with these words Spinoza devalidated *fundamental* (consensual) virtues of traditional Christianity. In what follows I shall not address the general problem of historicity and the relativity of moral substances, not even the contradictions between abstract and concrete moral norms, but shall confine myself to the matter of responsibility in the light of changes in moral substances.

To begin with, I return to *prospective responsibility*. If I am 'in charge', I have responsibilities, obligations. I must live up to these responsibilities without fail. Failure to meet any obligations involves an aggravating circumstance of retrospective responsibility. Now I add that this is true *unless* I deny this fulfilment of obligations by taking recourse to a moral principle, idea or abstract norm which *reverses* the moral content of my obligation: what resembled good now appears as evil. This act will be viewed in two opposite lights. Those who have put me 'in charge', as well as all those who believe that the obligation is good, will regard my act as *betrayal*. Those who share my conviction that the obligation lacks goodness, has become irrelevant, or is even evil, those who believe I have acted for the good of those under my charge in violating this obligation, will regard my act as *supererogatory*. Luther married and defied thereby one of the obligations of a Roman Catholic priest. During the First World War certain officers allowed their troops to fraternize with the enemy in flagrant violation of their obligations, and thus contributed to the sudden ending of the war. Under the reign of Nazism, those who forged documents to help persecuted Jews violated the code of officialdom. Ibsen's heroine Nora, who rejected her obligations as wife and mother in order to affirm herself as a personality, stands as a person for all those women who have done the same. All these acts can be, and indeed were, viewed in the twofold manner mentioned above.

These test cases have been selected to exemplify what is at stake here. It is clear from the start that the choice involved in defying obligations from the viewpoint of an idea, a principle or an abstract norm is precisely the kind of choice I have described as *'taking our chance' as our destiny*. Interestingly, Weber referred to a special kind of ethics premised upon the gesture of taking our chance, terming it the 'ethics of responsibility'. Since all possible ethics are ethics of responsibility, one may wonder why Weber thought of attributing responsibility as *differentia specifica* to a relatively rare and controversial type of action pattern. In Weber's view responsibility is taken for the consequences of action. Whether or not there is preliminary reflection upon these consequences, a *kind* of consequence must be borne by those who 'take their chance', and by these people alone. In such cases it is not simply or even primarily the consequences of our particular action that really matters, but rather the consequences of the *value choice* itself. If the norm, value or principle constituting the standpoint of defying our own obligations does not prove to stand higher than the norms of obligation thus defied (both in form and in content), our act will not be supererogatory, but morally controversial and problematic from the standpoint of the *successors*. If the norm, value or principle which constitutes the vantage point of defiance proves to be of *lower* standing both in form and substance, or even only in substance, than the defied norm of obligation, the act will be *evil*, and the person will be regarded by subsequent generations as the repository of this evil. The problem here is that of *evil maxims*. However, if actors 'taking their chance' do so on the basis of maxims which prove to be *higher* in form (more general, more universal) and at least of *equal* (equally good) substance compared to the defied maxims, then the act will mark the *beginning of moral progression* in that aspect of social life in and for which the action occurred. These are the terms under which people can 'take their chance'. Given that in doing so they can introduce a new good or a new evil into the world, the responsibility involved is enormous. Thus I term responsibility of this kind *enormous responsibility*.[2] If someone is not certain that his or her chosen values stand higher than the obligations defied, this person should not assume 'enormous responsibility'. If the normative content of obligations is open to public discourse, it is always advisable to engage in such discourse, wait for the outcome, and then collectively alter certain obligations, instead of just going ahead and infringing them. Of course, even under the most liberal circumstances, certain obligations may not be able to be and even should not be changed, for the simple reason that nothing is wrong with them except under *specific conditions*. As long as armies exist and wars occur, one cannot recommend that obedience to the commanding officer should be abandoned. And yet the Americans who defied their officers at My Lai assumed an 'enormous responsibility', and a supererogatory one. One cannot recommend as a general rule that officials should forge documents, but Raoul Wallenberg, the Swedish consul in Budapest who in 1944 distributed thousands of forged documents to persecuted Jews, also assumed an 'enormous responsibility', a supererogatory responsibility *par excellence*. The obligations of women as wives and mothers have changed since *A Doll's House* was written, but women like Nora spearheaded this change, and without them it would not have happened. What we call 'civil disobedience' is only a subcase of the taking of 'enormous responsibility'. But taking such an enormous chance also requires enormous care.[3] Shakespeare was as aware of this as he was of almost every facet of our moral make-up. Both Juliet and Edmund rejected *filial obligations*, but Juliet was a heroine and Edmund a murderous rascal.

'Enormous responsibility' is the most conspicuous phenomenon of the diachronic model of responsibility. All things being equal, the more one rejects 'taken for granted' norms, the less one respects and observes consensually valid norms and the greater one's own responsibility becomes. There is, however, an *apparently* contrary trend at work here. Suppose that in a given community *no one* subscribes to any norm, and, further, that everyone in this community agrees that moral norms *per se* are invalid. Or, considering this to be a very unlikely event, let us suppose that a considerable majority within this community defy all traditional moral norms and values, where the notion 'traditional' stands for the sum total of normative *inheritance* and thus involves general and universal norms as well. In such a case, responsibility will not be 'enormous', but will rather be close to nil, or so it seems. And as such a situation can only occur in modernity, we should not be surprised that Balzac discovered the problem. He asked, 'Who is responsible for collective crimes?', and answered, '*No one* is responsible for them.' (Let us keep in mind at this point that Balzac speaks here of collective *crimes*.) Yet a crime can only be a crime if it is viewed as such. So *who* defines actions as crimes, if the people who commit them do not view them as such because they have no yardstick for distinguishing good from evil? Who provides this yardstick? What kind of yardstick is it? If God is the provider of such yardsticks, then in our age they cannot exist because God is now forsaken. Well, is the yardstick that of our predecessors, as Balzac believed? Or is it the yardstick of those contemporaries who do not participate in collective crimes? Or is it the yardstick of our successors? Or of each and every matter just mentioned? But if we believe that there is a yardstick – and there must be, for otherwise we could not conceive of collective *crimes* – can it be true that no one is responsible for collective crimes? And just what does the notion 'responsibility' mean in such a context?

Indeed, no one is responsible for collective crimes if no one must *answer* for them, if no one asks the proverbial question 'Where is your brother Abel?' With Hitler and his cohorts, the question was put a posteriori, and the chief surviving culprits had to answer. With Stalin and his hangmen, the question was never asked.

Yet the statement 'No one is responsible for collective crimes' is only true, as the above distinction indicates, if 'responsibility' is viewed within the framework of a synchronic model. If we shift to a diachronic model, 'responsibility' appears in a new light.

Collective crimes have never been committed by *every member* of a given group or perpetrated *to the same degree* by every actor in such a crime.

Let us begin by examining the first statement. If we assume the presence of morality in every complex society, and we should assume such a presence, we *know*, even where no empirical evidence is available, that some people have always *queried* the validity of certain norms. Where such a questioning can occur, the fact that *no norms* are related to one or another kind of action can also be questioned. And we not only propose the devaluation of certain norms from the standpoint of morality, but we also propose the validation of certain norms not yet in sight. And, since the modern world is under analysis here, it is fair to say that both the upheld traditional norms and the proposed new norms are related to or brought into harmony with *universal* values and universal/abstract norms. Collective crimes are *never committed*, not even where actions *have become crimes* from our viewpoint alone, without the presence of those who have rejected such crimes on normative grounds. People such as these have usually been marginalized, sometimes punished, and almost always isolated in societies of 'collective crimes'. They have to answer for not being criminals in the same way as if they were criminals. Sometimes non-participation in collective crimes implies punishment (under Stalin, very often the voluntary death of the non-participant); sometimes it implies only the resolve to do what one deems good or noble. People of both these groups take their chance, they take responsibility: responsibility for Good. However, taking responsibility for Good amidst collective crimes is *not the same* form of taking responsibility for Good as we encountered in our synchronic model (doing the right thing in accordance with the norms of our world). This responsibility is taken for the Good trampled underfoot. It is a responsibility to keep Good alive. It is responsibility taken for the *world*. For this reason I term this responsibility *world-historical responsibility*. 'Enormous responsibility' and 'world-historical responsibility' may overlap, although they form two distinct types of 'diachronic' responsibility.

Let us now put the second statement – that not everyone commits collective crimes to the same extent – under scrutiny. Moral norms live through their application; so do non-moral norms. Some people are reluctant fully to apply evil maxims. They 'make exceptions' while listening to their moral sense, their moral feelings (which are not principles). Other people can overdo crimes by giving free rein to their worst inclinations. Even if collective crimes taken in their entirety were attributable to a particular group of people, they could not possibly be attributed equally, attributed to the same extent, to every single actor within this group. I have ascribed responsibility to the *voluntary* character of acting ('I did this'; 'I was the one who did this'). Everyone does what he or she does through voluntary acts. Only what you have done as a person can be fully ascribed to you. Against this, one could argue that in an atmosphere of collective crimes it is more a matter of luck than the result of voluntary decision whether someone becomes a murderer, an accessory to this murder, or is simply seen as a witness to a death. But this is a faulty and irrelevant argument, for two reasons. Whether accidental or the result of a deliberate decision, the doing of a deed (or abstaining from it) can only be ascribed to the person actually doing it (and abstention to the person actually abstaining from it). Secondly, non-participation in collective crimes can be regarded *purely* as a matter of luck or chance, if we view the characters of all the actors involved as at least *uniformly* 'moral-indifferent', and this is never the case.

Positional responsibility ('responsibility A') exists in every case where such a crime is attributable to 'collective actors'; that is, to a group of people. The taking of positional responsibility (the leadership role) stems from choice, and one is responsible for this choice. Finally, collective crimes are *initiated*. Whether the initiator is known and can be caught or found out, or unknown, is of no major importance. If there is no 'initiative' and there are no initiators, 'collective crimes' do not exist, even retrospectively.

Those taking a position of power among collective actors, and particularly those initiating collective crimes, 'take their chance' to the same extent as those rebelling against such crimes. In doing so they also take responsibility: responsibility for Evil. Theirs is the responsibility for keeping Evil alive, and this too is a responsibility taken for the world. For this reason I also term this kind of responsibility, this responsibility-for-Evil, 'world-historical responsibility'. 'Enormous responsibility' for Evil (acting via evil maxims) and 'world-historical responsibility' for Evil (initiating collective crimes) may overlap, but, again, these are two distinct types of 'diachronic' responsibility.

Who is responsible for collective crimes? No one? *Everyone is*, yet not every person to the same extent. Initiators of collective crimes bear 'world-historical responsibility' for Evil; their following is responsible in proportion to their own, personal, voluntary action, each person for his or her own deed. A person who does not participate in a criminal action is not responsible for the crime,[4] but may still bear liability. But those few people bearing world-historical responsibility for Good, and who in dark times do not allow the light of morality to be extinguished, can perform such an everlasting service to the world coming after them that for their sake even the mild guilt of the bystanders can be forgiven and forgotten. If it was not for the trials and tribulations such people bear for themselves and for others, how would we learn just what human beings are capable of in their resolve for goodness?

5

The Problem of Consequences

The distinction between the synchronic and diachronic models of responsibility, on the one hand, and between responsibility A and responsibility X, on the other, serve as guidelines for passing moral judgements in that they disclose something about the amount and quality of responsibility – something, but by no means everything. It appears obvious that those volunteering for a position of specific obligation and those 'taking their chance' in shirking such obligations or defying altogether the traditional norms of their world take a greater amount of responsibility than do others, for better or for worse, for good or for evil. Yet even this correlation is more complex than it seems. To understand the complexity of this problem, certain traditional issues in moral philosophy must be closely examined.

Whether a person is responsible for the consequences of an action, and to what extent this person is responsible, whether unintended consequences which follow the action mitigate or aggravate the moral judgement passed on the actor, whether the possible consequences must be assessed by actors prior to action, whether one can formulate guidelines and principles the observance of which might ensure good or at least acceptable consequences: these are all interrelated, though distinct, problems, their common denominator being *temporality* of a particular provenance – what I shall term 'congealed temporality'.

Action is a consequence of decision, decision is a consequence of deliberation, deliberation of a particular kind is a consequence of our character traits, and so on. Yet the kind of temporality under consideration here amalgamates this *flow* into a single time element, the *absolute present of the action*. Action influences the world from its very beginning (if such a beginning can be traced at all), and continues to influence the world until its very end, until the action is fully accomplished (if, again, such an end can be traced at all). The effect meanwhile goes on, accelerating or slowing and increasing or diminishing within and beyond the control of the actor, both during the action and upon its completion. What is termed 'consequences' is the congealment of this steady flow into the *state* of a supposed 'end result'. This 'end result' is then traced back to the particular act – that is, to the congealed absolute present of 'now acting' – and a *causal* sequence is established between the two congealed 'moments'. Thus the end result (the congealed future) is connected with the act (the congealed absolute present) in that the latter serves as the *sufficient ground* of the former.

Without the categories and causal procedure of congealed temporality no particular responsibility for consequences can be considered at all. Once we 'uncongeal' or 'dehomogenize' the congealed absolute present in order to distinguish between character, deliberation, decision, choice, action and the like, we reintroduce the assessment of intentions in passing moral judgements. We usually perform both these judgemental procedures, for we switch from the judgemental standpoint of congealed temporality to 'dehomogenizing' the absolute present, only to switch back from there to the judgemental standpoint of congealed temporality. Fair moral judgement comes from such a constant switching of judgemental positions because we cannot simultaneously congeal *and* uncongeal the absolute present. The congealed *future* can also be dehomogenized in a process of assessing the constant flow of the results of such actions as had previously been congealed in the end result. In so doing we are intent on assessing factors other than those of the actor, factors which have also contributed to the end result of the action. Thus we must dissect the end result, analyse it in its complexity, and insert it into a chain of multiple causality; but, then again, we must switch back and treat the end result in its congealed form or we are no longer dealing with the end result of that particular action. Without this 'to and fro' pattern our moral judgement cannot be *just*. Clearly, the simultaneous congealing and uncongealing or dehomogenizing of the consequences is impossible. What then is the difference between uncongealing the absolute present and uncongealing the end result? The first procedure must establish the *quality* of responsibility in terms of *freedom*, whereas the second procedure must establish the *amount* of responsibility in terms of *causality*. A wrong done with good intentions does not have the same quality as a wrong done with the intention to harm. And yet the quantity (the amount) of responsibility can be greater in the former than in the latter case if devastating harm accompanies the former and insignificant harm accompanies the latter. This is also true with the obverse case (where good results spring from good and bad intentions respectively).

I have referred to action as the congealed absolute present tense, and to the consequence of an action as the congealed end result, alias future tense. However, responsibility can be taken for consequences, and people can be made responsible for consequences both prospectively and retrospectively. In both cases we pass judgements, but judgements different in kind.

Moral judgement passed from the standpoint of consequences is *retrospective* if the congealed end result of an action can be referred to in the past tense (though again it is a matter of judgement as to which consequences can be regarded as end results). This is the position of the 'owl of Minerva': the consequences have already set in. We need not ponder the factuality of the end results, because we are familiar with them in their factuality, and so are others. Taking full responsibility for the consequences of my action can be summed up in the following formula: 'This is the result of my action; I take all the blame', or 'This is the result of my action; I take all the praise.' Such a formula indicates that we are confronted with *actions*, alias *voluntary* acts. Thus the question 'Who did it?' should be answered in the following straightforward manner: 'I did' or 'You did.'

Moral judgement passed from the perspective of consequences is *prospective* if the congealed end result of an action can only be referred to in the future tense. In other words, the end result has not yet set in. We have no knowledge of it, for the future cannot be known, and this is precisely why we try to gauge it. The actor is intent on gaining a mental picture of the possible consequences of an action before taking it. Speculation about likely and unlikely consequences is included in this deliberating. The shouldering of responsibility for these consequences can be summed up in the following formula: 'I have considered the foreseeable consequences of my action, and so I take my chance to act thus.' The actor thus passes a *practical* and a *theoretical* judgement simultaneously. The practical judgement is passed upon the result (as in the case of retrospective judgement); the theoretical judgement is passed upon the circumstances and upon the chain of causality to be triggered by the action. The theoretical judgement can prove wrong without the practical judgement proving wrong, and *vice versa*. Consequently, if the evaluation of the intended result is the same for the person passing judgement and the person being judged, *making someone responsible* for the future consequences of an action can also be formulated thus: 'You have/have not considered the foreseeable consequences of your action, so you are right/wrong in acting.'

But what if this evaluation is not shared?

Whether the judgement is retrospective or prospective, end results must be, and indeed are, evaluated. We credit or debit a person for the end result of an action depending upon whether we assess this result as good or bad. Similarly, taking the position of the actor-to-be-judged, in trying to determine whether to chance an action which in all probability will produce a particular outcome, we first must know whether this outcome is desirable or undesirable. On the grounds of what criteria do we evaluate results? Are there any objective criteria available for such an evaluation? Are success and failure such criteria? But, one might ask, 'Success in what?' and 'Success for whom?', and, equally, 'Failure in what?' and 'Failure for whom?' Both successes and failure can be adiaphoric. If X is a successful writer and Y an unsuccessful one, should X be *morally* credited and Y *morally* debited for their respective successful and unsuccessful writing? Or, to mention another aspect, should a successful tyrant and mass murderer be morally credited? Clearly, there are forms of success deserving moral disapprobation and forms of failure deserving moral approbation. 'Good consequences' and 'bad consequences' indeed have some relation to 'success' and 'failure' respectively, but 'good consequences' cannot be automatically associated with success, and 'bad consequences' cannot be automatically associated with failure.

There are 'good values' (*Güterwerte*) of different types. Equally, there are states of affairs or products of *negative* value content (*Unwerte*). This is the starting point of Aristotle's ethics. An increase in the amount or quality of particular (not all) good values is the result of actions, and actors can be credited for their success in this. But moral credit only comes from the promotion of particular values: namely, those which are to be reinforced, kept alive and actualized by moral (virtuous) activity. This is clearly a circular argument, and Aristotle was protected from this predicament because he could, and indeed did, argue precisely that the good value to be promoted by moral action is that which is good for *everyone*. All goods closely linked to the supreme good (the good of the state) are goods for everyone. Promoting such goods is behaviour to be morally credited. Success in promoting such goods is therefore good success, good end result, good consequence. But has the circularity of argument really been overcome by this kind of thinking? For Aristotle it certainly has; for us it certainly has not. Aristotle generated a full catalogue of main virtues: those who practised these virtues could not fail to promote good values. For those unfailingly promoting good values there is no need to evaluate the end result of their own action or the action of others to know the right thing or to do the right thing. Pre-evaluated end results are handed them together with the very virtues the practice of which will promote both the good of the state and their own happiness. Of course, even here prospective judgeement poses a problem. We need to gauge the foreseeable consequences of an action before embarking on that action. We carry a moral responsibility for the proper theoretical use of our reason. Ignorance of facts or circumstances can lead us astray. True knowledge is a precondition of good action. Yet we know in advance what a good result and what a bad result is, and we all know it. And, for all of us, which results are good and which results are bad is the same.

Of course, dissent in evaluating consequences was not unknown in ancient times: good result for the Greek was a bad result for the Trojan. Yet this fact alone did not pose a moral problem. The positing of a consensus concerning major good values within a given community was sufficient to dismiss the issue. If diverging views appeared, all but one of them could be and were dismissed by philosophers as 'mere opinions'. True enough, Euripides aired this problem as a problem more than once, whereas the Roman dictum attributed to Cato the Stoic ('victrix causa diis placuit sed victa Catoni') tells an altogether different story. But pluralism in values was regarded as indicative of 'decadence', of the erosion of communal ties, rather than a sign of the normal and desirable state of affairs.

In the modern age, a decisive shift towards value relativism has occurred. It was to this shift that Kant reacted with the dismissal of the viewpoint of consequences in moral judgement and deliberation. Yet, despite this shift, the consensus concerning certain good values (*Güterwerte*) did not completely vanish. It is still present in everyday commonsense thinking, and is present whenever people act in accordance with 'rationality of reason'; that is, in accordance with taken-for-granted norms and rules. Since this is still true today, the traditional method of attributing end results to actors survives. Within certain more or less well-defined frameworks, we still agree on the 'good' or 'bad' quality of consequences. If the end result of an occurrence is not group-specific, as for example with a bushfire, consensus can automatically be taken for granted. There is no question that a bushfire is a 'bad' result and that the person who started it can be made responsible: this person could and should have been cognizant of the foreseeable (possible or probable) consequences of this action. Here the degree of responsibility is determined through the general procedure of 'dehomogenizing' the congealed end result and the congealed act. The questions asked in this process include the following: 'Was it an act of arson or of negligence?'; 'What were the relative proportions of foreseeable and unforseeable consequences?' The saving of lives is always considered within a group as a good end result and is credited in the same way as a bushfire is debited. If a good result was intended, 'making someone responsible' carries a heightened credit, and, if a bad result was intended, 'making someone responsible' carries a heightened debit, whereas with unintended results both credit and debit are proportionally decreased. A most frequently and vehemently debated case – namely, whether someone can be proportionally credited for a good result if his or her intentions were to the contrary, or whether someone can be debited for a bad result if his or her intentions were pure and good – cannot be discussed on the level of structural abstraction. So many variables are involved here that any answer would be a sweeping and illegitimate generalization. There is only one relationship that holds true in every case; if the intentions are pure and good, and the result is bad but unforeseeable, this result can be debited to the actor, but only by the actor himself. Yet even self-accusation of this kind can be disputed on the grounds that it is comprised of *irrational* feelings of guilt.

Although, as mentioned, the shift toward value relativism did not make the traditional method of attributing consequences obsolete, it did make this procedure increasingly problematic. Moral assessment from the perspective of consequences must become problematic, even detrimental, from the moral point of view. What is the *better* consequence: to keep myself and my family out of trouble, or to rescue someone else? What is the *better* consequence: to become wealthy through business or to practise the profession I am dedicated to and remain poor? What is the *better* consequence: to lie and save my skin or not to lie and perish? What is the *better* consequence: to climb high on the rungs of power where I can boss others, or remain in a position where I shall be bossed? What is the *better* consequence: to help a few and in doing so harm others, or not help and thus not harm anyone? If moral judgement is to be based on the assessment of consequences in a world where consensus no longer exists, will not *everything* be permitted? Will not *every* result be considered 'good' in so far as it 'suits us'? Will not success of *any* kind be viewed as crediting the actor? It is obvious that Kant had more than sufficient reason to 'purify' morals by dissociating them from the dubious yardstick of consequences.

So far we have discussed the single consequences of single actions, assuming throughout that we can identify the good and the bad consequences. I have added that, in so far as we can disagree about 'good values' and about the goodness and badness of end results, ascribing single consequences to single actors will be not only perplexing, but also downright irrelevant. In the midst of this confusion two solutions present themselves. First, we can seek a universal standard with which to evaluate end results. Secondly, we can shift the problem of consequences from the traditional model of 'act A – consequence X' to the model 'all acts A – all consequences X' by building generalized and universalized consequences into the maxim of action. This is precisely what Kant did. If you act such that you can wish that the maxim of your action should become a universal (moral) law, then the maxim of your action has already posited the supreme substantive good. Once you enter into the *causality* of freedom in your capacity as a *noumenal* being, *you are the cause of that supreme substantive good.* Were everyone to act according to universal maxims (by the causality of freedom) in their capacity as a noumenal being, the outcome would be the supreme substantive good (the best possible world), the only universally and absolutely good consequence one could imagine. Yet Kant fully knew that by shifting the problem of consequences back into the realm of maxims he excluded the traditional problematic of consequences ('act A – consequence X') from moral philosophy. Yet certain neo-Kantians lack this degree of awareness. In particular I have in mind Singer's bold attempt. In shifting Kant closer to ethical reality, Singer watered down the Kantian solution by formulating his famous 'generalization principle', which can also be reformulated as the principle of *consequences*. The generalization principle is based on the recommendation that in any situation we should act such that we could wish that everyone else (in a similar situation) would act likewise. The principle of consequences (as one of the formulations of the generalization principle) is based on the recommendation that before embarking on an action we should ask ourselves, 'What would happen if everyone did the same?' If we want the projected result of our action to come about (as the result of everyone's action), our action is good, if we decry the projected result, we must not act.

We all know that moral choices are invariably situated. Kant's recommendation was to disregard the situatedness of moral choice because within his system no moral choice existed. We can generalize (or universalize) moral maxims, but we can neither generalize nor universalize a situated moral choice or action, as

Singer believes we can. Take, for example, Kant's famous and controversial answer to Considerant's challenge. Even if a would-be murderer is chasing his victim about our house, we have *no choice* between lying to him and telling the truth (that the person he is chasing is in our house). We do not ponder how everyone should act in this or a similar situation and then act, for we should be truthful *irrespective of the situation*. Kant did not argue that the situated choice should be generalized (or universalized), but argued that the universal maxim should be observed regardless of the situation.

We could argue against Kant that we still have a choice because we can choose between *two universal maxims*, and that our action should be guided by either the first, or the second. We can choose the maxim 'Tell the truth' or the maxim 'Preserve innocent human life.' Kant would of course reject this interpretation, as these maxims are not on the same level of universality. Even if we could wish that everyone should preserve human life, failing in this aim does not imply a logical contradiction, as lying does. To make a solid case for the maxim 'Preserve innocent human life', we must first reject the argument of non-contradiction. And, even if we do reject this argument, as I do, *Kant's reason* for introducing it cannot be circumvented or simply dismissed. In obeying the maxim 'Tell the truth', we clearly know *what* to do and also *how* to do it. In obeying the maxim 'Preserve innocent human life' we also know *what* to do but we do *not* at the same time know *how* to do it. The 'how' is situated; the 'how' and the 'how best' of the act must be calculated. But, suppose that a choice exists between acting according to the maxim 'Tell the truth' and acting according to the maxim 'Preserve innocent human life.' In opting for the first or the second, can we *really* be guided in our choice by the 'generalization principle'? Can we really claim that *everyone* should, in this or a similar situation, act likewise?

If I save an innocent human life by lying, can I really say 'I do it *because* I wish that everyone should act thus?' What if other people choose to remain silent? What if yet other people choose to *fight* the would-be murderer to preserve innocent human life? Since the maxim leaves the problem of 'how' open, the *acts* performed under the guidance of the maxim can be *different in kind*. I cannot claim that everyone should act likewise, only that everyone should act according to the maxim 'Preserve innocent human life.' I cannot recommend that everyone should lie in order to preserve human life. I can only assert that lying in such a situation is *permitted*, and this is less than a recommendation.

Now let us have some less extreme examples. A person concludes that a lost cause he has stood for is also a bad cause. The choice is then between two maxims (for one's action): 'No one should stick to a bad cause' and 'No one should desert a sinking ship.' But whether he sticks to the cause or quits it, this person cannot wish that everyone should act likewise. First, not everyone may share his conviction that the cause was (or is) bad. Also, people who drop a lost cause might feel a moral obligation not to pressure those who stay with it. A woman can decide to leave her husband under the guidance of the moral maxim 'No woman should tolerate humiliation.' But she cannot wish that every woman in the same situation should do likewise. For example, some women would be capable of remaining and 'educating' their husbands. Moreover, no two situations are completely alike. Even further, many different factors may equally be considered here. Some women would, upon becoming divorced, see their children left at the mercy of a brutal father. Others would have to live with the probability, or at least the possibility, that their husbands will commit suicide. In a situated choice, probable and possible consequences cannot be left unconsidered.

Situated choices (and all concrete moral choices are situated) are very complex. Sometimes we face *two* moral maxims that we regard as valid – what is more, as equally valid – but cannot act in any way without infringing one or the other. These are the situations of *tragic moral conflict*. There is no conflict (or contradiction) *between the maxims themselves*. This conflict is only located in the choice-for-action. Kant, who considered only the maxims, and not the action itself, could legitimately claim that there are no moral conflicts (no moral choices). But, once we endorse a principle of generalization in action choice (in situated choice), we can no longer circumvent the problem of moral conflict. On what grounds do we normally make decisions in cases of moral conflict? Sometimes we listen to our moral sense, and then favour one maxim over the other. Sometimes we ponder the possible, probable and foreseeable consequences of our action. If both maxims carry equal weight with our moral sense, we normally prefer that action the consequences of which look morally more promising. Considerant's example was extreme because both our moral sense and the matter of consequences favoured the acceptance of the maxim of preserving innocent human life. And there are yet more controversial and difficult decisions to take.

We can claim universality (or generality) for our *maxims* of action, but not for the actions themselves. I term this the *dilemma of morals*. Every time we act true to a universal maxim, our action is *morally permitted.* Yet it is not perforce mandatory. Other people can act true to another universal maxim, and this act is equally morally permitted, and is not perforce mandatory. Only where a choice is made between an act in accordance with a moral maxim or norm and an act in accordance with a non-moral or amoral principle of 'cleverness' (mere self-interest, illicit pleasure and the like) can we legitimately apply the 'generalization principle': we should then act in the way that anyone in this or a similar situation should act. Almost every Kantian example was taken from this list. No one should lie (for reasons of self-interest or pleasure), no one should murder (out of self-interest or pleasure), no one should cheat his customers, no one should embezzle money, and so on. Moral conflict is indeed absent in all these cases, because there is *no moral choice.* But do we really need the 'generalization principle' to find a reliable guideline here? I think that the old categorical imperative fully serves as such a guideline. If we are facing a choice *not moral* in nature (choice between observing moral maxims and norms *and* observing the maxim of cleverness), *the situation is morally irrelevant,* though the choice is situated. If a person has a wealthy father and cannot wait to inherit, it would be ludicrous to weigh the pros and cons of his murdering his father *in terms of a situated choice.* The question of whether an heir should murder his or her father out of an impatience to inherit should never be pondered, because parricide simply should never occur. The situatedness of choice draws its relevance from the presence of a moral conflict, but it is precisely the presence of a moral conflict that makes the generalization irrelevant. It is in the awareness of the 'dilemma of morals' that Goethe asserted that the actor is always guilty, and only the spectator is innocent. It is in awareness of the dilemma of morals that I have strongly emphasized that moral autonomy cannot be absolute.

Yet the problem of consequences has re-emerged in our discussion of the situated choice. If we can act whilst being guided by more than one universal (or general) maxim or moral norm, and must choose one over the other, we sometimes also consider foreseeable consequences in giving this preference. Yet the consequences, which we try to gauge in advance, are again *single* consequences of *single* actions, and not *general consequences* implied by the generalization of our choice. All this has not yet proved the irrelevance of the so-called 'principle of consequences' as proposed by Singer. To this problem I now turn.

The principle of consequences goes as follows: 'What would happen if everyone did the same?' Since this 'principle' is but one formulation of the generalization principle, some scepticism is not out of place concerning its general use. If we have in mind universal moral maxims alone, then the 'principle of consequences' is only a reformulation of the categorical imperative (you cannot wish that everyone should lie, or that everyone should murder, or that everyone should embezzle money, and so on). If we have in mind situated actions, where the maxim of action is chosen from among competing and equally universal (or general) maxims, then the 'principle of consequences' will be a shaky, fallible and fairly problematic guide. It can be considered a *good consequence* if every innocent victim is saved, a *bad consequence* if lying is mandatory in the service of a good purpose (the goal justifies the means). This is not to deny the advisability of considering the possible general consequences of actions ('if everyone did the same'). However, taking a factor into consideration, and accepting this factor as *the* guiding principle of action, are two very different things.[1] If no one waged wars, there would be no wars. Yet it does not follow from this that if my country is attacked by another I should not defend it. One could of course ruminate in the following way: 'What would happen if no one defended my country?' The decision, then, depends on the definition of 'no one' (which stands here for 'everyone'), and the definition of the situation. The situation may be defined in the broadest possible terms ('I am in the situation of choosing between participating in a war and not participating in a war'), in more concrete terms ('I am in the situation of choosing between participating and not participating in a just and defensive war'), and in completely concrete terms ('My expertise is needed in industry but I can volunteer to participate in a just war and go to the front'). *The more concrete the definition of the situation, the less I can rely on the principle of consequences*, for the simple reason that it is *unique* and cannot be deduced from a generalized principle. The upshot of this brief digression is, again, the dilemma of morals: maxims for action can and should claim universal (or general) validity, but actions cannot and should not. All actions are concretely situated. Before embarking on an action one must be aware of the specifics of the situation and include all those specifics in the process of deliberation. Obviously, the anticipated consequence of an individual action is one of the factors included in this process, and an important factor. Yet the principle of consequences is not a fraudulent principle, and can be put to limited use. The danger of defining our situation such that we opt for the least demanding action always exists. The principle of consequences helps us check whether our definition of the situation is the *result of an unconscious tendency* to choose the least demanding action. A check such as this is far from being foolproof, but with moral decisions nothing is foolproof.

There is only one type of situated action where the principle of consequence proves a reliable guide. This is when the *action itself* is morally indifferent (adiaphora) but the *situation* requires the *suspension* of such actions. The situation is defined by a *common goal* (to achieve a common good or to avert a common catastrophe), and the common goal is simultaneously every person's goal. For example, with a serious water shortage it is the common goal of all and the individual goal of every person to save water for drinking, cooking, and for the purposes of basic hygiene. In itself, nothing is wrong with watering lawns and filling swimming pools: the action is morally indifferent. But with a water shortage everyone must ask, 'What would happen if we all used water for non-vital purposes?' The consequences are completely predictable; everyone is familair with them. A similar situation is that where everyone working in a particular factory agrees to go on strike, and a picket line is established. The people crossing this picket line should first ask themselves, 'What would happen if everyone did the same?' (that is, take up work, which is in itself morally indifferent). But, if agreement cannot be reached in the evaluation of the objective in situations such as these, the principle of consequences will not serve as a reliable guideline even if the actions themselves are morally neutral. The first example above is the stronger one, for it is unlikely that anybody would value swimming more highly than a vital water supply. The disregarding of taxation regulations and laws against smuggling are matters closer to the second example just given, although here consequences of another kind (eventual legal punishment) must also be considered.

We can only conclude from all this what has been presupposed from the outset: that the principle of consequences offers no solution to the moral problem of passing judgements via ascribing certain consequences to those who perform these actions. Rather, it circumvents the problem itself. Either we return to Kant, disregard the situatedness of action and the situated choice altogether, and in a very un-Kantian manner *term* 'consequences' the universalizabiltiy (or generalizability) of moral maxims, or we address the problem of situated choice without hesitation and face the 'dilemma of morals' and the problem of single (individual) consequences, which no 'principle of consequences' can seriously tackle.

After this lengthy detour we are back to square one. If no agreement exists concerning the main good values, if a good result for some is a bad result for others, how can we pass even a relatively valid moral judgement on actors from the standpoint of the consequences of their action unless we pass judgement on the consequences in the first place? In the end, judging consequences is tantamount to judging a value: *it is a value judgement*. What is true of retrospective judgement is also true of prospective judgement. If I consider the foreseeable consequences of my action before embarking on it, I must first determine which of these are good consequences, better consequences, the worst consequences, and so on. Normally we are committed to values, and some of these values we take for granted, just as others take other values equally for granted. Am I thus obliged to judge my values, and, if so, how can I do this, and on what basis can I do it?

These and similar questions can be raised, but not answered, in the framework of general ethics. These answers can only be attempted in the framework of a moral philosophy. Yet it is worth restating the major problem we are facing, and I have said already that in the midst of value pluralism *two* solutions present themselves. First, we can seek a universal standard for evaluating end results, substantive or procedural. Secondly, we can shift the problem of consequences from the traditional model of 'act A – consequences X' to the model 'all acts A – all consequences X'. I have concluded that the second solution is not viable. If we do not discard the standpoint of consequences altogether, we shall present ourselves with insoluble theoretical problems. This leaves us with the first solution. Either we can locate certain universal standards for evaluating end results (for passing value judgements), or we should follow Kant and disregard common moral sense. *Tertium non datur*.

Since I have deliberately left open the problem of substantive or procedural universals, it seems that every relevant issue of moral consequence has been exhaustively dealt with except one. This is very misleading. Neither the difficulties we are facing in ascribing consequences to actors nor the difficulties we are facing in anticipating consequences stem from value pluralism alone. The more static and traditional a society is, the easier it is to anticipate consequences; the more dynamic, future-oriented and post-traditional a society becomes, the harder it is to anticipate consequences. Of course, there are unforeseen consequences even in a traditional society. Indeed, aside from predictable situations (such as a water shortage) the future is in every form of society full of surprise and uncertainty. Even if people agree about the evaluation of results, they can still disagree about action. The question is, then, whether actions contribute to these results, whether they promote them or impede them.

Throughout European history, which has been fairly dynamic even when attitudes have been mainly past-oriented, total repetitiveness has never been the case. Moreover, European history has increasingly shed whatever elements of repetitiveness it has had. During the Renaissance, in Italy and Western Europe at least, new lifestyles and forms of human interaction emerged and rapidly developed. The issue on the moral agenda became that of how to perceive that times were changing, and how to act such that action should not bring about an opposite result to that intended in this time of changes. Shakespeare's heroes and heroines struggle incessantly with this particular issue, sometimes with tragic results, sometimes with happy ones. Weber, who has given us the most brilliant analysis of the doctrine of predestination, did not raise the question of *why* people were so easily lured into accepting this unrewarding world-view. In my view, it was the awareness of the impossibility of anticipating the consequences of actions performed under subjection to concrete norms that contributed heavily to the emergence of Calvinism. The idea that we are predestined by God for salvation or damnation *irrespective of* our actions, and this is precisely why we must subject ourselves to all concrete norms without fail, without querying and testing them, must have expressed as well as reinforced the life experience of multitudes. And, ever since this point in time, Western society has undergone constant change, and change that has occurred at an ever-increasing rate. It has become a sisyphean task to anticipate the consequences of action. Hebbel's drama *Maria Magdalena* ends with the words of Master Anton, 'I no longer understand the world!' The old generation fails to understand the new generation, the friend the foe, even the friend the friend. The standpoint of a moral actor was never portrayed in ancient tragedy as doomed to failure *because* time passed by this person. Yet from the Renaissance onwards morality can be depicted as doomed to failure precisely for this reason, as can be mere subjection to concrete norms. The morality of Brutus in *Julius Caesar* is out of tune with the time, but so is the mindless obedience to concrete norms prevailing in both the Montague and the Capulet families. To achieve desirable consequences, the moral actor must be endowed with a 'historical sense', but, when historical events simply tear apart the moralists' norms, doom can be self-imposed. If we believed, as Hegel did, that Reason operates in History, we might share his preference for 'world-historical individuals' as against moralists who meet their well-deserved doom in pitting their subjectivity against the objective necessity of *Weltlauf*. Yet it has been precisely the *Weltlauf* of this century that has taught us a lesson appalling enough to make us reject Hegel's solution.

Hegel was bold enough to assert that good can be the result of evil. He was also bold enough to state that good morality can be evil if it thwarts historical progress. These and similar statements can only be refuted if they are first of all specified. If we accept that historical progress is by definition good, and if we further accept that the development of social factors of any kind can be called progress (a conception I certainly do not share), then and only then can we conclude that progress may indeed be promoted by evil. Even so, it depends on the definition of 'evil' whether or not one can subscribe to the Hegelian viewpoint that progress can be furthered by evil.

If every act *not* guided by the categorical imperative is evil, then every form of progress until now has been promoted by evil. Yet to my mind this is far too broad a definition of evil, because acts motivated by interest or desire can be value-neutral (adiaphoric). Nevertheless, even if we subscribe to the proposal that certain kinds of evil do promote progress, we have not as yet accepted the proposal that *good* can be promoted by evil. This only happens if we identify a progressive outcome with a good outcome, which is a matter of evaluation. Hegel's idea lends itself to another interpretation as well. Acts performed from the standpoint of morality are often rejected as evil by those endorsing mere concrete norms, and *vice versa*. But in saying this we must employ a different standard in assessing actors from that used in assessing the end result (the historically progressive outcome). We must be able to state that the actions of these people, actions rejected in their own times as evil, were instead good actions, and not merely because they promoted progress but, at least partially, were also good irrespective of any such effect. Furthermore, even if the statement that an action performed under moral guidance can have bad results is true, it does not follow that good actions cause bad results. Finally, just what is and what is not a bad result is again open to debate. Defeat can be a good result as well as a bad result: causes supported by strong moral efforts of particular types and which fail do not fade from our historical memory. And who knows the end results in history? *Are* there any end results in history? The more morality is historicized, the more good and bad become located in a universal 'course of the world', and the less we know just what end results are. And our ignorance is total in respect of actions performed on the stage of world history, which are exactly the kind of action Hegel had in mind.

All these controversial issues indicate that reckoning with the consequences of actions in the theatre of history poses more difficulties than reckoning with them in any other field of life. Precisely because the consequences of directly political actions are so weighty, for they are borne by many, and because responsibility in direct political action is always responsibility A, for anyone participating in such action is by definition 'in charge', *certain binding principles should be shared in this 'historical theatre'*, and cannot be chosen at random. The only principles that can be recommended as morally binding for all are those which can serve as the moral maxim for political action in general: *the democratic principles alone*. Foreseeable consequences should be considered, but only so far as the conclusive application of a good principle permits. The temporalization of morality does not relieve actors of the duty to attempt to come to grips with predictable consequences. Yet the more unpredictable the majority of consequences become, the more it is advisable to rely on firm and sound principles for action which should not be overruled by any speculation about a remote future. Taking our chance is, after all, a leap into the unknown. If it is not informed by democratic principles, it is a total leap into a darkness which might prove to be the ultimate darkness.

6

Moral Authority

Every time we act under the guidance of moral considerations, and every time we judge the action of another, the character of another, our own action, our own character, our own impulses or even thoughts, and do these things also under the guidance of moral considerations, we subject ourselves, as well as others, to *moral authority*. There are authorities of different types – political, social, legal, professional and so on – which may or may not simultaneously carry moral authority. And there are actions performed and judgements passed without recourse being taken to any authority, moral or non-moral. For the moment I shall only discuss moral authority and those aspects of actions performed and judgements passed which come under the guidance of that authority.

Norms and rules themselves are carriers of moral authority in so far as they command or suggest that we do something or avoid doing something. Yet norms and rules perform the function of norms and rules only if they are *binding*. And they are binding in so far as they are legitimized and authorized by meaningful world-views, transcendental powers, tradition, other human institutions, or reason alone. The actors who keep norms and rules 'alive' by formulating, observing and teaching them can always refer to the above phenomena if their normative world comes under threat. If all norms and rules are traditional, authority is taken for granted, but it is invariably in the name of *someone* (or something) that norms and rules are binding. This 'someone' must be present, must be living, thinking, interfering, acting. The dead god has no authority, only the living god has. Consequently, norms and rules have authority because they are carried by norm-enforcing human – and, incidentally, superhuman – persons who make them binding. All gods wield authority, but not all of them wield moral authority. That celebrated question 'In the name of whom?' can be divided into three distinct questions: 'In the name of which group of people or deity do we speak?'; 'Are there indeed moral norms and rules, carried or commanded by those in whose name we speak?'; 'Are we *authorized*, by those groups of people or those deities who are carriers of these norms and rules and who command their observance, to speak, act and judge the way we do by virtue of belonging to these groups, by virtue of having chosen these authorities or having been chosen by them?'[1]

If people subject themselves to every concrete norm of their group or community without employing selection or double-quality reflection, moral authority is fully *external*. The term 'external' refers not to a lack of internalization but to *the source of the authoritative content of norms*. Since norms are specified and concretized by the community at large, the individual obtains all his or her normative content from external sources, without adding anything to or extracting anything from this content. What you take, you give. Here, the question 'In the name of whom?' is not yet raised. Every unit is a single instance of the general. Every person speaks in the name of the community of which this person is a single representative. Thus it is that *moral judgement* resides in the *eyes of others*. This statement appears to be metaphoric, but it is not. These eyes follow you in all your acting and doing; they rest upon you, gaze at you. You are under the spell of this gaze just as others are under the spell of your gaze. If you do something you should not, if you fail to do something you should, the eyes of others make you feel *ashamed*. Shame is one of the most tormenting and humiliating feelings. When put to shame, you want to run away, sink into the earth, disappear – all in order *to rid yourself of this gaze*. Shame is an affect (like anger, fear, disgust), the only inborn moral feeling we can speak of. As I have argued elsewhere (in *The Power of Shame*), we have reason to suppose that shame, unlike most other affects, is not the remnant of an instinctual 'consummatory behaviour'. The genesis of this affect is to be sought in the process of human self-domestication. At any rate, shame, as an empirical human universal, is the involvement of the Self in the approval and disapproval of the external authority of judgement (the eyes of others). Shame affect, with its accompanying facial expression of the blush, can still be observed in pure form with infants, and sometimes even in the case of others who have subjected themselves to a fully internalized external authority. Shame affect normally undergoes modification during the socialization process. None the less, in the final instance even this modified sense of shame retains the same involvement of the Self in the approbation or disapprobation of the external

authority of judgement as did the pure, innate and naked shame–
affect. As the *recognition* of others, whether it be of all others or
only of certain others, is one of the pillars of self-construction, we
avoid shame as much as we can. This affect is modified mainly,
though not exclusively, via the selection of *representative* Others.
Nowadays a morally healthy person cannot be shamed by just
anyone (the generalized Other), but only by a given person (the
representative Other). This is why a morally healthy person will *not*
feel ashamed if put under the gaze of people whose authority this
person has already rejected on moral grounds. A person incapable of
feeling shame is *morally insane*; a person shamed by everyone is
infantile; a person who is exclusively or largely shamed by non-
moral authority is *morally incompetent*. All three personality types
have an affinity with evil, but each has an affinity with a different
kind of evil. The morally insane person is a brute (a Caliban), the
morally infantile person is dangerously easy to mould, and the
morally incompetent person is power-mad (or the lackey of such an
individual) and, if sophisticated enough, the demon of reason. I shall
return to this particular matter later.

The standpoint of morality is the standpoint of practical reason.
As long as all concrete norms are taken for granted and thus
internalized, practical reason is still *in nuce*. This means that
practical and theoretical understanding are not yet differentiated,
and that neither of them can be called 'reason proper', as they are
merely *passive*. Passivity is not used here in an epistemological sense.
Since human action is always voluntary, and human understanding,
perception and speech are always intentional, the term 'passivity'
refers solely to 'taken-for-grantedness'. By understanding *what*
normative expectations are, and how others live up to them, we
already *know* what good action is, and what we must do to fulfil
these expectations. Obviously, we are dealing here with an ideal
type. It is very difficult to imagine a state of affairs where concrete
norms cover every possible type of application in every conceivable
situation. Even if all norms and rules are taken for granted, their
application can still presuppose the activation of both theoretical
and practical reason, and some differentiation between the practical
and theoretical use of reason. The emergence of practical reason
proper (as well as that of morality) can be witnessed if the
application of norms and rules is no longer an exceptional event,
where it becomes the regular *task* of an actor to apply norms and
rules on many consecutive occasions. It is thus that the actor is
authorized as the agent of proper norm application, and must
determine which (taken-for-granted) norm applies to which case,

and *how* it can *best* be applied. Thus practical reason appears as *phronesis*. It is a norm that people should act with phronesis (good practical judgement in action, implying norm application). However, phronesis itself is an *internal* and not an external agency, an internal and not an external authority. If the main norms and their hierarchic structure are taken for granted, practical reason becomes *identical* with phronesis. This is not so in modernity, though it was not even fully so when Aristotle placed such enormous emphasis on phronesis. Granted this, one should not hastily conclude, as do so many contemporary thinkers, that phronesis in its role as the agent of practical reason has lost relevance. After accepting norms as valid and binding these norms must still be applied, and this requires good phronesis in the same way and to the same degree as did the application of mainly traditional norms long ago.

The internal authority of moral conduct was not restricted to the *application* of norms in traditional societies either. Whether we look at the narratives of the Old Testament, the Greek tragedies and Greek philosophies, or the stories of Christian saints, to mention the texts best known to us, we invariably encounter cases of *supererogation*. Supererogation is the opposite of phronesis. Ismene, not Antigone, was the bearer of phronesis. Though one could correctly assert that supererogation was regarded by the ancient Greeks as *hubris*, this was not so with the ancient Hebrews, the Romans or the Christians. Not the external but the internal authority engenders the resolve to supererogation (otherwise no supererogation would be involved). Furthermore, norms, virtues and values were, in highly civilized traditional societies, more or less *open to interpretation*. Philosophical ethics offer a variety of differing norm–value–virtue interpretations, as do certain 'moral religions'. Even if everyone accepts that courage, piety, temperance, wisdom and justice are the *main virtues*, and that happiness is the *supreme good*, and so on, there still remain such (morally crucial) questions as *what real* courage is, and what it is not, *what* constitutes happiness, and what does not. Clearly, interpretative reason has nothing to do with phronesis, for we must determine *what* real courage is *to be* courageous, in order *to act* courageously as the time and place demands. Aristotle offered an ingenious combination of virtue–norm interpretation with phronesis in his theory of the 'middle measure' (*mesotes*). But he immediately added that it was only of restricted use. If we look briefly at the three distinct acts of internal authority, we see that practical reason mobilizes different kinds of theoretical reasoning in two cases (phronesis and interpretation), whilst in the third act it monitors action on its own, without the mediation of theoretical reason: the case of supererogation.

We are involved in internal authority to the same extent as we are involved in external authority. Involvement in internal moral authority is called *conscience*. Conscience is a *feeling* like shame but is more closely related to emotional disposition and orientative feelings than the latter. And it stands to reason why. The term 'conscience' has a relation to *knowledge (con-scientia)*, indicating that the moral feeling in question is vested with reason. Involvement in external authority must essentially be *reactive*, for it emerges in reaction to the approval or disapproval of the 'eyes of others'. The fact that we can feel shame while *anticipating* disapproval does not distinguish shame from other reactive feelings (affects). The affects of sexual desire, anger, fear, disgust, joy and sorrow can equally be aroused by fantasy (imagination). However, conscience is not visual; it is an internal *voice*. It speaks to us, warns us, advises us; it rewards and punishes us. In its cautioning and advising, conscience is an orientative feeling. Our conscience literally speaks to us, and if we do not listen we feel *pain*, and pain of a more tormenting kind than its bodily counterpart. On the other hand, if we heed our conscience, listen to it, we feel *joy*, satisfaction, felicity, peace, tranquillity and the like. In so far as it manifests itself in feelings of varying concrete quality, conscience is really an 'emotional disposition'. This complex character of conscience indicates that it is *not* an innate feeling like shame or an empirical human universal. As a cognitive feeling, as involvement in practical reason (the internal moral authority), it appears together with morality, with the emergence of practical reason proper.

Morals have been defined here as the individual's practical relationship to the norms and rules of proper conduct. In the wake of Hegel, I have termed the norms and rules of proper conduct *Sittlichkeit*, and the individual's practical attitude *morality*. Now we have gone further. The objective aspect of this relationship (*Sittlichkeit*) has been defined as external moral authority, whereas practical reason activated in the attitude of morality has been defined as internal moral authority. Further, shame has been defined as involvement in external moral authority, conscience as involvement in internal moral authority. Since morals are the *relationship* of morality to *Sittlichkeit*, moral deliberation, moral principles and ideas, moral feelings – in short, all the elements operative in the 'moral point of view' – have, in direct action or judgement (speech act), recourse to *two authorities*. The balance between external and internal authority can vary. Either can have the greater weight. The structure of their relationship also varies. But we can legitimately discuss the 'moral point of view', morals, ethics (or whatever other name we give to this phenomenon), *only if* recourse has been had to *both* authorities. Or, to formulate the problem historically, if practical reason is only *in nuce*, authority is exclusively external; there is *not yet* a moral point of view. And, if practical reason remains the sole authority, because people do not have recourse to *any* external moral authority in their deliberations, actions and judgements, *there is no longer a moral point of view*. No moral point of view can exist without a subjective component (morality), yet sheer subjectivity cannot be moral.

As mentioned above, in traditional societies internal moral guidance is by and large restricted to the application of norms, to supererogation, and to the interpretation of norms. Internal authority (practical reason) and involvement in that authority (conscience) are thus complementary, in that they complement the operation of external authority. I shall term involvement in practical reason in its role as the agency of norm application *applicative conscience*, in its role as the agency of supererogation *amplifying conscience*, and in its role as the agency of norm interpretation and reinterpretation *interpretative conscience*. In all three cases practical reason and conscience are but *complementary*. The more practical reason wields the authority of norm interpretation, the more elaborate becomes the distinction between the authoritative other and the non-authoritative other. People who hold 'mere opinions' in moral matters are no longer regarded as bearers of external authority; only those professing true practical knowledge are acknowledged as authoritative. The fixing of eyes on non-authoritative others cannot shame a person with an interpretative conscience. This person will juxtapose the approval of the internal voice to the disapproving regard, and will heed the advice of the former. Socrates remarked that Anytos and Meletos might kill him but they could do him no harm. Indeed, neither Anytos nor Meletos, nor any of those Athenians who credited their accusations, could shame Socrates over any action which did not elicit the protest of his *daimonion* (conscience). But there are always authoritative others, repositories of 'true moral knowledge' whose gaze can shame the man of conscience. Here, the gaze of external authority and the voice of internal authority reinforce one another. Normally, interpretative conscience accepts certain basic norms as fully borne by external authority (as Socrates accepted the authority of the laws of Athens), even if interpretative conscience distinguishes between the right and the wrong interpretation of those norms. People with interpretative consciences do not succumb to all regulations, yet they succumb to many, and in full awareness of doing so. Their moral autonomy is only relative, but, as we well know, this is always so. What distinguishes interpretative conscience from other kinds of conscience is the awareness and affirmation of this relativity. People with interpretative conscience do not even try to infer their moral norms from non-moral 'ultimate grounds' such as reason or nature. They do not claim that every occurrence that has a moral component must be thought through from scratch. Complementary conscience does not need to invent absolutely safe procedures for the grounding of norms. Anticipating the end result of my train of thought, I wish to state here that in my view no other (subsequent) type of conscience would be more subtle or wield a greater amount of real moral autonomy than interpretative conscience. At the very best, subtlety and autonomy appear in later forms of conscience to the same extent as with interpretative conscience, and in worse cases these qualities appear to a lesser degree or even not at all. Yet, because of the breaking-down of traditionalism and the fixed hierarchy of values, conditions under which an initial agreement concerning the supreme values, norms and virtues could be taken for granted, interpretative conscience can now no longer rely on the solid framework of a *Sittlichkeit*. Clearly, traditionalism did not vanish with one stroke. Even unreflected forms of shame prevail in niches of modern society, and not in childhood alone. All three pre-modern types of conscience are still very much in evidence. However, at this point the coexistence of a broad variety of moral attitudes is not of major interest. The slow but ever-accelerating transformation of the *structure* of morals is our overriding concern.

If conscience is interpretative, the procedure for testing and querying norms and rules which have been handed down to us is already very evident. When such statements are made as 'Not this is *real* courage but that is *real* courage', 'Not this is *real* happiness but that is *real* happiness', 'Not this is the good of the state but that is the good of the state', all such assertions should be read as saying, 'Not this is true and good but that is true and good.' But a strictly interpretative conscience is not yet nominalist, or very rarely so; not even 'mere opinions' are dismissed by it as 'mere names'.[2] In times of great upheaval new values and virtues encroach upon the old ones until an 'either/or' situation is reached (this is value choice). But even then bearers of both the old and the new values have recourse to their respective communities, to representative others. They subject themselves to the normative world of *their own Sittlichkeit*, sometimes completely. When traditional societies experience great upheaval, conscience only becomes nominalist in so far as it denounces the norms of others, those of the outgroup, as 'mere names' lacking essence. This implies that the norms of the ingroup are accepted in their substantive concreteness. Nominalism will never become a general attitude because it will never be extended to the norms of the ingroup. More precisely, the emerging new value system impedes rather than advances general nominalism, whereas the old and dying value system authorizes it. Despite frequent counter-tendencies, from the Renaissance onwards the opposite situation holds. The new world emerges under the star of nominalism. This is the first indication of changes in the structure of morals. Assertions such as 'X is not a value but a mere name' or 'Y is not a value but a mere name' are uttered with increasing frequency and emphasis. In this period, a new value can quickly be substituted for an old one (humility is no longer a value, while pride is). However, these substitutes need not be values or virtues of the same level of concreteness. Instead, practical reason urges us to proceed towards ever higher levels of abstraction, right to the universal stage. This process concludes in an extreme imbalance between external and internal authority. The devalidated values and virtues are fairly concrete, or if they happen to be abstract they are still open to concretization via interpretation. They are carried by communities and groups as bearers of 'ethical life'. The new, validated virtues and values are less and less concrete. If they become completely abstract they are open to several divergent interpretations. Some of these virtues and values are carried by groups; others are not carried by any existing human group at all. The increasingly abstract value claims, in their capacity as recommended substitutes for more concrete values and virtues, are appropriated and utilized by members of pluralistic social clusters. They serve as legitimizing devices supporting the emerging and extensive variety of patterns of conduct and interests which for their part could not pass the test of moral scrutiny in their capacity as concrete moral norms. Put simply, the more abstract the norms and values in whose name the old norms and values are denounced as 'mere names', the greater become the *ideological* implications of the procedure of practical reason. The theoretically clumsy Marxian suggestion that people should be judged on the grounds of what they do and not on the grounds of what they think of doing or claim to do pinpoints a real issue. As long as value and virtue claims of practical reason are supported by the 'ethical life' of a community, whether or not they are idealized and sanitized, there is no discrepancy between doing something and thinking of doing or claiming to do that same thing. Yet, as soon as concrete or even general–abstract norms and virtues are disqualified, and only highly abstract and eventually universal values and norms can pass the test of validity, the discrepancy between doing something and thinking of doing or claiming to do that same thing can become most striking. Formalism, the emaciation of value substance, permits the filling of the same formal claim with almost any kind of substance, a fact which gives rise to false consciousness; that is, to the *lack of awareness* of the *particularistic* propensity of the substance that fills the form. My proposal for a theoretical and practical solution of this dilemma will be made within the framework of moral philosophy. Right now this dilemma can only be outlined.

Modern philosophies began to respond to this challenge in the seventeenth century. As already indicated, they dismissed *Sittlichkeit* as the ultimate foundation of moral reasoning, and made a heroic attempt to infer universal moral principles – and, incidentally, also certain abstract moral values – from non-moral ultimate grounds (of reason or nature). The magnificence of such philosophical constructs notwithstanding, a special kind of false consciousness lurks behind this form of neat reasoning. Those very first principles supposedly derived from non-moral ultimate grounds had in fact been hidden behind those ultimate grounds by the philosophers themselves after they had borrowed them from a particular kind of *Sittlichkeit* and abstracted and distilled them beyond recognition. *External authority appears in these attempts to have been derived, when in fact certain claims of an external authority had been taken for granted in the first place.* The risk of such a procedure is obvious: the abstracted and distilled ultimate grounds could be moral as well as non-moral in character. Hegel, recognizing this danger, revitalized the ancient procedure in a historicized version. But he paid a heavy price for allocating the procedure of selecting norms to the development of the World Spirit (alias 'Reason in History'). In taking the idealized *Sittlichkeit* of his age not only for granted but also as the ultimate outcome of history, he reduced the standpoint of morality to the level of a merely accidental subjectivity.

Morals have been defined here as the individual's practical relationship to the norms and rules of proper conduct. The first structural change of morals occurred via the emergence of the subjective aspect of that relationship, through the differentiation of authority into external authority, and the differentiation of involvement in these two resulting forms of authority (shame, conscience). The second structural change in morals developed out of the increasing imbalance between external and internal authority. Yet this second change is not unidirectional. This growing imbalance can crystallize two distinct structures. Internal authority (conscience) can act as the *ultimate* arbiter in the choice of action and the judgement of human conduct. It can also act as *sole* arbiter in these matters. Although the second structure develops after the first, the first does not become obsolete, nor is it discarded, with this development. At least, this is my hope, and for the following reason. Whereas the emergence of internal authority as the ultimate arbiter in practical decision and judgement can be called an indicator of moral progress because at least one subcase of that structure contributes to moral progress, internal authority as the sole arbiter in action choice and the judgement of conduct represents *moral regression*. It is part of the dialectic of modernity that the moral contradiction it involves is neither a value contradiction nor a contradiction between abstract and concrete norms, but a contradiction *between the two developmental logics of its intrinsic moral structure*. These two logics should now be discussed.

1   Practical reason (conscience) is the *ultimate arbiter* in action choice and the judgement of human conduct if, in the event of norm contradiction and value contradiction, it is the subject who makes the final and binding commitment. Upon becoming an ultimate arbiter, practical reason cannot operate in the *modus* of phronesis, for it must determine not the application of norms but their validity. It cannot operate as interpretative conscience either, and for similar reasons: it is the guiding principle that must be established, not a pre-existing norm or virtue that must be reinterpreted. Double-quality reflection does not disappear in this structure. In fact the reverse is the case: the more universal the values which the person is for or against, the more prominent will be the quasi-transcendental component of double-quality reflection. If one posits universal values and then engages in self-reflection from the standpoint of these values, this reflection is supported by sense perception far less than in the case of complementary conscience.

At this level, no preference can be given to either a dialogical or a monological choice of values and norms. Whatever the importance of such a distinction may be, and whatever theoretical and practical implications the option for either the first or the second may entail, it has little relevance for the issue presented above. Internal authority is the ultimate arbiter, and equally so, irrespective of whether a person discusses the validity claim of norms and values with everyone concerned or accepts a maxim following upon intellectual intuition or speculation. Yet practical reason (conscience), as the ultimate arbiter, *always employs arguments*. Even if arbitration is intuitive and the new values are accepted with a gesture, a particular strand of arguments underpins the choice, and dialogue is immediately initiated – all the more so, considering that any devalidation of traditional norms and rules from the standpoint of validated norms and rules implies a procedure of argumentation. People justify both their value choices and their claims that certain norms and rules of their environment (or those of their ancestors) are invalid, are mere names, ghosts of the past, fancies, irrational constraints. This justification is directed towards others, for others, against others, but always in a reciprocal relation with others.

At first glance, the operation of conscience as an ultimate arbiter seems *deconstructive*, and up to a point it is. Bans are lifted, prohibitory signs are eliminated, and interdictions are annulled by this ultimate arbiter. Acts hitherto subjected to moral scrutiny are declared value-neutral. 'What is wrong with doing this?', 'What is wrong with doing that?' – these are the typical questions of the deconstructivist operation. And the answer is usually, 'Nothing is wrong with it.' Still, conscience as the ultimate arbiter is as much *constructive* as it is deconstructive. First, it engenders new and highly abstract norms, and constructs universal values and norms which are *binding*. Here, gestures of deconstruction are simultaneously gestures of construction, and concrete values are deconstructed as more abstract and universal values undergo construction. An example of this would be the statement that treating action X as a crime contradicts human rights.

Conscience as the ultimate arbiter stands for abstract and universal *taboos* which, if validated, sweep away a great number of concrete taboos. Contrasted to general taboos, concrete taboos are unmasked as handmaidens of social oppression and psychological repression. This brief account will suffice to show how the interpretative and applicative operation of conscience has been preserved, as well as grossly modified, within the new structure. I earlier set forth some sketchy remarks concerning interpretation with reference to the *ideological* use of universals. This ideological use aside, the interpretation of universals or of highly abstract norms requires great mental effort, if not necessarily a great amount of knowledge. The readiness to make this mental effort must be present in the individual so the new structure can stand as a *moral* structure. The reconcretizing of the new (abstract, universal) norms in a democratic legal system lends itself as a partial but not complete solution. Yet, if this reconcretizing fails to materialize or is insufficient, the balance between construction and deconstruction will be in grave danger of being upset. Application still requires phronesis, but it also requires something above and beyond this. Whether the action we initiate harmonizes with universals or contradicts them is difficult to determine unless we have some kind of crutch to lean upon in our decisions. Moral philosophies offer crutches of several kinds, but they are rarely used, or rarely used consistently. The individual, under the heavy burden of an excessive moral responsibility in this process of arbitration, finds it more attractive to shed the burden and yet keep the power of arbitration, or to shed the burden together with the power of arbitration. As we shall see shortly, these two attitudes are complementary.

Practical reason (conscience) as the *ultimate arbiter* in action choice and the judgement of human conduct made its appearance in many forms. We cannot do complete justice to the diversity of the phenomenon by merely distinguishing the major ideal types of this new moral structure, yet it could be said that roughly three *basic* attitudes appeared. I term these *bad conscience, legislative conscience* and *sceptical conscience*. Protestant (and in particular Calvinist) ethics, as analysed by Max Weber, forms the prototype of the 'bad conscience'. Here, the enormous emphasis placed on morality (on individual, subjective arbitration) is counterbalanced by the *concretization* of the new values and norms *within the private and intimate spheres*: in work (*vocation*) and in *sexuality* (which includes eroticism). 'Legislative conscience' emphasizes the abstraction and universalization of norms and values and concretizes them in the *political* and the *legal* sphere. 'Sceptical conscience' places more emphasis on deconstruction, whilst elaborating the constructive value of general tolerance in both the *public* and the *private* sphere where judgement is concerned, and mainly in the *private* sphere where the choice of action is concerned. What is astounding here is the subdivision of the same moral structure according to *spheric* concretization (private, public, intimate), a new phenomenon compared to the subdivision of complementary conscience. As we know from Weber, the political or public sphere and the actions performed in them were of no moral relevance whatsoever for the repositories of 'bad conscience', whereas the legislative and the sceptical conscience were busy eliminating the particularism of sexual taboos and of taboos erected through religious, artistic and similar patterns.

2 Practical reason (conscience) as the *sole arbiter* in action choice and the judgement of human conduct – in other words, the second moral structure of modernity – appears as the combination of two mutually supporting and reinforcing attitudes. On the one hand, this

combination sheds moral responsibility but retains the power to arbitrate; on the other, it sheds moral responsibility together with the power to arbitrate. Practical reason becomes the *sole* arbiter if every binding moral norm and rule is deconstructed and no novel one is constructed, hence when *no external moral authority remains in force*. No values or norms remain to be accepted unconditionally; no values and norms are there to be accepted as *binding*. Thus for the individual nothing is binding and everything is permitted, provided that the subject gives the go-ahead. Everything the individual *decides* will be desirable or good *is* good. One may protest against the use of the term 'practical reason' or 'conscience' in this context, but there is no basis to this protest. People do not say, 'I realize that I and the world may perish because i could not care less about norms.' They rather say, 'I realize that I and the world may perish, and *this is the norm* (this is good).' Assertions such as 'Whatever is in my interest is good', and 'The goal I have set for you will make you great, so all means of achieving this goal are good', are embedded in the same structure and follow exactly the same logic.

The premise 'Whatever I decide to be right is right' is the premise of *self-authorization*. If one asks, 'In whose name do you claim that what you do and the way you judge are right?', the answer will probably be something like 'In my own name', or 'Why should I bother about authorization at all?' The voice of conscience always suggests that you answer to yourself, but it never suggests that you answer to yourself *alone*. As long as external moral authority exists, even if this authority is represented by only a singular moral norm or value accepted by one as unconditionally binding, 'answering to myself' is tantamount to answering the question 'Did you act according to the norm you have accepted or formulated as binding?' If I answer to myself alone, and to no external moral authority whatsoever, 'answering myself' does not include but rather excludes *moral reflection*. The transcendental (or quasi-transcendental) aspect of self-reflection is gone, and success or failure, which are merely empirical results, become the only criteria of self-judgement. Thus *practical and pragmatic–instrumental action and judgement merge*. Practical reason as the sole arbiter in action choice and judgement is the final product of deconstruction, both logically and empirically. Individualism runs amok in breaching the protective dams and shedding the last vestiges of external authority. Yet in so doing it does not shed authority in general, but affirms new authorities void of any moral content.

Just how the logic of practical reason unfolds can best be

illustrated through the image of a spiral. In the beginning, practical reason is *in nuce*. External authority is the sum total of the concrete norms to which people subject themselves. If someone fails in this self-subjection, the eyes of others shame this person. Subsequently, practical reason and conscience emerge, and with these things morality, and the duplication of authority. Double-quality reflection makes its appearance, particularly in the structure of interpretative conscience. Next, the process of deconstruction takes place. The taken-for-granted character of concrete norms seems to vanish, and highly abstract and universal norms and values are established. The quasi-transcendental aspect of self-reflection is in full swing, and practical reason relies heavily upon the use of argument. Finally, we return to the first stage, in a form structurally higher but morally lower than that existing at the beginning. External moral authority is deconstructed, as is the moral component of internal authority. Double-quality reflection disappears once again. The 'others' become fully instrumentalized by the Ego (as a non-moral authority), and this Ego totally subjects itself to an external authority void of morals. Conscience as involvement in internal authority (practical reason) becomes an *epiphenomenon*, and the eyes of others become mere mirrors of the end result (success or failure) and repositories of naked power which in the gesture of avoiding shame the person is subjected to.

One can distinguish four main types of practical reason as the sole arbiter in the choice of action and the judgement of conduct: *narcissistic conscience, private calculative conscience, public calculative conscience* and *good conscience* (I have borrowed the last term from Nietzsche). Conscience becomes *narcissistic* if the person is exclusively preoccupied with mere empirical self-reflection. Neither moral norms nor values constitute the standpoint of self-reflection; the entire interpretative framework mobilized in self-reflection is extraneous to morals (being either psychological, or social in a psychologized sense). The dangerously low sensitivity to shame of the narcissistic personality should be explained not by weakness of character but by the *structure* of the attitude itself. *Private calculative conscience* represents the merger of two distinct pairs of categories of value orientation, good/evil and successful/unsuccessful, where success is good and failure is evil. It is in this situation that *pragmatic consequences* become the (non-moral) yardsticks of self-reflection. All other yardsticks disappear. Good motivation equals good calculation, and 'pangs of conscience' are only felt if calculation proves bad (and the result is failure instead of success). In contrast to the narcissistic conscience, and very much like other situations where conscience is the sole arbiter, private calculative conscience has a heightened, almost hysterical, sensitivity towards shame. Persons of private calculative conscience will often commit suicide rather than be exposed to the eyes of others when it comes to miscalculation and failure. *Public calculative conscience* represents another merger of two distinct pairs of categories of value orientation, this time between that of good/evil and useful/harmful. What is useful for a nation, a people, a class, a party, is good. The leader, the dictator or an elite of any provenance *defines* what is useful for the rest (the reference group), and it is presupposed that 'usefulness' is determined by proper calculation. Since 'useful' is defined as 'good', blind obedience to social authority, this fountain-head of calculation, is considered virtuous, while disobedience is a vice. Every means supposedly leading to desirable end results must be regarded as a 'good'. Yet the confirmation of *real* success is not required, as it is with private calculative conscience. Loss of faith in the Great Calculator itself is shameful. The eyes of others are expressions of naked power as well as accomplices in the wielding of this naked power, and so shame is mixed with fear, fear of being punished and fear of deviation. *Good conscience*, as nihilism accomplished and reversed, is the final bid for *deification*. If there are neither gods nor norms, I am god. Good conscience is private, if other people are used as mere means for the Ego's full self-realization. Here the Ego construes itself as Superman. But this Ego–god lacks the main attribute of God: immortality. The great fear, the fear of death, lurks behind the pretence of deification. Mortality, this 'great shame' of the self-deified Ego, cannot be overcome. Yet good conscience is rarely private. The Superman needs his following, the eyes of which reconfirm his 'divinity'. This following is nothing more than the mirror image of Superman. These people obey their Superman blindly. His approval is their honour, his disapproval their shame. And, whilst he obliges others to submit in blind obedience, he too depends on this obedience. People who are neither afraid of him nor shamed by him personally threaten and mortify this Superman.

There is no *moral* choice between the two structures, between practical reason as the ultimate arbiter and practical reason as the sole arbiter, for only two distinct *moral* options would represent a moral choice. Regarding the structure of morals, *we have no moral choice*. Commitment to practical reason as the ultimate arbiter of action choice and the judgement of conduct is the only *moral* commitment open to us. And I mean moral *commitment*. We cannot be assured of a further stage of moral development – namely, ours, which is by definition 'higher' than every or any preceding stage. The modern moral structure is not unidirectional, but bifurcates. The commitment of the actors determines which tendency will predominate. Unless the structure I have terms 'conscience as the ultimate arbiter' is *concretized* in the ethical world, unless it becomes 'taken for granted' by the denizens of ethical worlds (in the plural), the danger inherent in this structure cannot be overcome.

7

Just Judgements passed on Single Cases

I have included the 'formal concept of justice' with the empirical moral universals. The first (abstract) constituent of the 'human condition' was said to be the substitution of social regulation for instinct regulation. Where there is human life, there are norms and rules as well. Norms and rules constitute social clusters, and the norms and rules constituting a given social cluster must be applied to every member of that cluster consistently and continuously. In the event of an inconsistency or discontinuity, an *injustice* has been committed, irrespective of whether the norms and rules in question are of moral provenance. The emergence of morality brings about a new interpretation of justice: individual persons or whole groups of persons can reject the 'taken-for-granted' norms and rules as unjust and simultaneously claim as valid alternative norms and rules, norms and rules which to them are more just, or simply just. I have termed this kind of justice 'dynamic justice'. Dynamic justice itself is not an empirical human universal, yet the 'formal concept of justice' is: even dynamic justice must follow the patterns inherent in the 'formal concept of justice', though in a modified form.

Every problem concerning justice and injustice has a moral element, yet these problems are primarily social and political in nature. I have discussed all of them in my book *Beyond Justice*. Working within the framework of 'general ethics', I wish to concentrate on one particular issue of justice, on that of just (and unjust) judgements passed on single cases.

To be 'just' (in the sense of the formal concept of justice) is to manifest a virtue, and to be 'unjust' is to manifest a vice, for injustice *hurts* people who do not get what they rightly expect to get (according to the norms and rules). Regular unjust acts constitute an affront against society, and increase the risk that society will relapse into a state of chaos or absolute tyranny (though we can add to this, 'unless alternative norms and rules can be and are observed').

If we have in mind the moral content of an action alone, the process of *judging* has two closely interrelated aspects. If I embark on an action I must use good judgement to decide either how to apply norms in the concrete situation at hand, or whether the situation is one where rule X or rule Y applies. Of course, the judgemental process can be completely 'instinctual' and unnoticed if the situation is 'obvious'. The other aspect of judging involves decisions about the moral merit or excellence of *other* people and the fact of whether or not those people observed, or eventually infringed, the norms; whether they followed, or rather failed to follow, the rules. These two aspects of judging, though connected, can be separated, and indeed they often are separated, individually as well as socially. There are people who are bad judges in situations where they must make decisions about their actions, and good judges when it comes to assessing the actions of others, and *vice versa*. Not everyone is entitled to pass judgements on the actions of any other person. If people pass judgements – as speech acts – they are not entitled to pass, they are normally subjected to social sanctions. This is even more the case *if passing a judgement itself means applying social sanctions*. The people entitled to pass judgements (as speech acts) which involve social sanctions are termed *social authorities*. In certain cases (for example in some tribal societies), 'social authority' is identical with the whole of the adult populace. To give a modern example, the Catholic clergy is a social authority only for confessing Catholics, for the former's judgement carries social sanctions only for the latter. Legal sanctions are the kind of sanctions implemented by legal authorities on the basis of judgements passed by these authorities. If the distinction between legal and other social authorities is clear, which is not always the case, legal authorities are not entitled to implement sanctions if the judgement has been made by an authority other than legal, whereas other social authorities are not entitled to implement sanctions if the judgement has been made by a legal authority (even if they are obliged to inform the legal authority of the conditions under which legal sanctions can be implemented). Finally, laws prescribe the social sanctions that *should never be implemented* by any other authority but the legal. Yet the laws cannot prevent us from making a judgement. In this sense, public opinion has the right to pronounce that 'A, convicted by law, is innocent', or 'B, set free by the court (the law), is guilty.' But the public is certainly not entitled to set free the former or imprison the latter.

All this is obvious, and has been said only to support the

preliminary statement that the two aspects of judging can be, and generally are, separated from one another. It is important to substantiate this preliminary statement in order to justify as a reasonable enterprise the objective of this chapter, in which I restrict the discussion of just judgement as passed on single cases to the analysis of the second aspect of judging. Even if in most cases a right moral decision is impossible without making good judgements about the actions and behaviour of other actors, even if passing judgements on others includes on our part a moral commitment, even if implementing social sanctions requires direct action by us – even if these facts are undoubtedly true, the problem of *judging others* can be treated separately. And, if we do treat it separately, it is not purely because of methodological considerations, or, more precisely, because these considerations have the quality of verisimilitude.

The discussion of the *second aspect of judging* will concentrate on the *act of judging*. At this juncture I am not interested in what kind of social sanctions are involved in the judgements passed, or whether the judgements carry social sanctions at all. We do not distinguish between *moral* and *legal* judgement, since we view the latter exclusively from the perspective of the former.

It is possible to pass judgements on single persons with or without *overtly* making a comparison or ranking. (We always *covertly* make comparisons and rankings.) It should be mentioned that, if an overt comparison or ranking is *not* made, and the judgement is in the *affirmative*, we do not denounce the judgement as 'unjust', even if we consider it false (in that it is too positive). This is always so if excellence is being judged, and true to varying degrees if one passes a moral judgement on an action, or makes a judgement about character. If a, father claims that his child's drawings are excellent, we may politely overrule what we believe to be parental self-delusion, but we do not call his assertion an unjust act. If, however, the same father praises excessively his child's drawings whilst belittling those of other children who in our view draw at least as well, we unhesitatingly call him and his act unjust. If someone praises a person's character in a manner disproportionate (in our view) to the merits of this person, we call this judgement wrong (false) but not unjust, if it is made without overt comparison. Yet *negative judgements* are termed *unjust without overt comparison* if they are considered wrong (false). The father who asserts that his child's drawings (in our view skilful) are rubbish is called *unjust* without any recourse to an overt comparison and ranking. And, if a person's character is derided in our presence, we call the derider 'unjust' (if we believe the judgement false) irrespective of whether the abused person has been, overtly or covertly, compared to others. We take this distinction so much for granted that we never even ask why it is so. Passing positive judgements without open comparison and ranking *does not hurt* anyone, nor does it affront social norms and rules. If everyone passed judgements more positive than deserved, without overt comparison and ranking, neither chaos nor tyranny would ensue. Moreover, excessively positive judgements, without overt comparison, accord with the interclusteral moral virtue of *benevolence*. Finally, they lend *recognition* to a personality, and 'lending recognition to a personality' has in modernity become an interclusteral moral norm. However, the exceptional status of positive judgements without overt comparison only pertains unconditionally to the sphere of *static justice*. If one rejects certain norms and rules as unjust (wrong), *certain positive judgements* in respect of the actions or the character of a person who behaves in accordance with these norms and rules *can legitimately be called unjust.*

We normally judge actions after the event, but occasionally we also judge those which have not yet taken place (if a person's intentions are disclosed to us). We judge people on the grounds of actions already performed, and we assume by this judgement that the same person is likely to perform similar kinds of actions in the future.

We know that the statement 'Action X is just' or the statement 'Person A is just' is an evaluative statement deduced from statements of fact. So is the statement 'A's judgement is just.' The judgement of A is the fact. Before drawing the conclusion 'A passed a just judgement', it must first be known whether this judgement was or was not the case. But the conclusion 'A passed a just judgement' is only apparently a mere evaluative statement. It consists again of statements of facts from which the evaluation follows. This statement of facts consists of statements about the *circumstances* in which or about which the judgement (appraised by us as just or unjust) has been passed. It must be borne in mind that, if we evaluate a judgement as just or unjust, the statements of fact we must get right *do not include* statements concerning the *motivations* of the initial judgement. Put more succinctly, if I state, 'The judgement of A is unjust', I must determine, first, whether A has passed this judgement at all; secondly, which facts have formed the basis of that judgement; thirdly, under the guidance of which norms and rules the judgement has been made; and, fourthly, whether those norms apply to the case in question (the term 'circumstances' includes all these considerations). Even so, I do not need to determine whether A really wanted to pass an unjust judgement, or whether this just or unjust judgement was motivated by goodness of heart, envy, self-interest or the pursuit of justice. To speak with Schutz, both the 'in order' and the 'because' motives are left out of consideration here. I don't need to know what motivated A in passing his judgement in order to pass a *just* judgement on the judgement of A. Obviously, I can also state, 'A passed an unjust judgement out of envy' or 'A passed a just judgement out of self-interest', but here I make an unjust or just judgement on the character of the person and not on his *judgement about a single case*. Moreover, in order to pass a just judgement about the judgement of a person, and despite the need to be familiar with the circumstances and to be aware of my obligation to do my best to get all the facts right, I do not have to know *how* the person who has passed the initial judgement understood those very circumstances (whether he got them right or wrong). Whether A passed an unjust judgement because he got the facts wrong, or some of the facts wrong, is not a matter that must be settled before it is possible to pass the judgement 'A's judgement was right or wrong' (alias just/unjust). Certainly, one can also state, 'A passed an unjust judgement because he was uninformed', or 'A can only pass a just judgement instinctively because he is feeble-minded', but such judgements are also judgements of character, and not judgements about the particular judgement that A has passed in the given (single) case. (The statement 'Had A been properly informed he would have passed a just judgement' is a judgement of character.) All this relates to the fact, already discussed by Aristotle, that a person cannot be called 'unjust' merely on the basis of having performed an unjust act or passed an unjust judgement. This distinction clearly holds true of the person B who passes judgement on the judgement of A (for his judgement can also be unjust without his being an unjust person, or just without his being a just person).

Let us now discuss the judgement of A (the initial judgement). Let us assume that A passes a judgement on moral merit or demerit. In this case the judgement should be regulated by the idea of justice, 'to each according to his or her merit'. Since we restrict the analysis to the *act of judging*, the above-mentioned idea of justice regulates us as follows: 'Each should be judged according to his or her merits.'[1] Judgement is an evaluative action which should follow from a statement of fact, and should (in this case) take the following form: 'This act is meritorious (more or less meritorious) or wicked (more or less wicked).' And what are the facts to be known? Since they have been enumerated by Aristotle, I shall give only a brief account of them. One must know the norms and rules (whether or not act X is meritorious according to the norms); one must know the situation in which the action has taken place; one must know the actors for or against whom the action has taken place, the time and place of the action, and several other factors. All this knowledge should be true. In order to place the action on the two extreme loci of the merit/demerit continuum, it is unnecessary to have true knowledge about the motives ('in order to' or 'because' motives). None the less, it is necessary, in order to make a *just* comparison and ranking, in order to make *just* judgement about the 'more or less' aspect of the situation (more or less wicked acts, 'in between' acts), to know the motives of the actors, and to know what they knew and did not know when they embarked on the action being judged. This is a highly important distinction between the primary (initial) judgement passed – in this case, on merits and demerits – and the secondary judgement concerning the *justice* of the primary judgement. Each time we pass the judgement 'A's judgement was *unjust* (or just)', we assume that A drew the evaluative statement from *false* (or true) statements of fact. The motives of the actor whose action has been judged by A are *included* in the cluster of facts which ought to be got right. So if I assert that the judgement of Justice A is unjust, I can argue that this unjust evaluation has resulted from false statements about the *motives of the defendant*. However, *my* statement is passed independently of *my* knowledge or ignorance about the *motives of Justice A*, which are irrelevant.

To pass a just primary judgement, a *hearing* must be given to the actors on whose action judgement is to be passed. Just judgement presupposes communication with those whose action is to be judged. If a face-to-face encounter is possible, the hearing must be direct. The actors (who have performed the action in question) must have the opportunity to *justify* their actions as well as *explain* them. They must be free to refer to *anything* (force of circumstances, lack of information, motives and the like) in this process of justification and explanation. If a face-to-face encounter is not possible, the very person who passes the initial judgement must mentally place himself in exactly the same situation as that occupied by the person under judgement. Further, he must try to identify any alternative motives that may have influenced this person. On the other hand, the same person (who passes the primary judgement) must give a *hearing* to *all* fellow creatures who are, or can be, in the position of judging. Personal interaction is rarely possible with all of them, but is almost always possible with some of them. 'To give a hearing' means, then, to consult others who are in the position of judging, to find out what kind of judgement they would pass in this particular case. The two 'hearings', whilst equally indispensable, are completely different. The first hearing must be granted to the *singular*, the second to the *general*. It stands to reason that those consulted (in reality or in imagination) in the second hearing cannot refer to their *own motives, circumstances*, and the like, because what is to be determined by the second hearing is nothing but the *secondary judgement* in the state of *anticipation*. For my primary judgement can be just if I give total consideration to the case under judgement, *and* thereby anticipate that the secondary judgement passed on *my primary* judgement should be 'A's judgement was just', and that the statement should be *true*. The latter proviso is of the greatest importance. The statement that 'A's judgement is just' can be either true or false. In respect of static justice one can assume that, if every person, either virtually or actually, states, 'A's judgement is just', this statement is true. However, the same cannot be assumed under the conditions of dynamic justice.[2]

The first hearing is always performed critically. Clearly, neither the justifications nor the explanations of the actors who are to be judged can be taken at face value. To emphasize what is obvious, the testimony of witnesses must be equally considered (though also in a critical way). All the same, in the case of static justice the 'second hearing' is *not* performed critically, which does not mean that the primary judge must listen uncritically to all the concrete advice presented, though it does mean that the anticipated judgement of *all* possible secondary judges (of the same position) is accepted uncritically. This is not so under the conditions of dynamic justice. There, the second hearing too is critical, for the 'all' whose anticipated judgement you seek ('A's primary judgement was just') comprises only those with whom you share values, maxims and principles. And this 'all' can indeed be only a very few. You then anticipate that all those who do not share your values, maxims and principles will judge (or might judge) your judgemental act as 'A's primary judgement was unjust', while you are convinced this anticipated judgement is *false*.

Not every initial judgemental act (on matters of merit/demerit, excellence and the lack of excellence) is a *recommendation*. In respect of judgements passed on the merits or demerits of a single act (of a single actor or a collective actor), recommendations may take the following form: 'You have done well, do it again', or 'You should not have done this, you must not do it again', or 'You should have done better, so do better next time.' However, the judgements 'You did your best under the circumstances' and 'Your action was one of the possible good actions under the circumstances' are not recommendations, although they are positive judgements ('your action' is praised as meritorious).

Since the task of primary judgement is to consider motives and situations, judgemental acts such as this very often do not involve recommendation. If judgemental acts are simultaneously recommendations, but *only* then, the judgement is relevant for *all* actors, single or collective, in the same or a similar position, even if we pass it on a single case. (For example, 'You acted disrespectfully. Don't do it again. No one should be disrespectful to his father'; or, 'You acted bravely. Do it again. All soldiers should act bravely.') Even if those judging do not address the person whose act they are judging, comparing or ranking, their judgement may or may not involve recommendations. One can make the same distinction in judging fictitious characters. For example, in discussing the Shakespearean characters Goneril and Regan, we can justly make the judgement 'They should not have acted as they did', and then add, 'No one should act as they did.' Yet in passing judgement on Hamlet we might justly say, 'He acted as well as he could under the circumstances', though we could not recommend that everyone should act in the same way. However, in contrast to primary judgement, secondary acts of judgement are *always* recommendations. This statement is self-evident, following as it does from everything said so far about judgements passed on judgements. It is not possible to say, 'The best you could do under the circumstances was to pass an unjust judgement': unjust judgements are never 'best' (not even in a relative sense); *no one* should pass an unjust judgement.

I have argued that secondary judgement passed on the justice or injustice of a judgement excludes the judgement of character. I have also argued that in primary (initial) judgement (when the merit or demerit of an action is to be determined), motives must be considered, and consequently that judgement of character must enter the judgemental procedure. But, even so, judgement passed on a single action should not be *based* on the judgement of character (the latter can only increase or mitigate the severity of judgement). It is for the *good* sense of justice to find the proper *degree* to which judgement of character should modify (increase or mitigate) the severity of the judgement passed on a single action. To make such judgements dependent upon the judgement of character is by definition *unjust*, for this procedure *contradicts the formal concept of justice*. Yet the converse is not true. There are certain single actions where the magnitude and the type of moral offence perfectly justify a full and negative judgement of character, just as there are single supererogatory actions which might (though not always) justify a final positive judgement of character. People, unique as they are, cannot be either compared or ranked as wholes. None the less, the formal concept of justice enjoins us to compare and rank. Actions are comparable under the guidance of norms and rules. And characters are comparable (as 'good', 'less good', 'bad', 'wicked') on the basis of their *actions*, or even on the basis of a *single action*. The judgement of character as a whole can enter the primary judgement (altering it in either direction) if it is made on the basis of psychological and mental endowments, character traits and motivations, by which concrete actions can be *explained* (or we surmise that they can be). Even so, to include in the assessment the sexual habits of the actor when the act under judgement has nothing to do with sex, or to dissect his soul, to investigate all his opinions, would not only be to commit an outrage against his personality, but would be totally unjust. This point has been strongly and rightly emphasized by Foucault.

If the judgemental act includes recommendations other than 'Don't do it again', the demand or even the imperative of *rectifying* the action thus judged has also been included in this judgemental act. The demand or imperative addressed to the single actor of the single action is generalized as follows: 'Everyone who should have acted better than he/she has is *advised* to rectify what he/she has done', and 'Everyone who has done something that he/she should not have done *should* rectify what he/she has done.' Rectification, in whatever form it occurs, is the restoration of *social justice*. It stands to reason, then, that the very actions which *cannot be rectified* are always considered the *most evil*. The consequences of an action are considered in the primary judgement in so far as non-rectifiable acts are judged to be the most severe transgressions. Hart aptly remarks in his *Punishment and Responsibility* that the expression 'responsibility for action' stands for 'responsibility for the result of action'. To repeat his examples, X is responsible not for *gossiping* but for the *defamation* of Y's *character*, or X is responsible not for *killing* Y but for the *death* of Y. In other words the rectification of an act is tantamount to the rectification of the results of an act, for this is precisely what restores social justice. Of course, what actions (results of actions) can be rectified, and what actions cannot be, is a matter decided via the norms and rules of the society in which the deed has been committed. If X caused the death of Y, but causing Y's death can be rectified via the norms and rules of the society in which the act was commited (by X being exiled, by X paying compensation to the relatives, or the like), the killing of Y is clearly not regarded as one of the most severe transgressions. The death penalty (be it executed by the legal or any other social authority) is the expression of the fact that a person has committed an act which cannot be rectified (either in the present or in the future), and thus an expression of the belief that social justice can only be restored if this person is denied a place among the living.

As the 'rectification of an act' is tantamount to the rectification of the result of the act (which must take place according to norms and rules), the advice or imperative to rectify included in the primary judgement has nothing to do with the intention *to reform character*. Such an intention is only *implicitly* present in the recommendation 'You should act better in the future', 'You should never do this again.'

Certain conclusions can be drawn here. The recommendation included in the judgement 'You should never do this again' is a *moral* recommendation, in that it means, 'You should never do this again, *irrespective of social sanctions.*' For a statement such as 'You should never do this again *because* if you do you will be punished again' is clearly not identical with the *recommendation* 'You should not do it again'; rather, it is a *threat*. And so the intention of *reforming character* can only be expressed in a purely moral recommendation such as 'Don't do it, irrespective of social sanctions', and this is an implicit recommendation to reform one's character precisely in the sense of 'Don't do it, for the *merit of not doing it*, for the virtue expressed by not doing the deed, for the merit or virtue of doing something else', whereas nothing like this is implicit in a threat. Confusing a demand or imperative of rectification (which has nothing to do with the intention to reform character) with a purely moral recommendation aimed at the reform of character 'irrespective of social sanctions' is not just a logical blunder; it also constitutes moral mischief.

Do we have the *right* to judge (others)? Who, or what, has authorized us to judge others? In discussing only the pure model of static justice we can dismiss these questions as irrelevant. But after dynamic justice made its first appearance, and ever since, such questions have been raised, and the answers to them have always been of the greatest importance. The problem of the right to judge lies alongside that of the right to blame, censure, condemn, and in fact is tantamount to it. It is quite different from the 'right to praise', which has never been in doubt. Accordingly, in what follows, the 'right to judge' stands for the right to blame, to censure and to condemn. Moreover, since this chapter deals with just judgements passed on single cases, I shall discuss the 'right to judge' only where negative judgement (blame, censure, condemnation) is indeed passed on single cases, under the conditions of both static and dynamic justice. Obviously, the question of whether we have the right to judge does not include whether we have the right to pass *unjust* judgements, for no one has the *right* to do so (as this contradicts the formal concept of justice and therefore cannot be 'rightly done'). That we do so without having the right to do so is another matter. The question of whether we have the right to judge (others) takes the form 'Do we have the right to judge *others at all*?' In other words, the question is one of whether we have the right *to pass just judgements on others*. The same question can also be read as follows: 'Although we do have the right to pass *just* judgements on others, we do so only rarely and inconsistently because of the intrinsic faultiness (and sinfulness) of our nature; consequently, it is more meritorious not to pass judgements at all.' This second formulation does not query our *right* to pass just judgements, only our *ability* to do so, or to do so continuously and consistently.

No society could exist if everyone constantly asked this question and the question was constantly answered in the affirmative ('Truly, no one has the right to judge others'). However, conscience (practical reason proper and the involvement in it) could not exist if no one asked this question, and if no one ever gave the following answer: 'In *this particular case* I have no right to judge others', or 'In *this particular respect* I cannot judge others, though I have the right to pass just judgements.' In both these formulas, 'I' can stand for 'I as a person' and 'I as a member of community X'. In the case of pure static justice the right to judge is allocated to a social cluster, position or rank, and this is exactly why the question is never asked. The less such allocation takes place in a 'quasi-natural' ('taken for granted') way, the more the 'right to judge' must be at least co-determined by practical reason (conscience).

What does it mean that the right to judge is co-decided by practical reason (conscience)? How is such a co-decision effected?

Asking these questions is in itself tantamount to the *purely moral* recommendation that, before passing a judgement on an act of others, or before passing any judgement upon character, we must first pass a just judgement about ourselves. The recommendation is purely moral because it is made 'irrespective of social sanctions'; that is to say, the question of whether we have the right to judge tests and queries the validity of primary judgement as *primary* judgement. Since the question of whether we have the right to judge is only asked if judgement is passed on merits or demerits,[3] it entails the following (moral) recommendation: 'Any time we are about to pass judgement on the merits or demerits of others, we must first determine whether we have the right to pass such judgement in this particular case.' We can do this by transforming the primary judgement into a secondary judgement, which is itself preceded by a primary judgement passed upon ourselves. We must decide via primary good judgement whether we have committed acts similar in type and gravity to the act we are about to judge. If we have committed a similar act of greater gravity, we do not have the right to judge. If we have committed a similar act of equal gravity, we have the right to judge *if* we have rectified our mistake, fault, crime, or whatever. If I (as a person) judge *collective subjects*, I must pass the *same* judgement (a self-judgement) on the *collective subject* of which I am a member. I (as a person) do not have the right to judge the acts of any collective subject if the collective subject of which I am a member has committed the same acts, or similar acts of greater gravity, or similar acts of the same gravity, without subsequent rectification, unless I have passed the *same* judgement on the acts of the collective subject I was a member of *at the time* the acts in question were committed, in the first case; and retrospectively, in the second case. Obviously, if I pass such a judgement and was not alive or was a minor when identical or similar acts were committed by the community of which I am a member, the (self-) judgement passed on the community is, in both cases, retrospective.

This indicates that the question of whether or not we have the right to judge in a particular case is to be decided under the guidance of the *formal concept of justice*. This cannot be otherwise, the formal concepts of justice being the maxim of justice. The moral recommendation to make a preliminary 'self-judgement' before passing any primary judgement enjoins us to observe the norm of consistency in the application of norms and rules.

Granted this, it is possible to withhold judgement, not only because a person *does not have the right* to judge, but also because this person believes that in one or another respect he or she cannot *be* the judge of others. X can withhold judgement about the act of Y, not because X has committed similar acts of equal or greater gravity, but because *X does not know how he/she would have acted in Y's situation*. The formal concept of justice does not apply here (so we do not discuss the *right* to judge). The preliminary judgement of X to withhold judgement about Y's act is a self-judgement passed upon *character*. Yet I have already argued that no preliminary judgement should be based on the judgement of character. For this reason the decision to withhold judgement because of considerations based on the self-judgement passed on character does not annul the *right* to judge.

Every person who has not forsaken the right to judge has the right to judge due to membership of a community the norms and rules of which apply to everybody, this person included. One judges in one's capacity as an embodiment or repository of the norms and rules. Precisely because the right to judge is ascribed to persons as *repositories* of the norms and rules of their community, a person, *qua* single person, can forsake the right to judge if this person has infringed the norms in a similar manner to or to a greater extent than the person whose act is to be judged. For now the former cannot judge as the repository or the embodiment of the particular rule or rules concerned.

It is easy, at least theoretically, to determine who has the right to judge and who has forsaken this right, if dynamic justice only devalidates certain *interpretations* of values (norms), and not the values (norms) themselves. The problem becomes more complex if the person who judges and the person being judged observe *different norms*; where these two people are *not* embodiments or repositories of the *same* normative system. How, and under what circumstances, can we assert that a person belonging to a real or imaginary community has the right to judge someone observing the norms and rules of a *different* community? Such a right must be based on the *conviction* that the norms and rules observed by the party doing the judging are superior (better, fairer, more just) than those observed by the party being judged. The traditional, quasi-natural 'ethnocentrism' of human communities and cultures is based exactly on this conviction. For as long as the norms and rules of the 'other' culture have been regarded as inferior (barbarian, biased, wicked, callous), the persons observing those norms have without fail been judged and rejected as barbarians, biased, wicked and callous. Only when the normative system of a culture is undergoing devalidation, and the conception of a system of alternative norms *relativizes* the 'rightness' of judging and being judged in both the cultures, is this quasi-natural feeling of superiority lost. In this case only our membership in the community of ideal (imaginary) norms establishes our right to judge members of other cultures who are themselves supposed to live up to the imaginary norms of the ideal community. It is from the standpoint of 'legislative conscience', and from this standpoint alone, that one can raise the claim that every human being, as the repository of 'humankind', should have the right to judge every other human being.

So far I have discussed at some length whether, when and why we have the right to pass moral judgements on actions. I have not yet really addressed the problem of whether we have the right to pass judgements on *moral characters*. We know that we have the right to pass such judgements as 'The act of X was a moral blunder, an offence, transgression, crime, sin.' But do we have the right to assert, 'X is wicked, a rascal, a scoundrel, a criminal, the embodiment of evil'?

In the spirit of a certain Christian tradition we could say, 'No human being has the right to judge; we are all sinners, and judgement is with God alone.' Obviously, this emphatic standpoint does not deal with the problem of judging *acts*. It would be amoral (and *un*-Christian) to suggest that the murder of the innocent (or blasphemy, to give a strictly religious example) should not be judged. The imperative of *forgiving* would make no sense at all if single acts were not to be judged. I can only forgive an *offence*, and if there is no offence, an act the quality of which is established by judging, there is nothing to forgive. The suggestion that we should not judge our fellow-creatures refers to the *judgement of moral character*, or at least to the *ultimate judgement passed on a moral character*.[4] It is inconceivable that we should refrain from the judgement of moral character altogether, for a well-known and simple reason: although primary judgement passed on single actions cannot be *based* on the judgement of character, the judgement of moral character is co-constitutive in the process of passing such judgement. Besides, the judgement of *moral* character should be based on the previous *actions* of the person we judge. Thus if the judgement of moral character is impermissible, the judgement of single acts cannot be rationally performed. However, as I have suggested, the injunction that we should not pass judgements on moral character can also be interpreted as follows: that we should not pass *ultimate* judgements about a character, and we must not pronounce a *final verdict* on any fellow creature, because all of us are sinners, if not to the same extent. Only the One who does not know sin can pass the final verdict.

This suggestion is not only sound, but also humane, if we are all firmly convinced that the final judgement *will be passed*, and that the One who will pass this ultimate verdict will not only elevate the righteous but also humiliate the evil, condemn them to eternal damnation. But, if we do not all believe in the Heavenly Judge, and if only some of those who believe in Him are convinced that He will certainly pass this judgement, then it is left to us to pass verdict. We are still not entitled to dismiss altogether the moral lesson intrinsic to the injunction that we should not pass judgement on moral character, in that we should remain parsimonious concerning *final* verdicts. However, in certain cases even this is not avoidable. We are only human, and none of us is without fault. When we judge crimes which cannot be rectified, our judgement is a final verdict, but not necessarily the final (ultimate) verdict upon the moral character of the perpetrator. We can still feel some empathy for those who do not deserve it, for this matter concerns our own humaneness. However, if evil deeds are not only beyond rectification but also fully the doing of a particular person, passing ultimate judgement on the moral character of this person is not only a right but also an unconditional duty. If God is not the ultimate judge, we must be, for justice must be done.

The ultimate judgement of character is to be passed on individuals as members of the human race. This is why no one can be the *ultimate judge* of moral character, either as a single person or as a member of a particular community. It is only 'humankind in us' that can so judge. Passing ultimate judgement on character is not *condemnation*, but *damnation* – or, to use a lay term, *excommunication* from the human race. No one is permitted to bestow on the excommunicated any sympathy; it is a measure of our humaneness and dignity to deny such a person all compassion.

To my knowledge, the only person who has addressed this problem with the high moral seriousness that the subject matter calls for, and with a great determination to carry through the inquiry to the end, is Hannah Arendt, in her controversial work *Eichmann in Jerusalem*. Arendt wanted to determine *in whose name* a man such as Eichmann can be excommunicated from the human race, *who* has the right to pass *ultimate* judgement on his character, on what grounds we can claim that no one *should* bestow any empathy or compassion whatsoever upon him, because he is the embodiment of evil. When I excommunicate a person who is a repository or embodiment of evil, I do so neither as an individual actor nor as a representative of a single human community, but as a repository and embodiment of humankind alone. If God does not pass the ultimate verdict, only humankind can. The ultimate divine punishment is *eternal exclusion* from the company of the righteous and from the company of all sinners who can, at least in the other world, at least in everlasting time, still pay the moral debt and be readmitted to the company of the righteous. Similarly, the ultimate punishment of humankind is an *eternal and everlasting exclusion from the human race*. Arendt even invented the *formula* of excommunication: 'no one, that is, no member of the human race, can be expected to want to share the earth with you'.[5] Yet in my view the following statement of Arendt's is not correct: 'this is the reason, and the only reason you must hang'. It is not correct because someone who has perpetrated despicable crimes upon a body of a people can *rightly* be condemned to death solely on the decision of the survivors of this body of people. The right to the ultimate verdict (excommunication from the human race) and the right to condemn to death do not coincide. However, apart from this inconsistency, the formula of excommunication stands. The statement, alias verdict (*'no member of the human race* can be expected to want to share the earth with you'), refers not only to the living but also to the unborn, to all future members of the human race. Execution excludes someone only from the company of the living members of the human race (at least it does not exclude the possibility that future generations can live together in a conciliatory manner along with the memory of the condemned), whereas excommunication excludes this person from the human race as such, for everlasting time, for eternity.

If we cast even a cursory glance at Arendt's formula of excommunication, we immediately become aware that the right to pass an ultimate verdict upon a person via the authority of humankind is *not* a real (existent) right, *only a claim to such a right*. No common (existent) norm of humankind authorizes anyone to excommunicate evil from the human race. Even if we dismiss the completely irrelevant fact that most of the human race do not even know who Eichmann was, and suppose for the moment that every human being knew what he had done, it would still be highly unlikely that the human race *en masse* would favour excommunication in this case. And, indeed, there were many people who knew Eichmann, who knew what he had done, yet were happy to share the Earth with him, among them people completely uninvolved in his crimes.

There is of course a different approach to the excommunication formula. Should we read it as a formula pertaining to the *idea of humankind*, then it suggests that no member of humankind *who lives up to the idea of humankind* wants to share the earth with an embodiment of evil: the formula 'no member of the human race can be expected to want to share the earth with you' also lends itself to this interpretation.

If we do not share the belief that 'radical evil' dwells in 'human nature', not even in the nature of those who have become repositories of evil, then full responsibility for evil resides in the actors who have become evil, and they should be excommunicated from the human race. As mentioned earlier, these individuals carry the 'world-historical' responsibility for evil. Hannah Arendt's formula is based on this presupposition. So is everything that has been stated so far. Yet, if evil does not reside in 'human nature', what then is the source of evil? Is evil still eradicable? I shall return to this question in the final chapter of this book.

8

Knowing, Thinking, Feeling, Acting

'Virtue can be taught.' So goes the first premise of the first moral philosopher, a premise modified and restricted many times since, but never completely abandoned. Yet virtue cannot be *completely* taught; it can only be taught to a certain degree. Also, it can only be taught under certain conditions, and not everyone can be taught to the same extent. However, it *can* be taught. If virtue could not be either taught or self-appropriated, moral philosophy would make no sense. Pondering on morals with practical intent and advising people about how to act would be a vain and even downright senseless exercise if one believed these people could not heed this advice anyway, could not follow it even in some small way. The second premise of Socrates, according to which whoever *knows* the good also *does* the good, this blueprint of a fully fledged moral rationalism, is the strongest possible interpretation of the first premise. The weakest possible interpretation would read as follows: 'Whoever does not know what good is, cannot do good.' This weak formulation of the theory is the common denominator of moral philosophies. Undoubtedly, people can perform acts of merit blindly, almost by accident. However, though such accidents can be a concern of modern novelists, they cannot be of interest for moral philosophers.

How is knowledge of the good taught and how is it appropriated? Provided that norms and rules are taken for granted, the answer to this question is simple and straightforward. It is the adult who teaches the infant to distinguish the good from the bad. Language mediates knowledge; so does the 'example'. The adult explains, prescribes, advises, commands; the infant comprehends and imitates. The adult threatens; the infant learns to avoid. While learning to act and judge according to 'taken for granted' norms and rules, the infant learns to act correctly in a process of trial and error. *The capacity to discriminate* as an inherent quality is assumed to be present in every process of 'socialization'. One does not need a word for 'reason' to assume that every person is born with reason. 'Reason' is a complex philosophical category, and requires specification in order to be *attributed* to every healthy representative of our species. I have defined reason as the ability to discriminate according to the categories of value orientation (good/bad, Good/Evil, sacred/profane, true/false, beautiful/ugly, useful/harmful, pleasant/unpleasant, successful/unsuccessful, and the like). I have defined practical reason as the capacity to discriminate according to the *hierarchy* of the categories of value orientation ('Good comes first'). 'Teaching' morals means 'giving content' to the capacity to discriminate of the second type. Learning morals means internalizing that content.

All theoretical and philosophical differences notwithstanding, there is *basic agreement* between my conception and that of the philosophies of 'communicative rationality', represented primarily by Apel and Habermas. When these philosophies suggest that every speech act raises the claim to the *rightness* of our norms, they insist, much as I do, that practical reason is an empirical universal, and that it constitutes the ability to discriminate. For if we failed to discriminate between right and wrong (good and bad, good and evil), we could not posit the rightness of our norms.

Reason (as the ability to discriminate) is *not a mental or spiritual faculty*. When speaking about reason I do not mean *Vernunft* as against *Verstand*, *Urteilskraft*, and the like. Both when we are learning to discriminate and when we have become well-versed in discrimination, what we do in this process is mobilize several distinct mental faculties, such as logical thinking, problem-solving, applicative (determining) judgement and imagination. We also mobilize affects such as fear, disgust, anger, joy and sorrow, and especially our only innate 'moral feeling', the affect of shame. Moreover, our *orientative* feelings ('yes' feelings and 'no' feelings such as faith and doubt, trust and mistrust), as well as our *orientative emotional dispositions* (attraction and aversion, sympathy and antipathy, love and hatred), emerge in the process of 'trial and error' and become inherent elements of the ability to discriminate. If norms and rules are no longer taken for granted, then additional faculties are 'mobilized', such as pure speculative thinking, reflective judgement, theoretical reasoning. Complex emotions (first and foremost that of conscience, but also devotion, and enthusiasm or passion) also participate in the process of discrimination.

One knows what is right and wrong (good and bad) because one learns this. Yet how does one know that what one knows to be good *is* good? This question need not be given *conceptual clarity* to be answered. Meaningful world-views, particularly myths, include *narratives* about the establishment of the normative order in general and the establishment of certain concrete norms and rules in particular. The *genesis* of the normative order pinpoints the *legitimacy* of the normative order. You *vest your faith in the source of legitimacy* and *this is how you know that what you know to be good is really good.* Faith and knowledge are not contradictory, but rather support each other. And this remains so even when this question (the matter of 'how we know that what we know to be good *is* good') is given conceptual clarity. And the case will be no different if within the same culture different answers can be supplied to this question. What can and indeed does undergo change is *the source of legitimacy.* Although Weber did not have moral norms exclusively, or even primarily, in mind, he provided a clue of great importance for this matter. There are two basic sources of legitimacy in relation to moral norms: tradition, on the one hand, and reason, on the other. In other words, one can assert, 'I know that what I know to be good is good (right) because . . .', after which comes the reference to the ancestors, the 'myth of creation', the divine convenant, and so on. One can equally assert, 'I know that what I know to be good is good for it has been proved good by Reason/by the following reasons', and so on. There are subcases of norm legitimation as well: for example, legitimation through personal charisma or feelings. By using the term 'subcase', I do not mean to imply that norm legitimation via personal charisma or feelings is of small importance. In times of rapid normative change these forms of legitimation can even become predominant. This is precisely what happens when both traditional and rational forms of norm legitimation enter a phase of crisis. At any rate, where there is knowledge of the good, there is also the *faith* that what I know to be good is good.

Three further remarks must be made at this point.

First, the main types of (moral) norm-legitimizing agency or instance and the two types of moral authority (the external and the internal) *do not overlap.* True enough, if tradition and tradition alone warrants the truth of knowledge about good and evil, moral authority is external. Yet moral authority can be completely external even if personal charisma warrants the truth of that knowledge. If reason or reasoning alone warrants the truth of our knowledge (concerning good and evil), moral authority is internal, or in part internal. Yet moral authority can also be internal if the truth of our knowledge is warranted by insight, intuition, or revelation.

Secondly, I have pointed out that reason is an empirical human universal, and I have defined reason as the ability to discriminate according to the categories of value orientation. I have also defined practical reason as the ability to discriminate according to the hierarchy of the categories of value orientation ('Good comes first'). Now, if moral norms are legitimized by reason alone, it is not another faculty or ability, but the same capacity to discriminate, that is at work. It is the *attitude of reason* that changes dramatically. Discrimination will no longer be tantamount to observing, but to formulating laws. I have termed the two distinct attitudes of reason 'rationality of reason' and 'rationality of intellect'. 'Rationality of intellect' is tantamount to moral rationalism. It must be kept in mind that with moral norms *reason does not qualify* as the source of legitimacy; only *practical reason does*. In other words, the *good*, and no other positively evaluated category of orientation, must be the guiding idea in the process of legitimization.

Thirdly, if the differentiation among norm-legitimizing procedures is accepted, the theory of communicative rationality can immediately be subjected to the criticism that to deduce the claims of communicative rationality from the theory of speech acts is *illegitimate*. That the speaker claims rightness for his or her norms in every speech act has nothing whatsoever to do with the source of norm legitimization. The theory of communicative rationality presupposes that, in claiming rightness for our norms, we declare ourselves ready to make our normative claim good in discourse concerning the validity of this norm. However, this is definitely not the case. If the rightness of the norm we claim in the speech act is warranted by tradition, personal charisma, divine authority or insight (revelation), the normative claim excludes rather than includes the possibility of subjecting our norms to discursive testing. Even the assumption of an 'ideal speech situation' does not mediate between the two concepts. The speech-act theory backs the theory of rational communication *only in that special case* where 'rationality of intellect' is acknowledged as the sole or at least the major source of norm legitimization. In other words, the readiness for rational argumentation about the validity of norms is the *precondition* for the validity claims redeemable by such a procedure.

We do not think about things we know. Rather, we think about things we do not know, although we can think about things we do not know *in conjunction with* things we do know. As long as (or in so far as) moral norms and rules are 'taken for granted', we are *not permitted* to think of them because we must know them, and know them as 'good'. The questions of children, such a 'Why is this so?', 'Why is this right?', 'Why should it be like this?', are an irritation to the adults who dismiss them. Alternatively, adults may respond to such questions by repeating norm-legitimizing myths which are supposed to legitimate the 'thusness' of norms. The child learns to know; that is to say, the child learns that thinking about norms is something which is not done, which is to be suppressed and eventually eliminated. Yet one is always permitted to think *in conjunction with moral norms*, and in many cases this can even be mandatory. *Speculation and meditation* in conjunction with moral norms can be held in high esteem (as among Hassidic Jews). Besides, good norms must be applied in concrete situations, and this fact alone calls for reflection. One must determine which norms apply in this situation, which in that situation. One must determine the possible consequences of an action. One must think about one's own character in order to achieve better self-knowledge. Just judgement implies interpretation, and this, again, is a matter of thinking. In these, and in similar cases, *thinking* is thinking done in conjunction with moral norms, and not merely thinking that takes place about them. Put simply, thinking is, in all such cases, the *use of theoretical reason* in the service of practical reason. Theoretical reason *searches*, whereas practical reason *knows*. It happens exclusively in the case of *moral rationalism* that practical reason itself performs this 'search': the process of thinking. Or, to put it the other way round, we only encounter moral rationalism where the thinking process – and, what is more, the emotional involvement in this process and in the knowledge ensuing therefrom – is empowered to validate or devalidate norms. As mentioned, *interpretative conscience* is already the source and the result of moral rationalism of that kind. The active role of thinking in practical reason does not cancel the activation of theoretical reason in the service of practical reason, yet the thinking process itself bifurcates. To the extent that norms must be validated or devalidated by reason, theoretical and practical reason *merge*. To the extent that situations, character traits and consequences must be considered, theoretical reason continues to operate on its own in the service of practical reason. Yet not all kinds of thinking processes pertaining to the use of theoretical reason can merge with practical reason, and not all of them can be mobilized in the service of the latter. Aristotle distinguished several types of thinking. Yet he emphasized that only two of these, phronesis and wisdom, are of *moral* relevance, for only these two are activated when acting and judging in moral matters. It is of no minor interest to note that, while discussing morals, Aristotle reinterpreted basic moral categories (virtues, happiness, the good life) and thereby activated a mental faculty other than phronesis and wisdom. So did Socrates and Plato before him, to mention only philosophers. Thus we are not at odds with Aristotle if we add to his list a third kind of thinking of primarily moral relevance, and precisely that where practical and theoretical reason merge completely: dialectical reasoning about the validity of norms. However, one can accept Aristotle's recommendation that *nous*, *epistheme* and technical phronesis (thinking about the highest principles, scientific thinking, and technical problem-solving, respectively) are external to 'practical reason'.

Of the three types of thinking listed above, only *one* can be termed 'generative'. Neither wisdom nor phronesis can *generate* moral norms. Should we assume that any single mental 'power', ability, faculty, attitude can indeed generate moral norms, then, as far as thinking is concerned, only *dialectical reason* can apply for this position. The use of phronesis presupposes that we already *know* what the true and real virtues are. And wisdom presupposes a considerable amount of *experience* both in doing good and in passing just judgements: in other words, it presupposes 'preliminary knowledge' (such as 'knowing what' and 'knowing how') of the good. Subsequent to the first structural change in morals, dialectical reasoning occurs continuously, and this is particularly so in modernity. It is easy to comprehend how one or another moral norm can be validated by this type of reasoning, whether there are many participants in the discourse or whether such reasoning is conducted in the mind of a single person (the 'two-in-one' process suggested by Arendt). Yet generative thinking occurs in a 'moral environment' where certain norms are taken for granted. We cannot argue rationally without having a background consensus. But, if the norms involved in this background consensus have not been generated by reason, can we possibly know they are right and good? For, if they are not, our entire argumentation has gone astray. If we try to generate moral norms from the outset, without presupposing the validity of any value and norm, then indeed we do not know whether the newly generated norm can legitimately be termed 'good' unless we presuppose that 'something', a certain non-rational force, motivates reason towards the good in the first place. And so what is truly generative is not reason itself but this 'something' which guides reason silently towards the good: an impulse, a drive, a feeling, a mind.

This and similar questions arise when reason has already gone a long way towards undermining tradition and the divine command as 'the warrants' of the legitimacy of moral norms. Traditional norms are embedded in narratives and mediated together with these narratives. The *genesis* of moral norms is well known. If however, traditional and divine laws are discredited, *the genesis of the normative world* as such must be explained anew. And it must be explained rationally. Yet not all norms can be explained as having been generated by reason or reason alone. If they were generated by reason in the first place, they would have been completely rational, but they were not so generated. This problem and others like it have given rise to a great variety of solutions. Yet all these solutions have pinpointed one or another constituent of 'human nature' as the main agent of norm generation. It is around problems such as this that the theory of 'generative feelings' was constructed. Some authors attributed the capacity to generate norms to both feelings and reason; others attributed this capacity to one or another kind of feeling alone. It finally became clear that the idea of 'generative feelings' carried implications that extended far beyond the scope of the question it was supposed to answer in the first place.

I should like to return now to the truism that one must know what good is in order to practise it. Whether moral matters are discussed in an everyday setting or in philosophical discourse, this elementary truism must be presupposed. It must be equally presupposed that people can discriminate between the categories of value orientation. A third and similarly general kind of knowledge can be added to the above: that some people never come to know what good is, despite their ability to discriminate according to the value orientation category good/evil, and that there are other people who can discriminate properly – who know perfectly well what good action and good conduct are – yet who do not engage in this discrimination. Thus the question is posed, 'What *prevents* those who know what good is from practising it?' There is also a second question posed here: 'What prevents people from coming to know what good is even though they can so discriminate?'

Typically, there are four answers to the first question:

1   innate or acquired inclinations, affects, and the like, that cannot be controlled;
2   bad habits due to an inferior education;
3   ignorance, in matters other than the knowledge of the good, leading the person astray; and

4   the deliberate infringement of norms by the person, preventing him or her from practising the good.

There are also four typical answers to the second question:

1   the person's low social status (for example, being born a slave), and the resulting incapacity to come to know what good really is;
2   innate or acquired inclinations, affects and the like;
3   faulty thinking, in so far as people seek but cannot find the good, or accept mere opinion concerning good and bad; and
4   the deliberate rejection of both the search for the good and of discriminating between good and bad in general (a kind of intellectual *hubris*), a rejection that prevents people from coming to know what good is.

Now, if we take stock of this situation, it will immediately become clear that a certain type of *faulty reasoning* and the syndrome of certain *bad inclinations and affects* as chief sources of the morally bad or the evil appear in the answers given to both these questions. Conversely, it is normally assumed that proper thinking gets the norms right and is the reliable guide to practising the good we are already familiar with. It is also usually assumed that there are certain inclinations or affects which strengthen our ability to discriminate correctly and which facilitate correct action once we know what good is.

I have already distinguished between reflective reason and generative reason, or, more precisely, between the reflective and the generative use of reason, stating that 'phronesis' or 'wisdom' stands for the reflective use of reason, whereas 'dialectical reasoning' stands for the generative use of reason. I have also raised some doubts, and have echoed the doubts of others, about the claim that reason and reason alone can generate all moral norms. I have not pursued this matter further, yet I have mentioned the attempt to substitute the theory of 'generative feelings' for the theory of 'generative reason', or at least to complement the latter with the former.

Feelings were *not* normally considered as 'generative' in pre-modern moral theories, whether or not these theories were rationalistic in nature. In these theories, even if the 'true knowledge of good' is supposed to be grasped in a state of ecstasy, of mystical insight as revelation, it is not the insight, the ecstasy, that actually *generates* and thus legitimizes the norms. Rather, the divine authority discloses Himself and His commands to the person in this state. The man in the state of ecstasy, insight, intuition, or even in the state of dreaming (like Jacob), is but the vessel of the revealed truth.

All feelings are normally divided into those promoting the good and those preventing or hindering the individual from finding or practising the good. Indeed, philosophies discuss feelings in a complex manner which is rich in anthropological, epistemological, ontological and psychological implications. However, in such a brief account I must leave these issues unexplored. It is sufficient for the present purpose to refer to the most simple and trivial interpretations, such as 'Good moral feelings may motivate good moral actions better than reason', or 'Passions and desires are responsible for the persistence of evil', or 'People do wrong because they are driven by strong passions and desires', or 'Moral feelings are sublime virtues.'

Up to this point I have discussed two 'moral feelings' in some detail: shame, and conscience. Neither has been supposed to be a 'generative feeling' proper. Shame, as involvement in the external authority of moral judgement, was discussed as a typical reactive–reflective feeling. Conscience, as involvement in the internal authority of moral judgement (practical reason), was discussed as a *participant* in norm generation, not as an independent agency.

I have already expressed some doubts about reason as the sole norm-generating agency. I also have the same doubt in relation to feelings. Since there is no thinking without feeling, and no feeling without thinking (if we disregard the innate aspects of drives and affects, which are irrelevant for the problem under consideration), the distinction between norm-generating thinking and norm-generating feeling seems to me to be arbitrary. The obvious objection here is that one might heavily emphasize either the aspect of thinking or the aspect of feeling, and abstract from the 'weak aspect', regarding it as basically irrelevant. But for several reasons this 'concession' is still not sufficient. I mentioned at the outset that there is no knowledge (of the good) without faith. When reason is regarded as the main norm-generating agency, our faith is vested in reason alone. I have also mentioned that moral norms cannot be validated in the process of argumentation without a higher order consensus: at least one value, one norm, must be accepted in faith prior to the argumentative procedure. Yet clearly it is *not faith* that generates the norms in these situations. Furthermore, practical reason – the capacity to discriminate according to the hierarchy of the categories of value orientation ('Good comes first') – is also *moral sense*. This capacity is being activated when we learn what good is or where good can be sought. 'Good moral sense' develops *in experience*, as do all other kinds of senses. A 'sense of the poetical' cannot be developed if poetry does not exist and one has not had practice in listening to poems, while if these conditions are met one can easily distinguish between 'good' and 'bad' poetry. Similarly, one cannot develop a 'moral sense' without morals 'being around'. But, if this precondition is fulfilled, 'good moral sense' can help a person both to perform unprecedented good actions and to participate in generating new norms, yet without generating such norms on its own.

What types of feelings can be conceived as constituting the *fountainhead* of morals? Either feelings the *overall presence* of which can easily be detected, or those already *morally credited* as 'emotional virtues' of the highest degree. The feelings of *pleasure* and *displeasure* (pain) are good examples of the former, whereas *love*, and all those feelings associated with love (empathy, sympathy, compassion, benevolence), are good examples of the latter. Every person wishes to find pleasure and avoid pain, and, since every person does this, morals can be 'generated' from such elementary feelings. This is a typical case of a philosophical 'handstand', for *that which* we are pleased and displeased with cannot *be explained* by the feelings of pleasure and pain – not, at least, without a great deal of hair-splitting and speculation. Categorizing love and all the feelings associated with love as 'generative feelings' is a more simple and more promising undertaking, and one closer to everyday experience, but is no less flawed philosophically. And I do not wish to embark upon a discussion of such philosophical flaws here. Instead, I should like to make a case for the following hypothesis: that theories of generative feelings have discovered and expressed novel elements in moral and amoral feelings; that they have contributed to a certain differentiation of moral and amoral emotions in modernity, and that they have also contributed to an increased *psychologizing of morals*, a tendency that has gathered momentum during the last century. I shall address all three aspects of this hypothesis in turn.

It is not necessary to follow in the footsteps of psychological reductionism to entertain the idea that, early in the modern age, emotions and passions gained prominence as pains and pleasures in the process of delivering new values and norms. With Socrates, the simile of the midwife produced the credentials of reasoned speech. Everyone was supposedly pregnant with the true knowledge of the good, and reasoned speech assisted in delivering the brainchild. In this conception, heightened emotions or passions were not needed to make the delivery possible, or even to hasten it. However, once conscience becomes legislative, it can no longer be presupposed that everyone is pregnant with this knowledge of the good. It can only be presupposed that everyone possesses the ability to seek the good. Reasoned speech is no longer powerful enough to 'activate' this ability; only emotions can do so. As Hirschmann pointed out, it was this insight that allowed the celebrated theory of 'countervailing impulse' to become accepted far beyond the circles of the learned. It will suffice to quote Spinoza's laconic formulation: 'No impulse can be cancelled but by a stronger countervailing impulse.' And Spinoza was a moral rationalist *sensu stricto*.

Still, it is not only the theory of 'countervailing passion' that is novel and that discloses a newly emerging phenomenon. So is the theory which purports that love, or a version of love, generates the 'good'. The norm-generating power attributed to empathy, sympathy, benevolence and the like introduces a new element into moral theory. This conception is only remotely related to the traditional injunction that you should love your neighbour and even your enemy, for, if loving is tantamount to obeying a divine commandment, then the feeling of love cannot generate such a commandment. It is not for reasons of theoretical consistency alone that the idea of the generative force of certain moral feelings has been entertained. The atomistic vision of 'human nature', which made headway in epistemology and contract theories alike, matched well the experience of the most sensitive denizens of early modernity. Individuals became the 'building blocks' of the social edifice. Irrespective of whether one worked with 'facts' or one constructed utopias, it made sense to begin with the *psychological make-up* of the supposed building blocks: the individuals. It was equally reasonable to raise the question of *which* are the innate impulses and feelings that bind individuals – what is the cohesive force between individuals, what makes them turn to one another or act in concert. Love, as well as all the other moral feelings associated with love, were, so to speak, 'natural' contenders for such a position in our psychological make-up, particularly as the *moral significance* of love (and of all the other sentiments of 'sympathy') gained momentum in the life experience of the modern individual. The destabilizing and eventual breakdown of the traditional community freed the individual from the constant pressure of concrete norms, but at the same time placed the burden of choice on these same people. The feeling of *contingency* accompanies such a burden, and constant anxiety can be the result. To alleviate the distress caused by these feelings of contingency and anxiety, the individual had to be constantly reconfirmed *qua* person in his or her ipseity. The less tradition sets personal obligations, the more personal assistance is dependent upon feelings and inclinations. Personal help is given out of empathy, compassion, sympathy – in short, out of love. One needs to be loved in one's *ipseity*, although love is not *due* to 'ipseity' (as reverence was due to a master, a lord, a father). Your contingent personality must be affirmed irrespective of your position, and is affirmed by those loving you, those sympathizing with you, and those who, if things take a turn for the worse, will give you compassion and empathy. This was the particular life experience from which emotional dispositions, sentiments and inclinations came to be 'moralized' to an unheard-of degree. This was the particular life experience that gave impetus to theories of 'generative feelings'. Even Freud stands in this tradition. His 'Eros' and 'Thanatos' are also 'generative impulses' for the normative world. The Superego is supposed to be generated from precisely these impulses.

As mentioned, theories of 'moral sense' expressed as well as enhanced emotional differentiation. Emotions, sentiments, passions and moods became 'fashionable'. As long as and to the extent that certain emotions were regarded as 'virtuous', the ideas of emotions and sentiments could also serve as reference points in double-quality reflection. People 'discovered' in themselves sentiments of differing shades, cultivated these sentiments and thus created them. Public moral passion (enthusiasm) and private moral sentiment, if combined, could result in the exuberance of moralistic zeal. Virtue itself could become an *emotional issue* of the first order. Passionate self-abandonment to a chosen idea, on the one hand, and romantic love, sentimentalism and the cultivation of inwardness, on the other, made triumphant inroads into the modern emotional culture.

Yet both public passion and private sentiment are morally ambivalent if unaccompanied by critical reasoning supported by argument. Theories of 'generative feelings', if taken at face value, can clear the way for momentous development, though they cannot be held responsible for this development. If public passion vested in an idea is virtuous *per se*, the question of whether the *idea* itself meets moral normative criteria is relegated to the background. In the end, the question is no longer asked. And, in this atmosphere, any cause, any goal or any means goes. If private sentiment located in the 'good heart' is virtuous *per se*, even the adjective 'good' can eventually be dropped. 'Having a heart' as such will do. Being excessively filled with sentiment, passion and emotion can become the mark of superiority. The cultivation of 'sensitivities' of the Self becomes an end in itself. The aesthete of emotions, the narcissist, the irrational fanatic become accepted and sometimes acclaimed protagonists of the emotional world.

What begins as the *moralization of sentiments* continues as the cult of *sentiments as virtues in their own right*. And it seems that we finally end up with the *psychologizing of morals*. The latest stage in this unsavoury development appeared with the *colonization of the soul by scientific discourse*. I shall discuss in detail this particular problem in the next chapter. For now, a few remarks will suffice. The 'moralization of sentiments' means endowing certain sentiments, feelings or impulses with the power to generate moral norms. Yet norms, once generated, have an authority of their own. Although sentiments are supposedly the source of the legitimacy of norms, the norms themselves are binding in their own right. This holds not only in theories of 'moral sense', but also in philosophies wherein norms are supposed to be generated by the elementary feelings of pleasure and displeasure (pain). Hume 'deduced' the virtues of 'justice' and 'benevolence' from pleasure and displeasure, yet he had no doubt that a person *should be just and benevolent*. The 'psychologization of morals' means *explaining* moral norms and virtues as well as human goodness and badness by *psychological causes*. Morals, including moral norms, become *epiphenomena*. Since 'to be healthy' is good and 'to be sick' is bad, guilt becomes 'psychic disorder' and punishment is replaced by the goal of the 'cure'. Choice, moral autonomy, is thus negated and people are treated as machines – machines which, in the event of malfunction, are repaired by the professional mechanic, the psychologist.

In order to be good, people must know what good is. In a pluralistic moral universe, there can be more than one 'good way' of acting and living. Yet there must be certain moral norms we all share, otherwise we could not discriminate between good and bad in our relations with people who live and act differently from ourselves. The question of how norms are generated is a historical one, if it is raised in such general terms. I have given my answers to this question; others can supply their own. Even so, the major concern is to answer not this general question but another one: namely, 'How can we, here and now, generate certain moral norms deemed valid by everyone? And, further, how can we generate moral norms in and for our own particular way of life such that these norms can be accepted as *permissible* by everyone else?' Clearly, only moral philosophy is competent to answer this question. A theory of general ethics can only delineate the problem.

In the modern world, sensitivity and reason can be considered separately less than ever before, because in fact, practically speaking, they *are* separated to a lesser degree than ever before. It sounds paradoxical, though it is not, when we note that this is precisely why reason and sentiment have been juxtaposed to one another to a greater degree than ever before on the theoretical plane. Can this tendency be reversed? Is it inevitable that subjectivity, the individual in his or her single totality and ipseity, should be treated as a mere epiphenomenon, as a cog in the moral machine, or as the sheer embodiment of speech; or, alternatively, will a situation develop where intersubjective norms are dismissed, where the moral law and justice are viewed as mere 'externalities', as empty institutions, as agents of repression destructive of expressivity, sensitivity or pleasure? To be more explicit, can the idea of the self-development and expression of all our abilities and sensitivities and the idea of the rational constitution of norms in speech (argumentation) *be reconciled* in a moral philosophy, and consistently so?

9

The Division of the Norms of
Proper Conduct

A division of *Sittlichkeit* can be reasonably discussed if not everyone who is subjected to the *same socio-political rule* of a tribe, a city state, an empire, a nation state) is simultaneously subjected to *exactly the same moral norms and rules*. There has always existed a division of *Sittlichkeit*, and one still exists, and, regardless of whether or not it is conceivable, a withering-away of all forms of moral division is to my mind not desirable. In discussing this matter, I shall briefly address the following questions: 'What kind of division of *Sittlichkeit* dominated traditional societies?'; 'What kind of division of *Sittlichkeit* dominates modern (Western) societies?'; 'What kind of division of *Sittlichkeit* would be desirable?'; 'Why would the elimination of such a division be undesirable (though not impossible)?' Only the first two questions can be fully addressed within the framework of a general ethics.

I accept Luhmann's distinction between traditional and post-traditional societies. Traditional societies are characterized by a stratified division of labour, post-traditional societies by a functional division of labour. In traditional societies it is a person's stratification position that determines the social function this person performs, whereas in functionalist societies it is the very function performed that determines the person's position in respect to stratification. The changes occurring in the pattern of the moral division of labour express this transformation and are simultaneously the motive forces of this transformation.

The *gender* division of labour precedes social stratification, although as a rule stratified societies increase gender inequalities and so also magnify the gender division of labour. In contrast, the functional division of labour has the potential to reduce the gender division of labour. This potential can be realized if other conditions are also met.

To be able to proceed further, I must at this point sum up certain results of chapter 2. In traditional societies, moral norms, virtues and rules are divided both along lines of stratification and between the two genders within each stratum. The highest and most sublime virtues and norms regulate the conduct of the upper social stratum or strata. The virtues and norms of the upper stratum (or strata) were *termed* the highest and the best *because* they were the virtues and norms of this upper stratum, the virtues and norms of the level of domination. And these 'noble' virtues were indeed the best, at least to the extent that, the greater the freedom of the person, the greater the possibility of value choice and 'taking responsibility'. The 'master–slave dialectic'[1] is, however, of particular importance in moral stratification, first and foremost because, with the exception of the intermezzo of the Greek democracies, the *sense of justice* (a subcase of moral sense) is generally more developed in the lower strata (and in women in their relation to men), and this sense of justice becomes the catalyst of social change, and of change in moral patterns, in times of crisis. If this happens, certain *virtues* which were relegated to a lower stratum by the outgoing elite achieve the status of sublimity through the act of liberation. What Sartre termed the 'radicalization of evil' is a widespread phenomenon throughout several histories. Character traits once thought 'lowly' become accepted, are practised freely and with dignity, and in turn become 'sublime' and 'noble'. Jewish slaves turned the table on their Egyptian rulers; Christian underdogs on their Roman rulers. It is the gesture of choosing ourselves, this very act of liberation, that introduces a new kind of hierarchy of virtues into the world. And yet, until the end of the era of stratification and the dawn of modernity, the same cycle begins again, for social and gender stratification is reinforced even if values and norms change.

True enough, the term 'stratified societies', although apposite, may obscure certain important differences in the modes and methods of the moral division of labour. We can roughly – and only roughly – distinguish between virtue-oriented and imperative-oriented moral cultures.[2] Obviously, there are imperative norms in virtue-oriented moral cultures just as there are distinguished moral virtues in imperative-oriented cultures. Despite this, the distinction remains. If virtue-norms are paramount, the moral division of labour tends to be all-compassing. There can be little if any commonality between the virtues of free citizens and the virtues of slaves, the members of the highest caste and the members of the lowest, the untouchables, the warriors and the merchants. If imperative norms are paramount (irrespective of whether they are prohibitive or assertive), as in the ancient Jewish and Christian moral cultures, or, in a totally different way, in Imperial Rome as a result of the formalization of the legal system, there are always common norms and standards which the members of different strata and of both genders must observe equally and to the same degree. This fact does not annul the moral division of labour, yet it can cut some of its edges, for it allows the members of all strata and of both genders to have recourse to the *same* norms. In particular it allows both the members of the lowest strata and women to reject the downgrading of *their* morals as 'base' or 'inferior'.[3]

Morals are a Janus-faced phenomenon in stratified societies. To the extent that the moral division of labour expresses, reinforces, and legitimises the social and the gender division of labour, morals are a means of domination. To the extent that justice (a particular kind of moral sense) provides the imaginary vehicle of rejection and rebellion, morals are a means of liberation. Furthermore, the process of abiding by moral norms and rules may humiliate as well as elevate, may repress well-balanced desires as well as unruly passions, may crush as well as develop the personality, may lead to acceptance of the bad life without protest or make life a truly good life. It is here that the individual relationship to the already given norms and rules of proper conduct assumes tremendous importance. Blind subjection to the norms and rules of *Sittlichkeit* accompanies the unconditional acceptance of moral stratification, whereas the individual who takes the standpoint of morality can interpret moral norms in such a way as to query or even reject moral stratification, initially in its current form, and eventually in all its forms and modes. The heroines of Euripides' tragedies also challenge male virtues and customary norms from the perspective of morality, albeit not exclusively from this perspective. The 'cosmopolitan' idea, the first manifestation of moral relativism of a kind, as it appeared in Rome, was embedded in certain stoic and epicurean philosophies which had strong leanings toward individualistic moralism. Yet the decisive step in this direction occurred in modernity, when practical reason (conscience) became the ultimate arbiter in the judgement of human conduct. This decisive step signified that moral division along the lines of stratification had entered the stage of devolution.

This devolution of moral division based on stratification has been a long process, and certain vestiges of a traditional moral stratification are still discernible. The sociology of ethics can and indeed does discuss the delicate problem of the centuries-old coexistence of two kinds of division of the norms of proper conduct. This task cannot be undertaken here. I shall confine myself to sketching the ideal type of the new division of the norms of proper conduct, and in particular to the theoretical discussion which has revolved around it.

There is a general consensus among those theorists who draw upon Weber's heritage without being 'Weberian' that the *division of spheres* is the prime characteristic of the modern world as well as a main source of the dramatic changes that have occurred in modern morals. Although in the main one can agree with this conclusion, some caution is warranted. I have pointed out repeatedly that there has always existed two different spheres in all human societies, the sphere of 'objectivation-in-itself' and the sphere of 'objectivation-for-itself', to use my terminology. The norms and rules of the first sphere regulate action patterns, speech and everyday behavioural patterns, and are heterogeneous, whereas the norms and rules of the second sphere regulate practices different from, and considered to be higher than, the common practices regulated by the first sphere, and constitute a homogeneous medium. The norms and rules of this second sphere play an indispensable role in social reproduction in so far as they justify and legitimize the existing order of things and provide life with meaning. Roughly speaking, the sphere of the 'objectivation-for-itself' can, as it appears first, be termed the 'religious sphere', but only if we interpret the term 'religion' in the broadest possible sense. This is because the sphere encompasses the processes of creating things of beauty, productive practices, the modes of theoretical speculation, items of secret knowledge, the master narrative, and so on, with or without institutionalization proper, and with or without qualifications for admission or membership (for example, initiation or priesthood). In some traditional societies the division of spheres went even farther: a third sphere, that of non-everyday institutions (political, legal, reproductive and other institutions), was differentiated from the other two spheres. Sometimes the sphere of 'objectivation-for-itself' was differentiated into subspheres. However, the norms and rules of *all spheres* were at the same time the norms and rules of *Sittlichkeit*: that is, they were considered to be moral, or, at least, to involve a strong moral aspect. Human practices in all spheres were thus subject to ethical judgement. In short, all spheres contained a *common ethos*. Even in the Greek city states, particularly in the democratic ones, where the differentiation of the spheres was extensive, these spheres were still connected by a common ethos. Aristotle could already distinguish *techné* and *energeia* (the latter both as *praxis* and as *theoria*), the good man and the good citizen, and household economy and 'political' economy, and this was undoubtedly indicative of *spheric* differentiation. But Aristotle still rejected on moral grounds the lending of money for interest, he still ranked literary genres (tragedy and comedy) on an ethical basis, he still insisted that the best state is that promoting complete virtue, and he still linked *bios theoreticos* to sublime goodness.

As a result of recent debate, the view has emerged and become widely held that not Galileo but Machiavelli should be regarded as the founding father of the modern sciences. Thus the science of politics supposedly predates the sciences of nature. Indeed, the genius of Machiavelli should primarily be seen not in his advocacy of a non-moral or even immoral politics, a claim which has rather mistakenly been attributed to his work, but in the proposal to *understand* political action and political institutions from a theoretical viewpoint purified of moral preferences – and I mean *moral*, not *value*, preferences. Yet the dismissal of moral preferences from the study of politics amounted to the *rejection of the trans-spheric ethos*. The science of politics was not only established as a specific sphere; it was also claimed that the norms and rules intrinsic to this sphere could not be subjected, even conditionally, to a general ethos, whether it consisted of imperative norms or of virtue norms. It was the establishment of science as an *independent* sphere (independent from the ethos of the time) that prompted and gave impetus to the recognition and reinforcement of *other* spheric divisions. The political sphere as an independent sphere was constituted, or rather discovered, by political science as an independent sphere (in the aforementioned manner). Machiavelli did not assert that the independent political sphere has no norms or rules of moral relevance or provenance, but rather that such norms are *not identical* with the moral norms and rules of religion as practised in daily interpersonal contact. Moreover, Machiavelli did not assert that the norms and rules of the political sphere were given for all time, but that they depend on the constitution of a particular body politic, and that specific rules apply to a conquering political power and different rules to the maintenance of a settled political order. Politics requires political virtues which might roughly coincide with moral virtues, but which might also differ from or occasionally contradict them. But it is precisely political virtue that guides and should guide political action.

What Machiavelli did for politics, Mandeville did for economics. The philosophical background, the method of argumentation, was different, yet the result, at least from the viewpoint of the issue under scrutiny here, was the same. As Mandeville saw it, the science of economy must understand economic action and economic institutions from a theoretical viewpoint purified of moral preferences. Mandeville even went one step further – and to my mind one step too far – in his endeavour to constitute or to discover economics as a special or independent sphere: he argued that it is common *vice* which should be seen as the sphere-specific *virtue* in economics. To be brief, Kant was well aware of the danger inherent in taking a spheric division as a starting point. So, in order to make a case for the primacy of practical reason (morality) and at the same time preserve and reinforce the spheric division of the scientific, the political, the legal, the religious, the aesthetic and the 'everyday', he divided human capacities instead. Hegel, who claimed to express historical contemporaneity in thought, tried his hand at an intellectual experiment that was fairly out of date. While returning to a minute spheric distinction, he ventured to revive the idea of a common *Sittlichkeit* in a situation where a rather emaciated ethos was supposed to unify all spheres. The very fact that in the subdivision of the sphere of 'objectivation-for-itself' (absolute spirit) science was conspicuously absent, that Hegelian *Wissenschaft* reclaimed the archaic ideal of general *epistheme*, is telling in itself. Viewed from the twentieth century, this outmoded approach could also be described as *utopian* – certainly for those who subscribe to the concerns expressed in Husserl's *Krisis*. Yet I do not wish to press the point any further at this juncture.

A brief excursion into the history of philosophy cannot replace a detailed analysis of the modern historic constellation. However, philosophies pinpoint the startling changes in social structures, practices and imagery during the period from the late Renaissance to the mid-nineteenth century, changes characteristic of the world that began to identify itself as 'Western' in the course of this transformation. What happened during this period was that morals more or less ceased to be divided along stratification lines and instead became divided among spheres. A stronger and a weaker theoretical explanation were put forward to account for this historical tendency. The stronger asserted that every sphere but the religious had been emptied of moral content. Were I to subscribe to this version, the notion of the division of the norms of proper conduct would not make sense. I would say rather with Nietzsche that we arrived at the epoch of nihilism (passive nihilism), the age of decadence; and since God is dead anyway one could only overcome decadence through active nihilism. Yet I would rather subscribe to the weaker version of the theory, which is that the division of spheres, together with their increasing independence, brought about specific types of *Sittlichkeit* within each sphere. The norms and rules to be observed or followed within a particular sphere cannot be observed in other spheres, and should not be observed in other spheres even if they could be.

I shall discuss the spheric differentiation of morals in two consecutive steps. First, I shall examine the division of *Sittlichkeit* among spheres. After this I shall address the problem of the individual relationship to the spheric division of morals as such. The sequence of the analysis will be the same as that in chapters 2 and 3. In chapter 2 I discussed *Sittlichkeit* in general, and in chapter 3 the individual relation to *Sittlichkeit*: that is, morality and moral autonomy in general. In what follows I shall enlarge upon one area of this picture, and for a very good reason: this is the area in which we happen to live.

The same facts can be organized within the frameworks of different theories, and can often be organized to an equally successful degree. Yet sometimes they cannot be organized to an equally successful degree, because the *meaning* attributed to interpreted facts substantially differs. The vocabulary of a theory already indicates an affinity with certain solutions upon which one confers a particular meaning. Throughout this discussion I have spoken of a *spheric* division of morals, although it is by no means evident that the phenomena I refer to *should* be described as a 'spheric division'. One could just as easily have the same development in mind and describe it in the language of 'systems differentiation', arguing that modern *Sittlichkeit* is system-specific. Equally, one could simply discuss the differentiation of *institutions*, and argue that all institutions, large or small, 'have' a *Sittlichkeit* of their own.[4] Although theories are as numerous as innovative theorists, it could easily be demonstrated how the ideal type of a pure systems theory and the ideal type of a theory of institutions would address the issue under consideration. Since systems are self-generating and self-expanding, a pure systems theory would argue that systemic rules themselves are tantamount to the rules of moral conduct within every system. These rules cannot be changed or modified by the people who keep the system operating. Role performance is tantamount to mere subjection to inner-systemic rules, nothing more. A pure 'theory of institutions' need not attribute any degree of autonomy to the Self either, but will seek both ceremonial and expressive elements in the act of role-playing. Luhmann, who combines systems theory and a theory of institutions, insists that modern institutions, functional in character, regulate or monitor behaviour, but not motivation.

The notion of a 'sphere' is traditionally associated with the adjectival term 'cultural'. Weber discusses 'values spheres', thereby suggesting that spheric differentiations occur with the differentiation of the main 'cultural values' and of the practices therein. Whether or not one accepts the Weberian theory, it is obvious that, once it is asserted that a moral division is occurring among spheres, and not among systems or institutions, a far greater emphasis is being put on the differentiation within the sphere of objectivation-for-itself, within the sphere of meaningful world-views and cultural images. I would go even further and insist that, as far as meaningful world-views and cultural images are concerned, a pure systems theory or a pure theory of institutions falls short of a theory of 'spheres' in the dimension of interpretative power. There is a wide-ranging consensus that aesthetic, scientific and religious images have parted company in modernity, and that, in 'doing something aesthetically', in 'doing something scientifically', and in 'doing something religiously', one follows rules or observes norms that are completely different in kind.[5]

One can fully account for this fact by ascribing these three activities to three specific spheres of meaningful world-views and the practices therein. At the same time, it would be more than awkward to posit instead a 'system of religion' or a 'system of aesthetics', even if a 'system of science' would still make sense in a pure systems theory. The terms 'institutional aesthetics' and 'institutional religion' are empty generalizations, for there are many completely divergent institutions within the religious sphere and the aesthetic sphere; moreover, the main characteristic of such an institution is by no means its 'aesthetic' or 'religious' character. Even the term 'institution art' (a much narrower term than 'institution aesthetics') is, in my view, confusing. If an 'institution' is understood as a kind of objectivation which guides activity, involvement and creativity, the conceptual term 'spheres' will serve just as well. Yet the term 'institution' also has a negative connotation, a suggestion that something we might pejoratively call 'institutionalization' has perverted an otherwise pure life activity. In addition, it suggests that 'institution art' is *not artistic*, but commercial, bureaucratic, and the like. Indeed, several institutions of art are undoubtedly bureaucratic and commercial, yet to the extent that they are such they do not at all belong to the 'aesthetic sphere'. In so far as we describe modern differentiation as a differentiation of spheres and not of institutions or systems, we have already emphasized the *attitude* of the actors who enter into one or another sphere. In terms of a theory of spheres, not only the distinctiveness of norms in different contexts is emphasized, but also, at the same time, their distinctiveness in *kind*. This emphasis is at odds with a theory of 'institutions'. Goffman, a chief contributor to the pure theory of institutional differentiation, shows that people perform quite different roles while fulfilling different functions. There are roles for doctors, nurses, waitresses, lawyers, housewives, roles for boys and roles for girls, yet every role performance is *similar in kind* in that all role performances are 'dramaturgical actions'. You play one role and later you play another, but all the time you play in the same way. The theory of 'spheric division' does not exclude but rather includes the possibility that people acting within the same institution can perform according to the norms of different spheres in taking different attitudes. For example, literature is marketed in a thoroughly commercial manner, yet a writer can work according to the norms of the 'aesthetic sphere' or be guided exclusively by market rules. This is less obvious in the spheres, such as the economic, which best lend themselves to systemic explanation, yet even within the economic sphere attitudes other than economic ones can gain the upper hand, particularly political attitudes.

Clearly, no theory makes a plea for the complete autonomy of the spheres, systems and institutions, though some do make a case for the complete autonomy of *one particular sphere* (such as Marxism for the autonomy of the economic sphere), or for the greater autonomy of one particular sphere, system or institution than of others. All theories allow the vision of contemporary Western society as a (negative) 'totality', yet they also allow the vision of a conglomerate of systemic logics not completely fitted one to another, at variance with one another, incidentally enriching or impoverishing one another. However, the greater or lesser autonomy of a system or institution and the greater or lesser autonomy of actors within a particular system or institution are two quite different matters. Great autonomy can be attributed to the system and no autonomy at all to the actors within the system. In itself, the distinguishing of spheres instead of systems and institutions as the *primary* instances of rule and norm differentiation is no obstacle to holding the same view. Yet, since spheric distinction goes with the distinction of attitudes as one different in kind, the relative autonomy or heteronomy of particular spheres and the relative autonomy or heteronomy of actors within these spheres can easily be conceived of in concert. Although attitudes must change if a person or a group of persons acts first in one sphere and then in another, the attitudes pertaining to one particular sphere can still be employed in the *critique* of certain concrete rules pertaining to another sphere. Thus economic rules can be criticized from the viewpoint of political norms, political norms from the viewpoint of philosophical or scientific ones, scientific rules from the viewpoint of aesthetic ones, and so on. Of course, the critical potential of inner-spheric norms and rules can extend beyond its legitimate limits and be misused. This happens if the relative autonomy of a particular sphere is itself questioned and eventually rejected. At the other extreme, inner-spheric activity can cut itself off completely from other spheres and resign the critical use of sphere-specific norms and rules. For example, the aesthetic sphere can be illegitimately extended to the sphere of everyday life or of politics. Also, inner-spheric aesthetic activity can sever the umbilical cord connecting it with other spheres and pay for this with a loss of social relevance. However, at this point the question must be posed, 'Who extends the aesthetic sphere illegitimately to the spheres of everyday life or politics; *who* isolates this particular sphere from all others?' Spheres themselves certainly do not do so; only *human actors* do. Thinking in these terms, we must conclude that the relative autonomy of spheres and the relative autonomy of actors in all spheres can be conceived of together. The individual's relative autonomy does not lie in choosing or rejecting inner-spheric norms at random, or come about through preferences of taste, nor does it consist of being free to do things or refraining from doing things in accordance with the rules of specific institutions. Institutions are much too manifold and complex to allow people to make such conscious choices whenever they perform a particular function in the division of labour. The relative autonomy of the individual rests solely on the fact that *not all* inner-spheric norms and rules (and not all the norms and rules of a particular institution) must be taken for granted by this person. A single person and a group of persons can always make a plea for changing certain rules and norms, if not the inner-spheric specificity of such norms and rules.

Whether or not the theory of spheric division is superior to the theories of systemic differentiation or the theories of institutional differentiation, and whether or not the theory of spheric division can explain the same phenomena to the same degree or to a higher degree than can the latter, is an issue which the reader must decide. I must add that I cannot elaborate fully upon this problem within the present framework. At any rate, subscribing to the theory of 'spheric division' is congruent with my overall theory. I have already distinguished three spheres: that of everyday life (the sphere of objectivation-in-itself), that of the meaningful and meaning-rendering world-views (the sphere of objectivation-for-itself), and that of the sphere of social structure (the sphere of objectivation-in-and-for-itself). The sphere of everyday life cannot undergo further differentiation: it can only be emaciated. However, the sphere of objectivation-for-itself can be – and indeed has been – further divided (into the subspheres of aesthetics, religion, science and philosophy), and the same applies to the sphere of objectivation-in-and-for-itself, which has been divided into the subspheres of economics and politics. One can also distinguish a legal sphere. But it cannot be stressed frequently enough that morals does *not* comprise a sphere. This has been admitted by the most adamant of systems theorists. Luhmann remarked in his study of the sociology of morals that morals, and morals alone, cannot be grasped as a system: it escapes systemic interpretation.

It is the 'moral division' along spheric lines of demarcation, and *not* the evolvement of a specific 'moral sphere', that makes the division of the so-called 'cultural' spheres especially important for the purposes of the present discussion. As long as the spheric divisions are only present *in nuce*, there is a dominating world-view which permeates all of them, and it is this very world-view that provides life with meaning, everyday life included. This is why there is a *common ethos*. Values, norms and virtues are shared within one or another social stratum and should be observed in all forms of activity. Prior to the emergence of Western modernity, it was the religious (Christian) ethos that provided norms for everyday life, for the sphere of objectivation-for-itself, and for the sphere of objectivation-in-and-for-itself. The more that spheric differentiation increased, and the spheres began in turn to establish their intrinsic norms and rules of *Sittlichkeit*, the more religious ethics lost hold of the guiding activities in all but one of these spheres. This particular sphere is the religious subsphere itself, and it became a subsphere in exactly this process of differentiation. The remaining subspheres simultaneously *emancipated* themselves from religion and from the *ethos* of Christianity. Science, which established itself as a dominating world-view, provides life with a strong imagery (of production, progression, utility and the like), but it does not provide life with meaning, and it falls short as the provider of a common 'ethos'. The feeling and, what is more, the life experience that no common (shared) ethos remains at all, is gaining momentum. It would be difficult to deny that every sphere establishes a normative system (a system of rules) of its own, a *Sittlichkeit* confined to this sphere and unshared by the others. It would be equally difficult to deny that the differentiation *Sittlichkeit* can, along the spheric line of division, be legitimately termed *emancipation*. The expostulations that literature should not be subjected to the exigencies of religious morals, that politics should not be 'aestheticized' and the legal sphere 'politicized', that the political sphere should not operate according to the intrinsic rules of economics – that is to say, that sphere-intrinsic norms should not be extended to other spheres: this is what the 'emancipation' of spheres is all about. I have used the verb 'should' here. Where a 'should' extends to all spheres, if only negatively ('One should not . . .'), there must also be a common ethos of a kind. This means that the *norm* that the intrinsic spheric norms should be kept separate, the norm that no sphere should be subjected to the norms and rules of another sphere, is the 'minimum ethos' prevalent in Western modernity. This 'minimum ethos' is a defensive one, yet it can also take an offensive form. Battles are waged against the encroachment of science on philosophy, against the encroachment of economics on the arts, against the encroach-ment of economics on politics, against the encroachment of philosophy on art, against the encroachment of science on politics, against the encroachment of science, economics and politics on everyday life, a process termed 'the colonization of the life-world' by Habermas. This 'minimum ethos' is clearly not anchored in the spheres, for, if it were, we could not discuss the term 'ethos' at all. Rather, 'minimum ethos' is anchored in the *universal values* of modernity, in particular in the universal value of freedom.

The division of labour in modernity is functional. Where there is a division of labour, there is a functional division of labour. 'The division of morals', as it appears in the rationalized institutions of the division of labour alone, is depicted realistically by both systems theories and theories of institutions. Luhmann is absolutely correct in his account: within a rationalized institution it is only behaviour that matters, not motivation. Even Goffman describes certain features of this kind of division of morals in an apposite way: different institutions require different 'dramaturgical actions' with-out making demands on the unique Self and its moral or other motivations. Yet in the modern Western world with its democratic traditions, *transfunctional* action and discourse are not inhibited. And the transfunctional action and discourse of a democratic public life also generate a transfunctional ethos, this time a *positive* one applicable to all spheres, and to all of them equally and at the same time, without endangering the relative autonomy of specific spheres. It will suffice to cast a glance at the recent debates to discover how this positive, albeit weak, ethos works. Racism is now rejected in the public ethos, and this attitude has been extended to the use of racist language in literature, placing a *normative* constraint upon other subspheres of the 'aesthetic sphere' (painting, drawing, song and film) as well. The same prohibition has become a meta-norm for philosophy, scientific practices (as witness the controversy surrounding intelligence tests), and, as a matter of course, the political and legal spheres. It is a general expectation that 'human rights' should be granted in all spheres, irrespective of their inner-spheric rules. Consequently, what could be termed 'loose' ethos still exists, and in countries with democratic traditions there are no signs of it disappearing. The spheric division of *Sittlichkeit* rules out the possibility of *a prevailing 'dense ethos' as a meta-ethos binding for all spheres and for all men and women.* Yet this does not mean that a 'dense ethos' of a certain kind cannot gain momentum *within* particular communities (ways of life) in the sphere of everyday life. This is a problem, however, which I cannot explore here.

Up to this point I have only dealt with the Western form of modernity. But we must also reckon with that alternative form of modernity of great historical importance which first appeared in the Soviet Union and spread from there. The Soviet Union accomplished in almost one stroke what it took Western societies centuries to develop: namely, the substitution of a functionalist model for a stratificational model in the social division of labour. The ideologically motivated ban on traditions that was part and parcel of this rapid change, whether these traditions were religious or secular/ moral in character, assured the quick decomposition of those traditions in everyday life and secured the non-interference of these traditional moral norms in functional behavioural patterns. However, this was accomplished via the imposition of a *new dominating world-view* on society at large, a world-view which legitimized itself in modern terms (as *science*) but which performed the *function of religion* in determining a common ethos (*Sittlichkeit*) in all spheres, including the sphere of everyday life, and securing (propping up) this *Sittlichkeit* against all the questioning and rational testing procedures of morality through the use of force and indoctrination. As a result, powerful obstacles were put in the way of the evolvement of sphere-specific norms and rules. To take our previous example, that of literature, doctrinal norms of a political ideology were superimposed on both the form and the content of literature in order simultaneously to prop up the common ethos and suppress the sphere-specific norms and rules. Accordingly, a firm distinction between behaviour regulation and motivation regulation within institutional frameworks could not possibly develop (and where, in certain recent post-Stalinist situations, it could and has developed, a dismantling of the totalitarian nature of society has already been set in motion). The dominating world-view had become a lever for a new type of political domination that was all-encompassing (controlling all spheres). Consequently, all the specific spheres became but subspheres of the meta-sphere. And once it had accomplished its function, this same dominating world-view became increasingly symbolic and ceremonial, as well as pragmatic.

When such a process as I have just outlined takes place, the subjection of all spheres to the meta-sphere of political domination leads to constant crises in the subspheres. Everyday life becomes plagued by problems such as alcoholism, a decreasing birth rate and a lowered life expectancy. It is also characterized by the reappearance of an obscurantist traditionalism. And, although obscurantist traditionalism (chauvinism, racism, anti-Semitism, and in particular an upsurge of fundamentalist religiosity) can be harnessed to the cart of political domination, the symptoms triggering and accompanying it can cause alarm. And yet subspheric crises do not lead to a general crisis of society as long as the meta-sphere can be kept in good shape. The Soviet type of society is a *viable* version of modernity, and has the potential for continuous reproduction and generalizability. It is against this background that I have stressed the desirability of both the moral division of *Sittlichkeit* among the spheres (with the primacy of practical reason as a 'loose ethos') and the plurality of the moral forms of life.

I shall now proceed to the second major question: namely, the *individual's practical relation* to the division of *Sittlichkeit* in the form of spheric divisions. Weber, in his essays, 'Politics as a Vocation' and 'Science as a Vocation', addressed the problem of sphere-immanent norms and rules from the perspective of the *individual* who is at the point of deciding to *enter* one or another sphere. Such an approach fitted well with his action theory, and it was all the more warranted because Weber was addressing students, people who in his mind *were faced with precisely such a choice*. It would be too easy to explain away Weber's silence about the sphere of everyday life on the grounds that people do not choose to dwell in this sphere, but cannot help but dwell in it. Besides, on closer scrutiny, such an argument calls for further specification. With Weber, the choice among spheres is an *existential* choice, and as such is the choice of a *paramount way of life*. Everyday life can be chosen as the paramount way of life in choosing religion, and religious morality (the salvation of the soul) as the centrepoint of all life activities. Yet the religious sphere is not identical with the sphere of everyday life. What Weber had in mind (though his intention remained largely concealed) was that religion is the only sphere which can provide everyday life *qua* everyday life with meaning. The kind of everyday life which is *not a form of life*, which might be 'lived' but not chosen, and certainly not chosen *for its own sake*, was of no concern to him.

Before I return to the main problem under examination, I wish to make a remark on Weber's catalogue of the spheres. Weber omitted philosophy from this catalogue, and this might explain his insistence that religion alone can provide life with meaning. Also, although he did not list 'morals' among the spheres (as Habermas contends he did), Weber did mention an 'erotic sphere'. This lapsus can be accounted for by his biography, but a lapsus it still remains. An acceptance of Weber's proposal would first of all mean the restriction of the 'erotic' to the *avant* and the *après* of the practices of sexual intercourse, as well as to particular aspects of the latter. This is an untenable proposition, and not only because we live in the post-Freudian age; it would have sounded equally ridiculous to the Greek philosophers, who strongly emphasized the erotic dimension in friendship, in music and in philosophy. Kierkegaard, from whom Weber might have borrowed the 'either/or' of the existential choice, discussed eroticism *within* the aesthetic attitude, *within* the moral attitude, and finally *within* the religious attitude. Not theory but history holds the answer to the question of which sphere it is in which eroticism is mainly cultivated.

To my mind, Weber confused three very distinct problems while advocating the issue of existential choice, and confused them in a way and in a framework that obscured as much as illuminated the subject.[6] It would be profitable to look now at all three of these problems separately.

First, the Kierkegaardian legacy was carried by Weber beyond any degree of relevance. When Kierkegaard made a case for the existential choice, in particular for the choice between the aesthetic and the ethical forms of life, he did not have in mind a choice among spheres (nor did he refer to religion as a sphere when he included in his list the religious form of life). The *stages of life* are meaning-constitutive *attitudes within the everyday*. There exist *contradictory* life-constitutive attitudes and there is an absolute 'either/or' between them. One constitutes life either aesthetically or ethically, or religiously. And, since we are not discussing Kierkegaard at length here, one further remark will suffice. With Kierkegaard, the choice of an ethical form of life does not bar one from practising science or writing novels, even less from enjoying works of art, science or philosophy. The person dwelling in the aesthetic realm can pursue these same occupations without, however, having a *vocation*, and I mean here vocation in the Weberian sense, a steady pursuit throughout one's lifetime.

It was the young Lukács who attuned the theme of existential choice to the counterpoint of 'sphere versus life'. The observance of sphere-immanent norms and rules is not only warranted but also inevitable, and even binding. The sphere of everyday life calls for a moral attitude, whereas the sphere of art and philosophy (the absolute spirit) calls for an absolute self-abandon to its immanent norms and rules, norms and rules which Lukács argued are *not moral*. An existential choice must be made between remaining within the boundaries of everyday life and raising one's self to the sphere of philosophy and art. Either/or. To combine the spheres is to commit the gravest moral transgression. Life must not be measured with the yardsticks of beauty. The person who enters the higher spheres is banned from the sphere of everyday life, and should stay aloof, detached from everyday contact and practices. Dwelling in the heights of art and philosophy is a curse as well as a blessing, and the person who does dwell there should shun all contact with the 'living', for his touch is poisonous.

The young Lukács undoubtedly exerted some influence over his older friend. Yet Weber shifts the Kierkegaardian position even further. For Weber, 'either/or' is not a choice between ordinary life and 'Life' consecrated to higher objectivations. It is a choice between objectivations. What is preserved, however, is the ban against transgressing the 'boundaries', the boundaries between everyday (religious) morals and the morals inherent in the political sphere, the boundaries between science and politics, science and religion. But the Lukácsian theme of the 'poverty of spirit' is repeated, in a less tragic but certainly a more pessimistic tenor. It is the pursuit of science that is being depicted here as both a blessing and a curse. Weber's view is less tragic than that of Lukács because he does not insist that whatever is touched by the scholar in ordinary life is destined to perish. It is more pessimistic than that of Lukács because, while in Lukács the *Sinnfrage* is posed in the heaven of higher objectivations, in Weber the *Sinnfrage* cannot be posed, let alone answered, in the realm of science. The three problems which Weber illegitimately combines are the following: the choice of decisive attitudes within everyday life, the choice between a life devoted to higher objectivations and everyday life, and the choice between different (non-everyday) spheres. From the moral perspective these matters must be kept strictly separate from one another.

That the basic *attitude* in everyday life can be a matter of choice, and that this choice is existential (we choose ourselves in choosing an attitude), is a modern idea. The plurality of ways of life is not the ultimate issue here. Rather, the ultimate issue is the momentous fact that there *can be ways of life* void of all moral regulation. We have seen that Lukács and Weber reacted to this challenge in unison, contending that, even if everyday ways of life void of moral regulation are possible, no such way of life should actually come into existence. I should prefer to put this reaction in a more ontological manner: although ways of everyday life regulated by non-moral ideas and pursuits are possible, there is only *one existential choice*, that of choosing ourselves as moral beings. Yet I would add that, once the choice is made, we have chosen ourselves not only in the sphere of everyday life but in all spheres. No transgression of spheric boundaries, something that both Weber and Lukács legitimately wanted to avoid, follows from the above. But what does follow from it is that, once a person has chosen 'existentially', this person should maintain a *moral* perspective in every relation with an inner-specific norm or rule of *Sittlichkeit*. In my view, this is the only way a case can be made for the primacy of practical reason *without* eliminating spheric distinctions.

If what I have just said can be accepted, the Lukácsian tragic juxtaposition of higher (spheric) activity and everyday activity becomes irrelevant. Without one's existential choice of oneself as a good person, the destructive – and, let us add, fairly exaggerated – effect of 'touching someone' in ordinary life will not be the person's concern anyway. If, however, the existential choice (of ourselves as moral persons) has been made, this unleashes a dynamic in which a person will test and check inner-spheric norms and rules from the standpoint of morality (practical reason) and be able to 'commute' between the sphere of ordinary life and that of specific objectivations without running the risk of being destructive in the former or in the latter. It must be added that Lukács's image of the Self, as it appears in his earlier conception, is too rigid. A Self which is *either totally* absorbed by a 'higher sphere' *or totally* constituted in the everyday sphere is *monocentred*. Later, to some degree in his *Heidelberg Aesthetics*, and then fully in his *Aesthetics*, written in his old age, Lukács developed a concept of the Self that is more dialectical and has a greater degree of relevance. It is one thing that the Self is an identity as far as it has a 'kernel', a 'centre'. It is a different thing entirely to say that the Self is co-extensive with this 'kernel'. If we conceptualize the Self as neither completely lacking a centre nor fully absorbed by a centre, we can easily imagine the above-mentioned 'commuting' between everyday life and the sphere of higher objectivations.

The third problem touched upon by Weber (and here I am discussing Weber alone), the necessity of choosing between competing spheres ('deities'), as well as the existential character of that choice, requires further attention. Both the notion of 'deities' and the emphasis on the self-restriction imposed by the plurality of spheres remind us of certain well-known dicta of Goethe.[7] Problems of different import and range are being formulated here in one stroke. One of them has been repeatedly discussed here: that all spheres have their spheric-immanent norms and rules, which include norms and rules of *Sittlichkeit*. This is why the spheres must be kept separate from one another. It follows from this that one cannot serve two 'deities' with the same devotion, but it definitely does not follow that we should be monotheists. Weber is faithful to Goethe's premises but revokes his promises: the spheric division of labour, upheld with Weberian rigour, is the swansong of the multifaceted and harmonious individual, the ideal of German Classicism. In the Weberian spirit, choosing a sphere means choosing it for good, and resigning for good the notion of dwelling in any other sphere. This conclusion is a mixture of serious and responsible reflection and self-imposed reification. And the Protestant concept of 'vocation' serves both these purposes. Regarding the first, the strict division of the spheres expresses, as well as reinforces, the increasing complexity within every one of them. Coping with this complexity, particularly the complexity of the sphere of science, is a sisyphean task. Even if you nail yourself to the cross of science, even if you sacrifice your best years to science, you still die dissatisfied. The insatiable wish to attain the unattainable, the fully completed work, drives you day and night, and if you will weary of such a devilish ride you had better not choose science as a vocation. The Weberian ideal type of the scientist (and the politician) is extremely unromantic and yet romantic at the time time. It is unromantic because the sisyphean task appears in a prosaic, even pragmatic, garb. And it is extremely romantic because it is presented in absolutist terms: here the exception becomes the rule. All the same, without denying the relevance and sometimes the grandeur of exceptional attitudes, and without belittling the struggles and sufferings involved in such attitudes (which parallel Weber's own dramatic life struggles), I cannot see enough reason in them to declare them the rule. Why should people pursue only one vocation throughout their entire lives? Why should it not be possible for someone to be active in science and politics, as well as in art, and perform all these activities in accordance with their sphere-specific norms, without chasing after total perfection in any single one of them? Why should those who do not choose politics as a 'vocation' refrain from acting according to the norms of the political sphere? How would 'citizen action' be conceivable with such maxims? And, if a person does choose a major deity, should this person forgo the services of all the minor deities of his or her personal Olympus?

Finally, the fact that the choice of a sphere (against other spheres) as a vocation cannot be rationally grounded is presented by Weber as the *very locus* of the existential choice. That which I have termed 'self-imposed reification' is clearly at work here. In Weber's view, I choose *myself* in choosing myself as a scientist or in choosing myself as a politician, whilst in my view I simply *enter into a commitment* in making this or that choice. This commitment can be based on a previous existential choice, but it can also be a matter of taste, of pragmatic consideration, interest, talent, chance, or all of these things combined. Choosing a vocation is not more fundamentally 'existential' than choosing any way of life within the everyday life, if values are equal. The real moral issue is not the fact of choice but the 'how' of living up to the commitment once the choice has been made. It will be *disclosed* in this process of living up to the commitment whether or not the person has made an *existential choice proper* (the choice of morality). If this person has done so, he or she will enter any sphere chosen for any reason, carrying the commitment both to observe the sphere-specific norms and rules and to contribute to the *change* of inner-spheric norms if these norms contradict the imperatives of practical reason. If such a change cannot be implemented, the person will commit him/herself to another sphere.

Indeed, the modern imperatives of practical reason must be universal enough and general enough *not to interfere* with the relative independence of inner-spheric norms and rules. If they do interfere with this independence, fundamentalism will be the result, and this in turn will represent a violation of the value of freedom, the value which, in the end, modern practical reason finally stands for. Yet this fact neither annuls nor invalidates the claim of the primacy of practical reason: once the existential choice has been made (one's choice of oneself as a moral person), the ensuing vocational choice can and should be remade if the moral obligations which accompany it cannot be fulfilled.

To this point I have discussed the moral division of labour and I have made a preliminary case for the existential choice (of goodness) for the *moral personality* who can work out an *individual* relationship to all the sphere-immanent norms and rules of *Sittlichkeit*. I have also formulated the preliminary proviso that the norms of morality which guide us in checking, accepting and modifying the sphere-specific rules of *Sittlichkeit* must be universal and general in nature, for otherwise a moral perspective will be illegitimately superimposed upon the spheres, endangering the reproduction of their own *Sittlichkeit*. Yet thus far I have only briefly mentioned the pluralism of everyday ways of life.

The substitution of the functional division of labour for the stratification model resulted not only in the moral division among the spheres but also in the pluralization of *Sittlichkeit* within the sphere of everyday life. Although I agree with Weber and Lukács that everyday life should remain 'moral', ways of life can differ and still remain equally moral. The term 'should' as used by Lukács and Weber calls for some explanation. After all, everyday life is not void of morality. Only philosophers are bashful when it comes to discussing virtues; everyday actors still think in terms of virtue. Yet the moral content of everyday life becomes emaciated because the dominating meaningful world-view (science) falls short of providing moral norms for life. Weber was fully aware of this, which is why he made a plea for *religion* as the proper moral authority in the sphere of everyday life. In contradistinction to Weber (and to a degree to MacIntyre), I do not believe that only traditional religions and the vestiges of these religions can provide moral norms for life. Yet the danger discovered by Lukács (but not by Weber) of the intrusion of sphere-immanent norms into everyday life and their destructive impact on its moral fibre is a phenomenon that has gained momentum. It is from this trend that Habermas's thesis of the increasing 'colonization' of everyday life by non-everyday spheres draws its relevance. What Habermas has particularly in mind is the sphere of politics and economics, but along with Foucault we could add the sphere of science and the subspheres of art to the list. The most recent slogan of the 'decentring of the Self' indicates that the 'aesthetic sphere' has not ceased to be a 'colonizer'. The imperative that the sphere of everyday life should remain moral does not contradict the assertion that it still is moral up to a point. The issue at stake is not the protection of the remnants of a bygone *Sittlichkeit* against the intrusion of the other spheres, but the rethinking and re-exploration of the possibilities for a positive (offensive) recentring of lifestyles around particular types of *Sittlichkeit*. The plurality of everyday morals is an asset. It has an emancipatory potential, but only if it remains a plurality of *morals*. Otherwise, the person dwelling in it will no longer be capable of making the existential choice (of goodness) at all (no standpoint of morality – practical reason – will remain to test and change the sphere-immanent rules and norms).

Let me emphasize once again that it is not a regressive development that the all-encompassing 'dense' ethos of society has disappeared. But an all-encompassing *loose* ethos rooted in the universal values of freedom and life must still develop and grow beyond its present emaciated form. A loose ethos such as this would not revoke the division of *Sittlichkeit* among the spheres, and it would not hamper the coexistence and mutual recognition of diverse forms of life with their unique concrete systems of *Sittlichkeit*. A loose ethos such as this could be supported, reinforced and kept alive by the attitude of morality, by the individual's practical relationship to the fundamental norms. The term 'individual' stands here for both the 'individual person' and the 'individual form of life' of the community. If this were the situation, then the process of the division of *Sittlichkeit* along the lines of spheric differentiation could unqualifiedly be called a process of emancipation and progression.

10

The Good, the Bad and the Evil

Aristotle compared goodness to the central point of a circle: one can be wicked in many ways, the simile tells us, but goodness is of one piece, undivided. At a time when the common ethos has disappeared and metaphysical constants melt into the historical flow, this simile seems obsolete. It becomes a matter of course that norms of goodness constantly change, that people can be good, and equally good, according to different standards. Yet a thorough examination will not prove Aristotle's contention completely wrong (and I shall maintain this assertion despite my general insistence on value pluralism and normative pluralism). Aristotle's truth is borne out if we consider that one can recommend a *formal* definition of goodness which encompasses all those people who were good, are good or will be good in terms of any normative system, whereas it is impossible to discover or invent a similar *formal* definition of wickedness or evil. Rereading Nietzsche's *The Genealogy of Morals* from this viewpoint is quite instructive. Nietzsche clearly intends to make a case for an absolute historicist view of both good and evil, yet he fails to perform the operation on *both* counts. Concerning good, Nietzsche only shows that *norms* of goodness have been changing, and this is no novelty. However, regarding evil he concludes that it was the *gaze* of the good ones that constantly defined the Other in *structurally* different ways and forms, and that it was only the Jewish–Christian culture which substituted the idea of evil for the idea of bad. Good has always existed; evil has not. Whether or not we subscribe to the main theses of Nietzsche's *Genealogy* (and I do not), it is clear that the concept of good *resists* a totally historicist approach, whatever the effort. The fact that good and evil cannot be regarded as structural mirror-images of one another was a headache to Hannah Arendt, who was courageous enough to look the problem in the face. The 'will to evil', the

'Richard III syndrome', is a pretty rare phenomenon, she argued, but there is evil in the world which is many-faced and can even appear masked as 'banality'. Erich Fromm, who wittily remarked that evil has no horns, made a very similar observation. Everyday actors face the same puzzle. It is common knowledge that there are good persons; we recognize them; we know they are good. With Kant we can say that goodness shines as a jewel. We are also familiar with bad persons: for example, with hardened egoists who are totally indifferent to others or people who are regularly overcome by bad emotions. But when it comes to 'evil' we are at a loss. Since everyone 'has' certain 'satisfactory' character traits, no one, it seems, can be called 'evil'. And yet we know that evil is in the world, we know evil from its doings, and, since everything is done by humans, there must be evil humans.

And so what is evil? How, if at all, can we distinguish bad from evil? How, if at all, can evil be detected *before* irreversible harm is done?

To begin with, there exist a *broader* and a *narrower* notion of moral (ethical) evil, and a *moral* and a *non-moral* notion of evil.

Two structural changes in morals have been discussed in this book. The first structural change occurred with the emergence of *morality*, of practical reason and conscience as the internal moral authority regulating action and judgement. The second structural change (the modern) occurred with the breakdown of the moral division along the lines of stratification, with the subsequent emergence of the *spheric* moral division of *Sittlichkeit*, the universalization of certain values and the pluralization of concrete moral norms in the sphere of everyday life. In using the same quasi-historical ideal types we must conclude that *prior* to the first structural change there had existed *in nuce* a distinction between *moral* badness and evil. In that hypothetically conceived world, every infringement of concrete norms carrying social sanctions must by definition have been regarded as 'bad and evil' ('by definition' because in terms of my theory such a distinction could only emerge as a result of moral stratification and the separation of morality). But, even if this distinction between 'bad' and 'evil' existed *in nuce*, the vision of the *wrath* of suprahuman beings (for example, the spirits of the ancestors) provoked by acts of transgression, as well as the idea that these suprahuman beings will *destroy* the entire community unless the transgressor is 'cut out' of the body of the community, must have been, and certainly still is, widespread in so-called 'primitive' societies. Furthermore, the image of excessive moral transgression was at that time so strongly related to the image of non-moral 'evils' (all sorts of catastrophes, such as death, sickness, crop failure, volcanic eruptions, even the disasters of war) that the latter were normally seen as the result of the former. This was so even with certain forms of sorcery, in so far as this art was regarded as a means of exacting some sort of just retribution for transgressions committed against individual members of the clan or tribe. But there were also spirits who brought about evil gratuitously, and sorcery performed out of sheer malice. It is here that we can locate the first appearance of 'evil' in the narrower meaning of the term, as a *destructive* and *irrational* force. It is a destructive force in so far as it causes untimely death, sickness, starvation, and destruction through war, and an irrational force is so far as its workings cannot be halted by rational practices: namely, by the due observance of all concrete norms and rules. Such a destructive–irrational force fills people with *terror* but can also generate great *awe*. And the same can apply to the malicious sorcerer. Here we already witness the whole paraphernalia of evil: it is destructive (without moral provocation), it is irrational, it is a source of terror, and it is (incidentally) attractive, or at least the subject or object of awe.

The first structural change brought about the (relative) secularization and pluralization of evil. By 'relative' I mean that *humans*, who were not supported by suprahuman powers and did not possess abilities of suprahuman provenance, could be regarded as a source or embodiment of evil. All evil practices of human origin were thenceforth regarded as *morally* evil (moral transgressions of the most serious order), and so destructive. This can also be put the other way round: all practices supposedly destructive of the social fibre, the sacred order or the good life were defined as morally evil, and no greater evil (and usually no other evil at all) existed. Nietzsche's contention that aristocratic cultures were unfamiliar with evil does not hold water. These communities viewed the morals of the lower strata as base (bad) and not as evil, for they did not endanger but rather enhanced and reconfirmed the fibres of the moral order. Yet they did not doubt that *hubris* (for example parricide) should be regarded as evil.

By pluralization of evil I mean that evil practices became different *in kind*. One can easily discern two main types of evil. I shall term these the *evil of the underworld* and the *evil of sophistication*. The Atreides or the people of Sodom and Gomorrah are the embodiments of the 'evil of the underworld'. Old practices still operating *behind* the façade of a new civilization constantly endanger that civilization. They are seen by it as hubris of the greatest order. The underworld dwelling in 'man' can rebel against the sacred order (or the good life) at any time. Civilizations do their utmost to make the evil of darkness utterly repulsive, yet this is precisely why it attracts, why it becomes *demonic*. Euripides was daring enough to depict the demonic attraction of the underworld in his *Bacchae*. As Kierkegaard rightly remarked, it was Christianity that constituted *sensuality* as a principle, as the principle of the 'underworld', that of darkness. An evil was thus created which as such became attractive, became demonic. The symbiosis of terror and attraction is easily detectable here. But the same is true of the *evil of sophistication*. The evil powers of sophistication do not loom large behind the façade of civilization. They are created by that very civilization. (It is not possible to dismiss even the claim that they contribute to the birth of civilization, as the myths of the Fall and of Prometheus testify.) Challenging, testing and querying the norms and rules of a given civilization were considered hubris before the rise of modernity, coming to know what should not be known, solving puzzles humans are not entitled to solve, robbing nature or the gods of what properly belongs to them, penetrating the well-protected secrets of nature, challenging the knowledge of divine revelation – all this was evil because it threatened with destruction the very fibres of the sacred order (or of the good life).[1] The fear of desecrating nature or provoking the wrath of the gods by intruding upon the body of knowledge which is properly theirs, the fear of committing sacrilege by doubting the validity of norms or the hierarchy of values, or the correctness of lay or religious practices handed down by previous generations, is also coupled with an immense attraction. The quest for knowledge (as power), not ignorance, is the Demon. Ignorance harbours no temptation, though it is the ignorant who can be easily tempted.

The evil of sophistication has a Janus face. One of these faces is turned towards ever-increasing knowledge, the other towards less and less knowledge. One face expresses endless curiosity, the other the scepticism of disbelief. The quest for 'knowledge as power' overrules the primacy of practical reason. The defiant battle cry that all norms are invalid, puerile and ludicrous is aimed at ridding the quest for 'knowledge as power' of every constraint imposed upon knowledge by the principles of goodness, decency and justice.

Plato was the first and for a very long time the only philosopher who insisted that, in the last instance, evil is invariably the evil of *sophistication* (a term derived from *Sophists*). Evil is embodied in and disseminated by *evil maxims*. Yet it was precisely Plato's own philosophy that was regarded by many (for example by Isocrates) as the very source of such evil maxims. This was because of the tremendous 'charm' of the Platonic maxims, which contributed heavily to the destruction of the normative fibres of Athenian democracy. This paradox calls for some explanation.

If the evil of sophistication is tantamount to evil maxims, the question 'Which maxims are evil?' is automatically posed. Whenever someone advocates new maxims the dissemination of which endangers the normative pillars of society, the defenders of that order *define* such maxims as evil. But what about the normative order itself? From the viewpoint of the new maxims it is the old order that can be seen as evil, and the valid norms that can be regarded as evil maxims. Voltaire demanded, 'Ecrasez l'infame', and it was the *infamous tradition* he had in mind. Therefore, is the evil embodied in maxims always *relative*, being evil for those who defend a normative order and good for those who rebel against it? Or are there maxims which can properly be termed 'absolutely evil', termed 'evil' without any form of specification? I am convinced that there are such maxims. Moral maxims, moral principles and moral ideas were born together with *morality*. From the standpoint of morality, the maxims that aim at the destruction of a concrete *Sittlichkeit* can be regarded as evil, but evil of this kind is relative. However, maxims aiming at the *destruction of morality as such* are absolutely evil. These are the 'maxims for action' which directly or indirectly overrule all moral normation – directly, in so far as they induce us to go beyond good and evil, and indirectly, in so far as hypothetical imperatives, regardless of their content, are raised to the status of the supreme maxim. In Plato's dialogues, Callicles formulates an evil maxim of the first kind, Trasymachos an evil maxim of the second kind.

The 'evil of the underworld' can simply 'burst out' from behind the façade of a civilization, but without the supporting hand of the 'evil of sophistication' it can only cause temporary and limited harm. This support takes the form of the 'evil of the underworld' getting the green light or the go-ahead from the evil of sophistication. A plague is then in the process of spreading, and evil enters the body and the mind of the ignorant as well as infecting those previously morally healthy.

Science as the dominating world-view of modernity has marginalized the belief, handed down from our forefathers, that the evils of life (sickness, death, starvation, defeat at the hand of the enemy) are either just punishments for misconduct or sin, or the workings of wicked spirits or wicked men endowed with suprahuman powers. But moral evil, the evil of sophistication which brings the evil of the

underworld into its service, still brings 'plague' upon us, is still the
harbinger of untimely death, and still destroys the fibres of any
social order in which moral values and virtues can be chosen from
the standpoint of morality.

The evil of sophistication can spread this plague from any
position, but the position of *power* suits it best. The demonic
character of evil, its force of attraction, has a connection with power
anyway. This can be the power of political position, the power of
knowledge, or the power of character (will). One need not consider
the atrocious symbols of evil powers such as Hitler and Stalin to
envisage the symbiosis of evil and power. We all come across people
who destroy every living being around them by awakening via their
evil maxims the 'underworld' of these people. It is only a matter of
chance whether or not such people are in the position to destroy
whole nations, races, social classes, or whether they practise their
destructive power within the confines of a small circle. Were evil
only sheer power, who could not resist it? But evil is also
temptation, and it is only those who can never be lured into the
acceptance of evil maxims because they consistently follow good
ones who can always resist temptation. Without good maxims, even
the good-natured can be fooled, if not won over, by evil maxims.

Why is it so difficult to detect evil? Why do we need the evidence
of Auschwitz and the Gulag in order to believe that we can meet evil
face to face? And why can evil look banal?

The evil of sophistication can never be contained if we are merely
concerned with detecting bad character traits. Many people have
some bad character traits, and some people have many, and it is
common wisdom that only a few people have nothing but bad
character traits. Being ill-tempered, vain and selfish does not make
anyone 'evil'; were it only for that, no one at all could be called evil.
On the other hand, an evil person can 'have' several good character
traits, even attractive ones. Look at the person who consistently
follows the maxim of his *own personal breakthrough*. In order to
achieve this, *everything is permitted* to this person in terms of his
maxim. Consequently, he would destroy people who get in his way,
but he would also recruit admirers, supporters, an entire retinue. A
person such as this must be charming as well as reckless; moreover,
he will be sincere in both these roles, or at least will be capable of
being sincere. Or look at the person who follows the maxim of the
breakthrough of a cause. Again, in order to achieve this goal,
everything is permitted to this person in terms of his maxim. Yet, as
long as another person can be committed to the same cause without
qualification or vacillation, he or she will find in the 'man of a cause'

a good master or a loyal friend. Both absolute cynics and absolute fanatics can appear to others as 'nice blokes', 'sincere persons', 'generous' or even 'heroic souls'. If we run across someone whom no one likes, we can safely assume that we have met the bad but not the evil.

The evil of the underworld is easier to locate. Although I do not agree that something of the barbarian dwells in the soul of every one of us, it does dwell in the soul of far too many. Still, this is not yet evil. To infringe norms through a destructive or self-destructive impulse is bad enough, but this is not evil. None the less, if the *horror* of shedding all norms *grows attractive* precisely because all norms are being shed, and the urge to rend norms, human beings, our own selves, becomes a source of *pleasure*, then the person possessed by the underworld *is* evil. The term 'possessed' stems from ancient lore. The idea that an evil spirit or the Devil can 'enter' the body of a person and also be exorcized from it may sound abstruse, but this imagery is appropriate if stripped of its mythical connotations.

The evil of the underworld very rarely posseses someone just by chance. If this happens, mental disorder rather than evil should be assumed. For the evil of the underworld is *evoked in and by a social setting*. Such a setting can be well organized and even distinctly ceremonial. Yet these days it is only the evil of sophistication that prepares a setting for evoking the evil of the underworld. Sade and Dostoevsky knew all about this. It can happen that the wielder of the evil of sophistication wishes to cause others to be possessed by the evil of the underworld, or it can happen that this situation is a mere means on his route to achieving another and wider goal. It can also happen that one and the same person can be the repository of both the evil of sophistication and the evil of the underworld.

Evil, to repeat, is a plague. It is power, and it is contagious. I have already mentioned in this vein the power of position, the power of knowledge and the power of character (the evil will), and I shall add here the power of numbers. The greater the number of subscribers to an evil maxim, the greater the number of people possessed by the evil of the underworld, the greater will be the power and the demonic attraction of evil. This is how evil spreads. Imagine for a minute a person who, under the spell of evil, becomes evil himself. Imagine the same person in a different setting: his demon has lost power, the evil of sophistication which evoked his underworld has gone. The person who has been possessed by evil, who was evil, who performed evil deeds, will, all of a sudden, lose all 'symptoms' of evil. He will no longer be possessed; his evil maxims will disappear. In short, evil is among other things an *opportunist*. If the plague has gone, the opportunity has gone, and so has the spell. This is the solution to the riddle of the 'banality of evil'.

Evil is far from banal, but banal people can be possessed by evil, perform evil deeds and be evil. The Eichmann who spoke in the courtroom of Jerusalem was *not the same* Eichmann who masterminded, with obstinacy, cunning and ingenuity, and when time was running out for him, the deportation of Hungarian Jews. The man who played cat-and-mouse with the members of the Hungarian Jewish Council whilst indulging in his absolute power with a sadistic and quasi-aesthetic pleasure *was absent* from the courtroom in Jerusalem. Eichmann *became* banal, for he was no longer possessed, for he had lost the power (which in his particular case was neither the power of knowledge nor the power of character but that of position and numbers) which constitutes evil. He was no longer dreaded, he could no longer exert attraction, he was the empty shell of the person he had once been. Most evil people become banal once their power is spent. However, the conclusion that *evil* is banal does not follow from this, which is a further reason why it is difficult to detect evil and more easy to recognize the good and the bad.

Although I have distinguished two types of evil and have stressed that the evil of the underworld is normally evoked by the evil of sophistication, I have added that evil is a plague. People can become evil during a plague who show little if any indication that they are susceptible to such a change, and when the plague is over this evil can depart from them leaving little sign of their ever having had the disease. I have also added that evil and power are intrinsically interwoven, and, further, that evil is an opportunist. What follows from all of this is what I indicated in advance: there is no single generalized *formula* in which the essence of evil can be grasped. Evil maxims appeal to different life experiences, situations, frustrations. One evil maxim possesses one kind of person, another a different kind of person. One person has a strong inclination for evil as well as sufficient sophistication to formulate evil maxims. Another needs to be striken by a fully developed plague of evil to be carried away by it. If the right opportunity presents itself, there is astonishingly little resistance to the demonic power of evil. Ordinary, 'normal', average and decent people can succumb to it and become its incarnations. Thomas Mann's short story 'Mario and the Magician' goes to the heart of the problem: it is not enough to say 'No', for those who only reject evil are always in danger of being possessed by it. The only effective counter is constantly to *affirm good maxims* and stick to this 'Yes' *absolutely*.

Indifference, egoism, self-interest and unruly passions can easily be understood and explained. But can evil be explained? Myths and religions have furnished us with the explanations of evil without which our minds cannot rest. Yet science and even philosophy enter alien territory when they attempt to answer this crucial question: Freud's Thanatos is no less a mythical image than that of Original Sin. For my own part, I plead ignorance on this matter. I cannot convincingly object to attempts at mythical explanation. I cannot explain evil. But this does not mean that I wish to explain evil away. Even if all our worldly institutions were to become, in the Kantian sense, 'republican', not every person would behave as a decent person, though those termed by Kant as 'evil' and by myself as 'bad' might behave decently. In a world with choice, in a world with morality, evil maxims can always be chosen and the evil of the underworld evoked. However – and here I conclude my discussion of evil on a note of subdued optimism – if all institutions were as good as is humanly possible, the *opportunity* for spreading evil would be minimal, and consequently the effects of evil actions would be curtailed. And a person whose wicked designs fail, whose evil doings are frustrated, cuts a *comic* figure. Fully democratic institutions imbued with and underpinned by vigorous democratic sentiments could turn a Richard III into a Tartuffe. Such was Lessing's utopian design in *Nathan the Wise*. The prelate who fanatically demands that all Jews should be burned is *comical* simply because nobody listens to him. Could all the potential Hitlers of the world become like this prelate?

Good persons exist. Norms and virtues change, but the criterion of *good morality* is always the same. It must be stressed in advance that what I am going to discuss here is *good morality* – the goodness of persons who have already developed an individual relation to the norms and rules of *Sittlichkeit*. In contrast to evil, such goodness can be defined by a general formula. This formula grasps the essential form (structure) of goodness irrespective of substance. We owe this definition to Plato, and, if we strip all the subsequent ideas of goodness of the ever-changing normative substance, we shall immediately see that the form of goodness (or morality) has never changed since. *A person is good if he or she prefers to suffer wrong than to wrong others.* Everyone who lives up to this formal definition is good. There are also more subtle forms of goodness. A person can choose to suffer for another person even if the alternative to this suffering does not involve to even the slightest degree the committing of a wrong, of any kind. Also, a person can choose to support another person in being good in addition to not wronging her or him in any way. These and similar cases are cases of 'supererogatory goodness'. I prefer to term such people 'trans-culturally good', for the substantive norms actualized and observed by persons of supererogatory goodness are in fact transcultural. However, the genius of morality, the saint, the moral hero, cannot serve as a yardstick for human goodness; the substantive exception, sublime as it may be, cannot provide the *formal norm that everyone should fulfil*. What everyone *should* do must be in principle *possible* for everyone to do. And in principle it is possible for everyone to choose to suffer wrong if, and only if, the alternative to suffering wrong is to wrong others (doing harm by infringing moral norms). To refrain from assuming this much in a theory of morals would be self-contradictory.

However, Plato did not stop at defining the morally good person. He wanted to prove rationally that it is better to suffer wrong than to commit wrong. This attempt failed, and failed in a representative way, for Plato manoeuvred himself into a moral paradox. What was supposed to be proven rationally, finally had to be accepted through faith. To summarize this matter, the premise that it is better to suffer wrong than to commit wrong *cannot be proved*. Good persons are in no need of such a proof: being good *means* that it is better to suffer wrong than to commit wrong. Those who are bad reject any 'proof' as irrational and irrelevant anyway. They *know* that suffering wrong is the worst position to be in and thus that committing wrong is to be preferred under any circumstances. And the majority of people, those who are neither good nor bad, will reject this 'proof' as an overgeneralization and thus irrelevant. These people resent sweeping generalizations: sometimes we feel better if we wrong others, sometimes if we suffer wrong instead – this is what these people can prove. Kant tried to circumvent the problem, insisting, and to my mind rightly, that moral goodness is tantamount to *moral autonomy*, and that good persons are worthy of happiness. Yet Kant too had to have recourse to faith when he wanted to shift his argument from 'being worthy of happiness' to a situation of real happiness.

I recommend the acceptance of the Platonian definition of goodness ('A good person is a person who prefers suffering wrong to committing wrong') in full awareness of the fact that the premise therein ('It is better to suffer wrong than to commit wrong') cannot be rationally proved. I believe this premise to be true; this is *my confession of faith*.

My grounding statement was that good persons exist. And there *are* people who prefer to suffer wrong than to commit wrong. We all know this. The statement refers to empirical evidence. In addition, the number of good persons around is not as small as the sceptics would have it. Goodness is indeed demanding, but not excessively demanding. There is nothing in the definition of goodness to prevent good people from pursuing their own interests and enjoying the pleasures of life, unless by so doing they violate moral norms. Good persons do not prefer to suffer wrong *unless* committing wrong is the only alternative open to them. Good persons have no penchant for being altruists; they are simply honest and decent. This is why I shall call those people who observe the criteria of goodness in the above definition 'honest', in order to distinguish their goodness from the transculturally (supererogatory) goodness of the saint, the altruist, the genius of morality. Everything asserted here about morals in general and morality in particular can be regarded as the *explanation* of the grounding statement. *How are honest persons possible? How have they been possible since the emergence of morality?* These are the questions I have been answering throughout this book. It is the good, not the bad, that calls for explanation. My genealogy of morals is essentially the genealogy of human honesty and decency.

Let me elaborate further on the above statement. We all know that bad people exist. A person is bad if he or she prefers (consistently and continuously) to wrong others rather than suffer wrong. Such persons are not excessively numerous. Even a child would assure you, after having passed through that short period where the world is divided into 'goodies' and 'baddies', that most people are neither good nor bad, but are usually 'rather good than bad' or 'rather bad than good'. Even being consistently bad is, by definition, far from being evil. A person who consistently wrongs others in order to avoid being wronged may not wrong others at all *in any other case or situation*. This person is bad because it is better for him or her to commit wrong than to suffer wrong. Such people are willing to concede that it would be better to be good if goodness secured power, wealth, a good position and the like. Yet, since this is not so, those who do not understand what life is all about are simply fools. People who are close to being bad, but are not bad outright, are people who, owing to their lack of any sort of consistency, normally lack authenticity as well. Such people prefer to believe that they are good, referring to external and internal constraints (the pressure of circumstances or the force of impulse) to make their bad acts appear excusable in their own eyes and in the eyes of others. They fail to take responsibility for their character. This is what can be called all-embracing heteronomy (moral and non-moral alike). Yet, clearly, neither the pressure of circumstances nor that of internal impulses *accounts for* a bad character. The pressure of circumstances or internal impulses becomes irresistible *if* a person does not take responsibility for them. Moral results should be accounted for by moral causes. It is quite understandable for an inauthentic actor to explain villainy and transgressions using non-moral causes, especially in terms of psychological make-up, but it is a bad sign if theorists do the same. True enough, it is not equally difficult or equally easy to assume responsibility for each distinct impulse. Also, I believe that the impulse for which it is most difficult to take responsibility is not the most rare or the most extravagant impulse but the most common one: that of *fear*. And in the final instance it is the fear of death that lurks behind all fears, at least in modern times. If we were immortal, who would prefer to commit wrong (apart from the evil ones)? If we had time for everything, we would readily suffer wrong for a while, for nothing that eventuated would be irreversible. Yet we live under the pressure of time, and we know that what we do not achieve now we may never achieve, what we do not enjoy now or in the near future we may never have the opportunity to enjoy. Normally we commit wrong not because of the fear of suffering but because of the fear of being left empty-handed, of missing our opportunities, of remaining powerless, poor, unknown, unacknowledged, of losing the 'opportunity' called life without making full use of it. That the concealment of Being-Towards-Death is at the very heart of inauthenticity was one of Heidegger's wise discoveries, although he missed its moral implication. The twin vices of petty natures, envy and vanity, those motive forces of so many wrongdoings committed against others, are also rooted in the inauthentic fear of death. So is the pursuit of pleasure to the detriment of other human beings.

In all this I do not mean to imply that the inauthentic fear of death is the only bad impulse for which we need to assume responsibility. Jealousy, for example, if properly distinguished from envy, has absolutely nothing to do with this kind of fear. It must also be borne in mind that in this context we are discussing the bad, not the evil.

This short excursus on fear is intended to lend weight to the initial thesis that moral results should be accounted for by moral and not psychological causes. The fear of death is our human condition, since consciousness makes us conscious of our finitude and yet good persons do exist. This very fact indicates the possibility of assuming responsibility for the fear of death, the possibililty of *suspending the pressure of time* when it comes to choosing between committing and suffering wrong. Every time we choose to suffer rather than commit wrong we act *as if we were immortal*, though we know we are not. One need not believe in the immortality of the soul or in resurrection to be familiar with this attitude. To act as if immortal, you need not be immortal. But, while acting as if immortal, you carry the promise of the best possible moral world on earth. The best possible moral world is the End, the ultimate Good which is posited by the life of every good and honest person. We do not know whether the best possible moral world is possible; we only know that it is *not impossible*, as long as good persons exist, as long as there are mortals who act as if they were immortal, although they know they are not.

The honest person prefers to suffer wrong rather than wrong others. Yet 'committing wrong' does not mean 'to cause suffering', and 'suffering wrong' is not equivalent to suffering as such. Rather, 'committing wrong' means 'causing suffering by infringing moral norms or values', and 'suffering wrong' means being 'made to suffer by people who have infringed moral norms and values'. An honest person can unwittingly cause suffering just as he or she can intentionally cause suffering if this course of action is *right* (if this is the only means by which the evil one can be destroyed, the bad punished). One can suffer from unrequited love, but not be 'wronged' thereby. Equally, suffering can be brought about through others noticing that one has not lived up to their expectations, though this kind of absence of recognition does not 'wrong' one.

It has been assumed in my analysis that the formal structure of goodness has not changed since the emergence of practical reason, of conscience, of the standpoint of morality, though the substance of moral norms has changed. By itself this fact would not raise difficulties either for moral theory or for moral practice. If abstract norms, virtue norms and at least some concrete norms ar shared, if the hierarchy of values and virtues is fixed, people know or can determine when they are going to wrong others and when they are going to cause suffering *without* wronging others, when they will suffer wrong and when they will suffer without being wronged. When Don Giovanni seduced Elvira, he knew that he had wronged her. He did not need first of all to determine whether or not for Elvira 'being seduced' meant 'being wronged'. Of course, conflict did arise around the interpretation of 'wronging' long before the advent of modernity, particularly in times of political change and general crisis. A conflict like this could appear in everyday life as well. Yet this was the exception rather than the rule. And, more importantly, the distinction between directly and indirectly wronging others was fluid (for example, doing wrong to individuals causes harm to the city, and doing wrong to the city is in fact betrayal and harms the very people I know). With the dawn of modernity all this changed, for it was not only the *substance* of norms that underwent change, but also the structure of morals.

Do we share any moral norms at all? How can we possibly know *when* we wrong others, given that others might conceptualize right and wrong differently from the way we do? How can we know *if* we have wronged others, if we do not *see* those we may have harmed? In Balzac's *Lost Illusions*, Vautrin asks Rastignac, if you could gain great wealth by pushing a button in Paris and thus killing a rich mandarin in China, would you push this button? So do we have any guidelines left to distinguish wronging from not wronging, to distinguish suffering wrong from suffering without being wronged? Can we still establish such guidelines and live up to them? Finally, should we simply allow that human goodness is antiquated? Wouldn't it be enough just to observe the sphere-immanent rules, do whatever one likes, and still be 'all right'? If it is so difficult to distinguish wronging from not wronging, wouldn't it be simply prudent to drop the definition of the 'honest person' and put it on display in a museum of morals? Perhaps the concept of the *transculturally good person* could still be upheld precisely because it is transcultural. We could still say that there are good persons just as there are good painters, good statesmen and good physicists. One genius is like another genius, and, since we cannot wish that a person should be a genius, we cannot wish that one should be good either.

For all of this, there are still good persons, alias honest persons. For all of this, there are still persons who *carry* the promise of the best possible moral world. For all of this, there are still persons who are *good* in a way and to a degree that *everyone* can be. And, let me add, these people are good in a way and to a degree that everyone *should* be. This is indeed a strong normative statement. To give reasons for the relevance and the validity of such a statement is to go beyond the authority of a general ethics. The question of *how* we *should* act, *how* we *should* live, can be reflected upon and answered by *moral philosophy* alone. Reflecting upon this question and answering it is an imperative, a *should*, in itself. It is not only a theoretical performance, but also a moral action. Yet doing moral philosophy is not a direct but an *indirect moral action*. It is a moral action because one carries *moral responsibility* for it, yet it is an indirect moral action because it is performed in the theoretical medium. The theoretical medium requires a theoretical approach. Thus the answer to the question of how we *should* act, how we *should* live, must be embedded in, although not deduced from, the *theoretical solution* of the problem all actors face and must solve for themselves in modern life. The problem is posed by this question: 'Honest persons exist *now* – how are they possible now?'

Notes

In this work I have kept references to classic and modern authors to a minimum. I have also attempted to remain with the main line of argumentation and presentation and not to digress. This serves to make the text as clear, concise and straightforward as the topic allows, and thus – I hope – also accessible to the non-academic reader. However, it is unavoidable that I should state my opinion, affirmative or critical, on certain typical positions taken up by philosophers, especially contemporary writers, and elaborate further on certain peripheral matters. The comments below serve precisely this purpose.

Introduction: the Three Aspects of a Theory of Morals

1 The term 'moral philosophy' stands for every philosophical work which mainly addresses moral problems or which departs from or arrives at the discussion of such problems. Moral philosophy *sensu stricto* is a modern invention. Traditional moral philosophies were embedded in metaphysics or politics or both, and they tackled epistemological and psychological issues as much as strictly moral ones.

2 It is the interpretative aspect of moral philosophy that allows for the greatest diversity in philosophical styles. Aphorism, genealogical narrative, sociological reconstruction, analytical meta-ethics and several other miscellaneous approaches can perform the same task, and, incidentally, can provide as satisfactory or as problematic a yield as the general, all-encompassing philosophical theories.

3 There are already serious problems with Kohlberg's theory (as put forward in 'From Is to Ought') at the interpretative–reconstructive level. Philogenetic reconstruction does not prove that the sixth stage of moral development evolved later than the fifth. To value life higher than property in cases similar to that of Heinz, and to base this preference on general evaluative considerations, is not particularly modern. As Aristotle remarks in the *Nicomachean Ethics*, 'all sensible persons would do that'. Yet I strongly doubt whether the arguments character-

istic of the so-called fifth stage of moral development in Kohlberg would
have even been understood, let alone raised, by all 'sensible' people in
Aristotle's time. True enough, the value of life is not universalized by the
simple fact that it is preferred to property. Yet the justification for
stealing the medicament (in the famous – or infamous – case of Heinz),
stressing the superiority of the value of 'life', has nothing to do with the
universalization of the value of 'life' either. Only a strong and, to my
mind, praiseworthy bias for universalism can attribute a higher
developmental status to a higher moral status, and only the same
laudable bias can ascribe universalism to judgement not requiring
universalism at all. Let me enumerate some additional philosophical
naïvetés in Kohlberg's theory. Casuistry always risks translating moral
action into the language of a merely cognitive–speculative inquiry. Even
in his time, Aristotle knew that judgement passed upon cases and
judgement passed in action are different kinds of judgement. The
representative cases chosen by Kohlberg are devoid of any real moral
conflict, though he claims to present models of moral conflict. Another
example forms an alternative to the Heinz dilemma, and is also a real
and not a speculative case. In 1944, a Jewish-Hungarian industrialist by
the name of Goldberger was offered his *life* by the Gestapo in exchange
for legal entitlement to his factories. If he legally transferred his factories
to the Hermann-Goering Werke, so the offer ran, he would be free to
leave Budapest for Switzerland. Goldberger rejected the offer without a
second thought, saying that he would rather die than transfer his
factories to Goering. He was deported and gassed in Auschwitz. Now,
should we take the Heinz dilemma seriously, we ought to conclude that
Goldberger had not reached Stage Six, because, had he done so, he
would have chosen to live. However, to my mind this is a morally
unsound judgement. Kohlberg only seemingly encompassed the realm of
moral choice and action, because he believed that merely cognitive
solutions are foolproof. Furthermore, he presented the Heinz case as a
case of justice, whereas the dilemma of whether to save the life of one's
wife or steal the property of someone else has absolutely nothing to do
with justice unless we understand the theft (the act of stealing the
medical drug) as a *punishment* inflicted on the pharmacist for his
meanness, inhumanity or greed.

4 Kurt Baier, in his outstanding book *The Moral Point of View*, suggests
that, instead of asking, 'Why are we moral?', we should rather ask,
'*Why are we not moral?*' If these were the only available options, I
would unhesitatingly follow in Baier's footsteps. It is obvious that the
question 'Why are we moral?' cannot be answered, just as the matter of
why we *should* be moral cannot be answered. In a moral discussion this
is a matter of course. This is why Toulmin proposes (in *The Place of
Reason in Ethics*) to relegate what he terms 'limiting questions' such as
'Why should one do what is right?' to the religious sphere, where they
can be properly answered ('Because this is God's will', etc.). Yet
subscribing to the view that the central *explicandum* in moral

philosophy must be the infringement of moral rules ('Why are we *not* what we should be?') does not avoid the very pitfall Baier wanted to avoid: namely, the problem of *determinism*. I am confident that, if we accepted as the main question of moral philosophy the query 'Good persons exist – how are they possible?', we could answer this question *philosophically* without entering the sphere of religion, and we should simultaneously rid moral philosophy of its entanglement in determinism.

Chapter 1   The Human Condition

1 I have discussed this problem at length in my book *On Instincts*.
2 'More humanized' can stand for 'more humane'. Yet what is the criterion for 'being humane'? 'Being humane' is a strongly evaluative term, and standards of 'humaneness' vary. Besides, certain very widespread standards of 'humaneness' rooted in contemporary 'historical consciousness' pass verdicts or make judgemental comparisons which repudiate rather than confirm the thesis of the 'increasing humanization of our internal nature'. Who were more 'humane', the Australian aborigines, or those modern men who hunted them down like wild animals?

The question of which society, period or gender is 'closer to nature' is yet another controversial issue derived from and giving support to the metaphor of 'human nature'. Women are supposedly 'closer to nature' than men. (Even Adorno believed this.) What does this assumption mean? In modernity, women are obviously not as well positioned to perform merely instrumental actions within a rationalized framework, and one can suggest that something in their own tradition makes them uneasy in developing a merely instrumentalist attitude. But, if this is true, then it is a case of *one particular culture* facing *another culture* and not one of 'nature' facing 'civilization'. Bao-yu, the male hero of the classic Chinese novel *The Dream of the Red Chamber*, assures us repeatedly (in his capacity as the mouthpiece of the author, Cen Xiuhan) that girls are refined, cultivated and intelligent, whereas males are barbaric brutes. In his view, then, males are the ones 'closer to nature', and this is not meant as a compliment.

Furthermore, why should we subscribe to the idea that the *power of the body* is 'more natural' than the power of intelligence? It was the power of intelligence and not that of bodily strength that made our species the master of *the* animal kingdom in the process of *natural* selection. If only with our genesis in mind, we could conclude that the 'power of knowledge' is as close to, or, if you wish, as far away from, so-called 'nature' or 'human nature' as the power of bodily strength.

The polemic against the 'denaturalization' or 'desensitization' of modern men refers to *real problems*. The recommendations that we should not spoil the environment, our 'habitat', and that we should not *reverse* the modern development, which is heading towards the unfolding of all kinds of human sensitivities, are sound and vital ones. Yet the former has nothing whatsoever to do with the 'denaturalization' of humans, nor has the latter. Why would the full development of our sensitivities be 'natural'?

Analogies of this kind were hatched by philosophies of history which made a case for progress. Sceptics and anti-historicists such as Elias (in *The Civilizing Process*) and Foucault (in *Discipline and Punish* and *The History of Sexuality*) concentrate instead on examining the *types* of control, which have indeed increased in number since the period of the Enlightenment. Neither Elias nor Foucault claims that the human body (or soul) has been put under greater pressure in modern times; rather, they analyse the changes in the technologies of power and modes of control. Even so, irrespective of the emphasis placed on either the increase in a certain kind of repression or the increase in the manipulation of knowledge as power, narratives of this kind do not have in mind 'humanization'. It is well known that Freud, Heidegger and Nietzsche told similar, though not identical, stories. I incorporate the fruits of the anti-historicist tradition in my own position to the extent that I share with it the view that the same human condition can accompany controls and self-controls of varying provenance, with none being 'closer to' or 'farther from' 'nature' than any other. On the other hand, I subscribe to the tradition of the philosophies of history in so far as I do believe that there are stages of factual development and that modes of control and self-control exist which can be legitimately called 'better'.

3 The idea and the self-experience of *homo clausus* are modern, and strictly Leibnizian–Cartesian. Yet this does not mean that the distinction between *my* experience and that of *others*, or the distinction between 'internal' and 'external' is modern. One cannot imagine a hunter who could not, when hunting, distinguish *seeing* an animal from a report of *another's seeing it*, and who, therefore, would not be able authoritatively to state, 'It is not here. *I* do not see it.' Everyone can distinguish his own headache from the headache of someone else and can communicate this experience.

Romain Rolland, in his famous letter to Freud, referred to the 'oceanic feeling' as his own dominant self-experience. Freud did not deny the possibility of such an experience, and even tried to explain it. But he added that he had never had such an experience. Hannah Arendt remarks (in *The Life of the Mind*, vol. I. *Thinking*) that the soul always remains young, while Kierkegaard discloses that *his* soul was always old. We must lend equal credence to Kierkegaard's and to Arendt's introspectivity.

Foucault contended that the soul is manufactured by the disciplining practices of knowledge and power. Obviously, the kind of soul constructed as the subject–object of psychology, psychiatry, criminology, modern pedagogy, *is not the same soul* as the 'immortal soul' constructed by Christianity. Foucault put his finger on the dominant theoretical idea (on science as the dominating world-view of modernity) which construes self-experience as well as the experience of others in terms of *determination*, and does so in a specific and peculiar way. However, to my mind Foucault has made too strong a point. First, even the psychological construction of the soul occurs in a pluralistic way. Secondly, since science has no *moral* normative power, it does not and cannot prevent *alternative* self differentiations from occurring. (Were it otherwise, Foucault could not have written his books.) Berger and Luckmann, in comparing Budu belief to psychoanalysis in *The Social Construction of Reality*, have convincingly discussed how world-views become the major factors in *typical* processes of 'soul differentiation'.

4 In the writings of Goffman, in particular in his famous book *The Presentation of Self in Everyday Life*, the dialectic of the created and the creative self has been short-circuited. The only activity Goffman attributes to single persons is the strenuous process of concentrating on the 'performance' of role-playing. Meaning is thus never created, only received. But *who* constitutes meaning, if it is only received by so many 'empty pegs'?

Chapter 2   Sittlichkeit: *the Norms and Rules of Proper Conduct*

1 One can distinguish between the *types* of regulations in different ways. For example, Singer (*Generalization in Ethics*) discusses moral principles on the one hand and rules on the other, as well as subdividing rules into fundamental moral rules, local moral rules and neutral norms. Gert (*The Moral Rules*) distinguishes between moral rules and moral ideas. Yet neither Singer nor Gert is interested in the process of norm and rule differentiation. Instead, they categorize what they see as the final outcome of this differentiation or, alternatively, what they see as the general pattern of all possible morals (the two approaches usually overlap). For his part, Gewirth (*Reason and Morality*) simply glosses over the historical or quasi-historical dimensions of ethics. My aim here is not to criticize but to underscore the divergences between these approaches and my own approach, divergences which at least co-determine the categorical distinction in relation to the same or similar action patterns and regulative occurrences.

2 Nietzsche completely disregarded this distinction. The 'master moral' attributes moral perfection to sublimity, to 'greatness'. But whoever is great can still be bad, even evil, and judged accordingly. We are not aware of any culture where the members of the 'master caste' were not obliged to observe the norms of their own caste, and where those who infringed these norms and rules were not regarded as bad or evil, and punished accordingly, without this culture losing its aura of 'greatness'.

3 Gert argues that all the rules he terms 'general rules' are attached to specific values: for instance, 'You should not kill' to the value of life, 'You should not steal' to the value of property, and 'You should not lie'

to the value of truthfulness. I would go a step further and claim that *all norms* (including virtue norms) are related to values, and all concrete norms to concrete values.

Chapter 3   From Voluntary Action to Moral Autonomy

1   The tradition of interpreting action as by definition 'voluntary' goes back to Aristotle. Phenomenology, and in particular the work of Schutz (*Phenomenology of the Social World*), distinguishes action from behaviour on the same ground, as does Wittgenstein (in *Zettel*). According to Wittgenstein, action is voluntary if it makes sense to ask (or command) the actor to *repeat* it. It makes sense to tell an actor, 'Strike again', irrespective of 'motivation' (whether the actor struck out in cold blood or in a rage). It makes no sense at all to tell someone, 'Let your heart beat' (Wittgenstein's example). I am aware that such an interpretation of the term 'voluntary' might strike the everyday language user as strange. In everyday understanding, we normally refer to action X, as 'involuntary' if we have reason to believe that, had a *normal* situation been the case, action X would not have occurred, whereas, since an unusual situation did arise, action X did occur. Goffman's example (in *Behaviour in Public Places*) is the following: if an invited guest fails to turn up without sending an apology beforehand, and we discover that a member of his family has suddenly fallen ill, we regard his failure to come as an involuntary action and do not take offence at it. On the philosophical plane, however, such an action cannot be interpreted as 'involuntary': it was not the action but the offence that was involuntary. The action, whatever the situation, can be fully attributed to the actor. In the example just given it would be totally irrelevant to add, 'Yet the offence cannot be fully or even partly attributed to him.' Very simply, the offence ceased to be an offence the moment the circumstances were clarified.

2   When I use the term 'free choice' in the sense of *liberum arbitrium*, I refer to a philosophical tradition which addressed the same problem in terms of its own vocabulary. Thus *liberum arbitrium* is the case if the choice is made by a totally disinterested will in a state of 'equilibrium'.

3   Robert Nozick makes a similar point in his *Philosophical Explanations*. In his view, we do not always act on what was a previously existing stronger preference. A preference can *become* stronger in the process of decision-making, and *will have* a greater weight in future decisions. Preferences can be established *by choice*. Nozick distinguishes, as I do, *random* choice from *free* choice: the non-random character of a chosen option will be disclosed in the life which is going to be built upon it. Where I disagree with Nozick is his definition, to my mind heavily essentialist, of 'intrinsic value' as 'organic unity'. In his conception, humans make the existential choice in choosing the 'intrinsic value'; in my conception, the existential choice is tantamount to choosing

ourselves as good persons. Nozick follows the great tradition of philosophy in trying to *prove* that it is better to be good than not to be good. Yet, if we *could* prove that it were better (for us) to be good than not to be good, there would be no existential choice (leap) at all, for people would choose to be good (prefer a life of intrinsic value) *because* of the rational proof presented on behalf of that choice.

4 The concepts of autonomy and moral autonomy have been hopelessly confused by certain illustrious writers of our century. More problematically, only the issue of autonomy now remains; the question of moral autonomy has disappeared completely. Horkheimer and Adorno, but also Heidegger and Sartre, are guilty of the same neglect. One can detect the powerful subterranean influence of Goethe in all of them. The claim to an absolute autonomy, on the one hand, and the indictment of what is alleged to be the total heteronomy of our age, on the other, express both an aspiration and a *Lebensgefühl* from which the 'moral point of view' has disappeared.

Hannah Arendt assigns absolute autonomy to the 'life of the mind alone', and insists, without the slightest degree of resignation, that in *vita activa* autonomy cannot but be relative. Although she too does not differentiate moral autonomy from autonomy, she suggests that maximum autonomy be defined as 'personal distinction', and this is precisely the kind of interpretation of autonomy that best fits into a modern theory of moral autonomy.

5 Lying, cheating and pretension are regarded as moral offences if the deceit involved *decreases the autonomy* of a person whose freedom of decision should not be tampered with (according to moral rules and norms). Many cultures, such as ours until recently, have permitted the deception of children, and deceiving the enemy has generally been regarded as proper. Certain games can involve typical forms of cheating or pretending in their rules. Since everyone is supposed to know the rules, 'cheating according to the rules' or 'pretending according to the rules' does not decrease the autonomy of the players; they are not deceived. The 'merciful deception', the withholding of the truth from, or lying to, someone in order to spare that person shock, grief, or the pain of the fear of death, is always a morally ambiguous act. At the very least it involves a conscious choice between two moral norms to the detriment of the norm of truthfulness. *Ironical* pretension can be permissible if the ironical actor brings about the self-enlightenment of the person subjected to this irony. The person whose opinions are treated ironically becomes disoriented, and as a result may find his or her way toward greater autonomy. Similarly, someone whose inauthenticity is treated ironically might thereby achieve authenticity, thus increasing his or her autonomy. However, questioning the validity of abstract values and of general and abstract moral norms can be detrimental to and destructive of moral autonomy.

Chapter 4 Responsibility

1 Gewirth discusses a case – the contractual situation – where obligation is unrelated to 'taking up the responsibilities' of a position. The debtor, Gewirth argues, has an *obligation* to the creditor. If you avail yourself of credit, you behave like a person who takes up a position. In fact, you do take up a position, that of a debtor. You take the responsibility which accompanies this position (the obligation to repay the debt) without, however, being 'in charge' of anyone in particular. This is a 'limit case'. In the great majority of contractual situations, 'taking up responsibilities' implies 'being in charge' (such as with a marriage contract, and all kinds of professional and vocational contracts). If everyone who enters into a contract is at the same time in charge, each person so contracting is indeed in charge. This is the underlying idea of the theory of 'social contract'.

2 In chapter 3 I pointed out that Hegel (in *The Phenomenology of Mind*, and later and even more explicitly in *The Philosophy of Right* and in *Reason in History*) identified the attitude of morality with a subcase of morality – namely, with 'pure' morality, abstract subjectivity. If this is in fact the case, *enormous responsibility* is also the case. Hegel paid particular attention to the dialectics of abstract subjectivity. Abstract subjectivity, being in itself an abstract *negation*, will be *negated*, destined to defeat, while contributing willy-nilly to the establishment of a new *Sittlichkeit*, and thus be preserved as a 'moment' of that *Sittlichkeit*. Hegel subordinated abstract subjectivity (alias morality) to his meta-narrative (the unfolding of the World Spirit). The *offence* of (modern) abstract morality is not an offence committed against universal norms or normative external authorities of any kind, but one committed against the unfolding of the World Spirit, *Weltlauf*. The *failure* of a standpoint of morality is the proof of its insubstantiality. If one professes to know the (positive) outcome of world history, such a solution may seem satisfactory. If, however, one believes otherwise, one's judgement of the virtue attached to abstract morality must have a different basis. Within the Hegelian framework, historical *responsibility* as enormous responsibility cannot be seriously dealt with. The celebrated 'cause of the victims' does not please Hegel: they are victims of their own moral folly. To find out whether the victims' cause pleases us, we need to examine the *substance* of their 'folly' using the yardsticks of universal values in their universalistic interpretations. Only then can we ascertain whether they have carried enormous responsibility for good, or for evil writ large.

3 One must be extremely careful before taking such an enormous chance and, if possible, careful also during the process of action. Caution is certainly warranted *prior to action*, because taking an enormous chance is like sleepwalking: once embarked on your course you follow the path in something akin to an almost unconscious state of mind, led by a quasi-instinct of good or ill provenance. Caution is also called for *in the*

process of action, because taking an enormous chance is similar to walking a tightrope: you had better watch your step throughout.

4 I owe this distinction to Jaspers, who put the question of whether the German people as a whole were responsible for Nazi crimes. Jaspers' answer was that the actual criminals were responsible, and that everybody else was liable but not responsible.

Chapter 5   The Problem of Consequences

1 Robert Nozick (in *Philosophical Explanations*) makes a strong case for the proposal that maximizing good is not tantamount to maximizing the good of the resulting consequences. Nozick states, 'The different acts available in choice situations often will involve different verbs, that is, different relations to different end states, rather than the same verblike relationship to different end states. For example, one will be a bringing on, another a preventing, one a causing, another an allowing to happen. Since these different action relationships will involve different degrees of unity with other people in end states, the goodness of the acts need not vary directly with the goodness of their consequences' (p. 497). Thus Nozick makes a plea for a combination of the teleological and deontological aspects of deliberation, with the primacy of the deontological aspect. My view is similar to this, though my philosophical vocabulary is different.

Chapter 6   Moral Authority

1 Lyotard's recurring example of the Cashinahua narrative (for instance in *Le Differend*) presents the simplest case of authorization, the merely traditional one. The speaker, himself a Cashinahua, tells the stories of the Cashinahua to an audience of Cashinahua (the addressees). All Cashinahua are *authorized* to present and represent the *norms* of the Cashinahua (as legitimized by the stories) to all other Cashinahua. Thus authority, addressee and the carrier of authority coincide.

2 It is another matter that the standpoint of interpretative conscience can be interpreted by *modern man* as merely nominalist. The mainstream interpretation of Socrates has been dramatically changing from the nineteenth century onwards. Whereas during the Renaissance Socrates was still understood as a pagan Christ ('Holy Socrates, pray for us'), in modern times, and particularly in the post-Waterloo period, he became the twin spirit of Faust. Representative interpreters of Socrates had no difficulty in coming to grips with the claim to double authority. He was seen on the one hand as the first 'nihilist', the mere negativist, the 'ironist', on the other hand as the 'moral preacher' – and was accepted in the first capacity (Kierkegaard) and rejected in the second (Nietzsche). At any rate, even those with balanced views, such as Hegel, extensively *subjectivized* the moral aspect of the teaching and personality of

Socrates. Rejecting Socrates and returning to pre-Socratic philosophy or to an idiosyncratically interpreted 'orientalism' accords either with the rejection of all subjectivity or with the rejection of rationality in morals, and sometimes with both.

Chapter 7   Just Judgements passed on Single Cases

1   The logic of judging is the same regardless of which idea of justice regulates our action. If the regulative idea of justice is 'to each the same', *no judgement should be passed at all.* Secondary judgement can be passed if initial judgement has been passed; but then the *fact* of judging must be rejected as 'unjust'.

2   In the pure model of static justice we take all norms and rules for granted. This is a consensus unmasked by dynamic justice as a *false* consensus. Even if the subjects who are the repositories of 'rationality of intellect' can conclude that people, under the conditions of freedom and equality, would consent to their judgement, they cannot presuppose that people do so under the present conditions.

3   In judging excellence (or the lack thereof) where 'excellence' has no moral implications, similar (though not identical) questions can be asked about our authority to judge (if I know nothing about mathematics, I am no authority in respect of being a judge of excellence in this field).

4   Judgement of character is one of the most fascinating topics in ethics and in the history of cultures. How and in what form the judgement of character is permissible, advisable or avoidable are questions relating to the small number of ethical problems frequently discussed in everyday life, and the answers vary from culture to culture. What makes someone a good (or bad) judge of character is an additional but no less important question. Unfortunately, the framework of this study does not allow for a discussion of these matters. I would also add that writers of fiction are better at this job than theorists.

5   Hannah Arendt, *Eichmann in Jerusalem*, p. 256.

Chapter 9   The Division of the Norms of Proper Conduct

1   In the famous chapter 'Master and Slave' in his *The Phenomenology of Mind*, Hegel discusses the dialectics of super- and subordination from the perspective of work (labour), not from the perspective of the sense of justice. Without questioning the relevance of the Hegelian approach, I have not followed him, and for several reasons. The most decisive of these is that the Hegelian model does not and cannot encompass the male–female relationship.

2   Pascal heavily emphasized this distinction. In his *Pensées* he frequently returns to the contention that the Old Testament is superior to Greek–Latin philosophy because the Jews obeyed *laws* and not simply virtue norms. Of course, there is nothing novel in the idea that the Law

(the Torah), especially the Decalogue, is superior to all other laws. The interesting feature of Pascal's view is the distinction between the two cultures.

3   It was exactly this circumstance Nietzsche referred to (in *The Genealogy of Morals, Beyond Good and Evil* and elsewhere) as the moral institutionalization of *resentment*. With Nietzsche, to resent is not to grudge, nor is it equivalent to the impulse to let loose frustrations in a constantly recurring, sometimes effective and sometimes ineffective, hatred. *Equality* is institutionalized resentment, and the demand to *equalize* different and unique human qualities, from any viewpoint, be it moral, religious or political, is imbued with resentment. Nietzsche is not the first or the only person to pinpoint resentment as the core of egalitarianism: he is only the most outspoken person on this issue. Kierkegaard had already identified equality with resentment in *The Present Age*, and Marx, in *The Paris Manuscripts*, made the point that egalitarianism is nothing but generalized envy (which is in fact resentment). Yet, if there is inequality of freedom and of the opportunity to exercise it, then, as long as this is the case, the demand for equality cannot be conceived of or described in terms of resentment, and not because this might run counter to my own moral taste or that of anyone else, but for reasons of principle. To be brief on this point, if there is inequality of freedom and of the opportunity to exercise it, the demand for equality has nothing to do with the demand to equalize everything that is unique or different in kind. Just the contrary, it has to do with offering a broader area for such a uniqueness to come about – for everyone. However, in so far as demands for equality are not concerned with opening up a larger area for freedom and life chances for everyone, but are concerned with equalizing unique human persons by any other standards in order to annul distinctions, they indeed embody resentment.

4   Peter Berger and Thomas Luckmann (in *The Social Construction of Reality*) recommend that all reciprocal action patterns and behavioural patterns be regarded as institutions, provided these are repeated with some kind of regularity. For example, if I meet a friend once on a Friday, this is not an institution; if we meet regularly on each and every Friday, this is an institution. I find this understanding of what constitutes an institution too broad to be theoretically useful or illuminating. If we accept it, we are led to conclude that all of our diverse interactions with each other in everyday life are but so many mini-institutions (the 'institution' of having breakfast with my parents, the 'institution' of driving my child to school, and so on), whereas all our equally repetitive but not reciprocal actions cannot be regarded as institutions. According to this distinction, if I regularly watch television by myself every evening, this does not constitute an institution, but if a whole family watches television together regularly, this does constitute an institution. The distinction seems to me artificial. I would not deny that new institutions sometimes emerge from the regular repetition of a

chance interaction, but, even if all institutions were to come about this way (which I very much doubt), the above definition would still remain too broad.

5 It was Foucault who discussed with the utmost radicalism how scientific discourse (science as the dominating world-view) encroached upon everyday life in modernity, and among other things upon 'sexuality', a concept which has in fact been constituted by this discourse. One need not accept all of Foucault's points or his conclusion in order to agree with him by and large. The story narrated by Foucault exemplifies the conflict between the two dominating world-views of religion and science, from which the latter was to emerge victorious. Science in its capacity as the dominating world-view and a subsphere *lifts* moral restrictions, on the one hand, and *reifies* its object (in the example given by Foucault, human interaction), on the other. The *norms* of so-called 'sexual behaviour' cease to be moral and become 'scientific'. Instead of the 'good–evil–sin' juxtaposition, science operates with the 'normal–abnormal–pathological' distinction. That which is termed 'sexuality' is no longer understood and assessed via the categories of freedom (free will) but via the categories of causality.

6 The question that haunts intellectuals – in particular the leftist intellectuals of the last century – of whether or not to participate actively in political parties and institutions, of whether to subject theoretical pursuits to political exigency or to shape politics according to these theoretical ideas, is a question incorrectly put. We have seen that Weber's suggestion of an obligatory choice between politics and science (theory) is a romantic exaggeration, but so is the contention that a theorist's theoretical commitment should perforce be accompanied by a commitment to a particular political party or institution. A theorist may or may not operate and work as a member of a political institution. Yet, to the extent that a theorist does work in the theoretical field, he or she is obliged to think and argue and write according to the inner-spheric norms of social theory, and, to the extent that this person acts in the political arena, he or she is obliged to act according to the inner spheric norms and rules of politics. Political rules should not encroach upon the theoretical pursuit, and theoretical rules should not encroach upon the political action pattern. But what must *unify* both activities and endeavours are the main values and the main (abstract) moral norms the *person* qua *person* stands for. The person *qua* person must *check* both the internal rules and norms of the science (theory) he or she practises *and* the internal norms and rules of the particular political institution he or she is about to join with the *same* moral standards and principles. The idea that this person must live up to is not that of the existential choice or that of the superimposition of one set of inner-spheric norms and rules upon another, but the subjection of all activities to the guidance of a 'loose ethos' and advocating the general acceptance of such a 'loose ethos'.

Here the objection could be made that it is unjustified to term such sphere-immanent rules or norms *sittlich*. What is *sittlich*, one might ask, in doing science according to the (rational) rules of science, or doing art according to the immanent rules of the aesthetic sphere or any of its subspheres, or doing commerce according to the immanent rules of the market? (Similar questions will *not* be asked about the legal or the political spheres.) These three spheres have not only been differentiated, but their own *Sittlichkeiten* have also eventually become emaciated. Yet there still exist norms and rules relating to 'proper business conduct', norms and rules the observance of which evokes approval and the infringement of which evokes disapproval, irrespective of the success or failure of the business venture in question. And the same holds true of science: conscientious conduct, reflection before publicizing a discovery, the acknowledgement of the contributions of others and much else besides are matters of 'decency', and thus *sittlich* in a proper sense of the term. The 'aesthetic sphere', though only sparsely normative compared to other spheres, has generated a powerful norm that did not exist in previous ages, the norm which prohibits 'plagiarism' in a very broad sense of the word. Since the work of art is held in esteem as the expressive form of a unique individual, the nexus between this individual and this work must not be tampered with.

Despite these critical remarks, I am not prepared to underwrite the interpretation of Weber by Leo Strauss (in *Natural Right and History*). Strauss does quite an injustice to Weber in accusing him of nihilism. He treats Weber's statements committed to paper at different stages of his life (for example, in *The Protestant Ethic* and *Science as a Vocation*) and concerned with entirely different problems (for example, value in social sciences, on the one hand, and the choice between different value spheres, on the other) as if they constituted a homogeneous and structured moral theory. They do not constitute such a theory. Weber employed his enormous theoretical thrust in the defence of moral standards in facing all the difficulties which had emerged in the modern age. For Weber, Kierkegaard and Nietzsche had indeed been the greatest 'challengers'. Weber struggled with this challenge and did so with the utmost sincerity. Whether or not he succeeded in this struggle is a matter open to discussion. Yet I am convinced that the statement that Weber finally did not (or could not) recognize *any* moral standards whatsoever is simply false.

7 'Der Wissende muss sich beschränken'; 'Wer Wissenschaft und Kunst besitzt, der hat Religion. Wer diese beiden nicht besitzt, der habe Religion.'

Chapter 10   The Good, the Bad and the Evil

1 The salvation from primordial evil must have been regarded as an act of goodness in the post-archaic Greek civilization. The original message of the story of Oedipus thus had to be translated into the spirit of the new

age. *Knowledge* and *sophistication* (the solution of the riddle of the Sphinx) came to be seen as being to the merit of the protagonist, and not as a transgression. The hubris of Oedipus (parricide and incest) was no longer punishment for the 'transgression of knowledge', but was rather explained by his *ignorance*, his ignorance about the circumstances of his actions. It was this transformation of the myth that fitted the story into the imagery of the Greek enlightenment as we see it in *Oedipus at Colonus* by Sophocles.

Bibliography

Arendt, Hannah, *Eichmann in Jerusalem: a report on the banality of evil*. Viking Press, New York, 1964.
——, *Lectures on Kant's Political Philosophy*, ed. Ronald Beiner. Chicago: University of Chicago Press, 1982.
——, *Thinking*. New York: Harcourt Brace Jovanovich, 1977.
Aries, Philippe, *Centuries of Childhood: a social history of family life*. New York: Vintage Books, 1962.
Aristotle, *Nicomachean Ethics*, tr. with introduction and notes by Martin Ostwald. Indianapolis: Bobbs-Merrill, 1962.
——, *Politics*, tr. T. A. Sinclair, rev. and re-presented by Trevor J. Saunders. New York: Penguin, 1981.
Baier, Kurt, *The Moral Point of View*. Ithaca, NY: Cornell University Press, 1958.
Berger, Peter L., and Luckmann, Thomas, *The Social Construction of Reality: a treatise in the sociology of knowledge*. New York: Irvington, 1980.
Descartes, René, *Descartes' Philosophical Writings*, sel. and tr. Norman Kemp Smith. London: Macmillan, 1952.
Durkheim, Emile, *The Elementary Forms of the Religious Life: a study in religious sociology*. London: Allen and Unwin; New York: Macmillan, 1915.
——, *Suicide*. Glencoe, Ill.: Free Press, 1951.
Elias, Norbert, *The Civilizing Process*, tr. Edmund Jephcott. New York: Urizen, 1978.
Fischkin, James S., *Beyond Subjective Morality: ethical reasoning and political philosophy*. New Haven, Conn.: Yale University Press, 1984.
Foucault, Michel, *Discipline and Punish: the birth of the prison*, tr. Alan Sheridan. New York: Pantheon, 1977.
——, *The History of Sexuality*, vol. II: *The Use of Pleasure*, tr. Robert Hurley. New York: Vintage Books, 1986.
Freud, Sigmund, *Civilization and its Discontents*, tr. and ed. James Strachey. New York: W. W. Norton, 1962.
——, *The Complete Introductory Lectures on Psychoanalysis*, tr. and ed.

James Strachey. New York: W. W. Norton, 1966.
——, *The Future of an Illusion*, tr. W. D. Robson-Scott. London: Hogarth Press and Institute of Psycho-Analysis, 1928.
Fromm, Erich, *The Anatomy of Human Destructiveness*. New York: Holt, Rinehart and Winston, 1973.
Gert, Bernard, *The Moral Rules: a new rational foundation for morality*. New York: Harper and Row, 1970.
Gewirth, Alan, *Reason and Morality*. Chicago: University of Chicago Press, 1978.
Habermas, Jürgen, *The Theory of Communicative Action*, vol. I: *Reason and the Rationalization of Society*, tr. Thomas McCarthy. Boston, Mass.: Beacon Press, 1984.
Hart, Herbert Lionel Adolphus, *Punishment and Responsibility; essays in the philosophy of law*. New York: Oxford University Press, 1968.
Hegel, Georg Wilhelm Friedrich, *The Phenomenology of Mind*, tr. with an introduction and notes by J. B. Baillie. London: Sonnenschein; New York: Macmillan, 1910.
——, *The Philosophy of History*. New York: Colonial Press, 1900.
——, *Hegel's Philosophy of Right*, tr. with notes by T. M. Knox. Oxford: Clarendon Press, 1942.
Heidegger, Martin, *Being and Time*, tr. John Macquarrie and Edward Robinson. New York: Harper, 1962.
Heller, Agnes, *Beyond Justice*. Oxford: Basil Blackwell, 1987.
——, *On Instinct*. The Netherlands: Van Gorcum Assen, 1979.
——, *The Power of Shame*. London: Routledge, 1985.
Hirschman, Albert O., *The Passions and the Interests: political arguments for capitalism before its triumph*. Princeton, NJ: Princeton University Press, 1977.
Husserl, Edmund, *The Crisis of European Sciences and Transcendental Phenomenology*. Evanston, Illinois: Northwestern University Press, 1970.
Kant, Immanuel. *Critique of Practical Reason and Other Writings in Moral Philosophy*, tr. and ed. with an introduction by Lewis White Beck. Chicago: University of Chicago Press, 1949.
——, *Fundamental Principles of the Metaphysics of Morals*, tr. Thomas K. Abbott, with an introduction by Marvin Fox. New York: Liberal Arts Press, 1949.
——, *Foundations of the Metaphysics of Morals*, tr. Lewis White Beck, ed. Robert Paul Wolff. Indianapolis: Bobbs-Merrill, 1969.
Kierkegaard, Søren, *Either/Or*, tr. David F. Swenson and Lillian Marvin Swenson. Princeton, NJ: Princeton University Press, 1971.
Kohlberg, Lawrence, 'From is to Ought', *The Philosophy of Moral Development: moral stages and the idea of justice*. San Francisco: Harper and Row, 1981.
Lessing, Gotthold Ephraim. *Nathan the Wise; a dramatic poem in five acts*. New York: Ungar, 1955.
Lévi-Strauss, Claude, *The Savage Mind*. Chicago: University of Chicago Press, 1966.

Luhmann, Niklas, *The Differentiation of Society*, tr. Stephen Holmes and Charles Larmore. New York: Columbia University Press, 1982.
Lukács, Georg, *Die Eigenart des Asthetischen* I, II. Neuwied: Luchterhand, 1963.
——, *Heidelberger Asthetick*. Neuwied: Luchterhand, 1974.
Lyotard, Jean François, *Le Differend*. Paris: Editions de Minuit, 1983.
MacIntyre, Alasdair, *After Virtue: a study in moral theory*. Notre Dame, Ind.: University of Notre Dame Press, 1984.
Machiavelli, Niccolò, *Discorso o dialogo intorno alla nostra lingua*. Padua: Antenore, 1982.
——, *The Prince*, tr. with an introduction by George Bull. Harmondsworth, Middx: Penguin, 1981.
Mandeville, Bernard, *The Fable of the Bees*, ed. with an introduction by Phillip Harth. Harmondsworth, Middx: Penguin, 1970.
Marx, Karl, *Economic and Philosophic Manuscripts of 1844*, ed. with an introduction by Dirk J. Struik, tr. Martin Mulligan. New York: International Publishers, 1964.
Mead, George Herbert, *Mind, Self and Society from the Standpoint of a Social Behaviorist*. Chicago: University of Chicago Press, 1962.
Nietzsche, Friedrich Wilhelm, *Basic Writings of Nietzsche*, tr. and ed., with commentaries, by Walter Kaufmann. New York: Modern Library, 1968.
——, *On the Genealogy of Morals*, tr. Walter Kaufmann and R. J. Hollingdale. New York: Vintage Books, 1967.
Nozick, Robert, *Philosophical Explanations*. Cambridge, Mass.: Harvard University Press, 1981.
Pascal, Blaise, *Pensées; Notes on Religion and Other Subjects*, tr. John Warrington. London: Dent, 1973.
Plato, *Euthyphro, Apology, Crito, Phaedo the Death Scene*, tr. F. J. Church, rev. with an introduction by Robert D. Cumming. Indianapolis: Bobbs-Merrill, 1956.
——, *Gorgias*, tr. with notes by Terence Irwin. Oxford: Clarendon Press; New York: Oxford University Press, 1979.
——, *Phaedrus*, tr. with an introduction and commentary by R. Hackforth. Cambridge: Cambridge University Press, 1952.
——, *Philebus and Epinomis* tr. with an introduction by A. E. Taylor. London and New York: Nelson, 1956.
——, *The Republic*, tr. Allan Bloom. New York: Basic Books, 1968.
Sartre, Jean-Paul, *Critique of Dialectical Reason*, tr. Alan Sheridan-Smith, ed. Jonathan Ree. London: Verso, 1982.
——, *Men without Shadows (Les Morts sans Sépulture)*, in *Three Plays*, tr. Kitty Black. London: Hamish Hamilton, 1963.
Schutz, Alfred, *The Phenomenology of the Social World*, tr. George Walsh and Frederick Lehnert. Evanston, Ill.: Northwestern University Press, 1967.
Singer, M., *Generalization in Ethics; an essay in the logic of ethics with the rudiments of a system of moral philosophy*. New York: Russell and Russell, 1971.

Spinoza, Benedictus de, *Ethics. Preceded by On the Improvement of the Understanding*, ed. with an introduction by James Gutmann. New York: Hafner, 1949.

Strauss, Leo, *Natural Right and History*. Chicago: University of Chicago Press, 1953.

Toulmin, Stephen Edelston, *An Examination of the Place of Reason in Ethics*. Cambridge: Cambridge University Press, 1950.

Weber, Max, *Economy and Society: an outline of interpretive sociology*. New York: Bedminster Press,1968.

——, *Selected Works*. Atlantic Highlands, NJ: Humanities Press, 1976.

Wittgenstein, Ludwig, *Philosophical Investigations*, tr. G. E. M. Anscombe. Oxford: Basil Blackwell, 1953.

——, *Zettel*, ed. G. E. M. Anscombe and G. H. von Wright. Berkeley, Calif.: University of California Press, 1967.

Index

anthropological reductionism, 2
Apel, and 'communicative rationality',
  132; and determination, 55
Arendt, Hannah, and evil, 166; and the
  'human condition', 17; and just
  judgement, 128; and morality, 61
Aries, P., 11
Aristotle, 34, 39, 50, 54, 73, 74, 148;
  and ethics, 85; and goodness, 166;
  and 'human nature', 14; and just
  judgements, 118–19; and moral
  philosophy, 1; and morally relevant
  thinking, 135; and phronesis, 101;
  and virtue-norms, 33
asymmetric reciprocity, 39
autonomy, 50–1; absolute, 60; and
  Kant's notion of moral goodness,
  175; moral, 52, 54, 60–6, 68, 91,
  102, 143; relative, 60, 64; and
  responsibility, 68, 75

Balzac, H. de, and 'collective crimes',
  79, 179

courtesianism, 2
Castoridis, 7, 42
Cato, 86
causality: and judgement, 84; and
  Kantian freedom, 88; and
  responsibility, 83
cognitive surplus, 36
collective crimes, responsibility for,
  79–81
competence, 35
conduct, theory of, 11
conscience: and goodness, 178; and
  modernity, 147; and moral authority,
  102–3; and moral autonomy, 103;

and practical reason, 47–8, 135; as
  practical reason, 60, 103, 107–11,
  124, 139, 147, 178; in relation to the
  structural change of morals, 8–9,
  102; and responsibility, 71; and the
  right to pass judgement, 124; and
  traditionalism, 104; as the ultimate
  arbiter in the judgement of conduct,
  107–10, 147; see also practical reason
considerant, 89, 90
cultural surplus, 22, 27, 30, 36

determination, 51–5
Dostoevsky, F., and evil, 172
Durkheim, E., and general ethics, 10–11
dynamic justice, see justice

Eichmann, A., 173
Elias, N., 11
Epicureanism, 12
ethics: components of, 7; as the
  condition of the world, 31, 40;
  general, 5ff, 10–11; and the judging
  of consequences, 94; and progression,
  43; and traditional society, 148
ethnocentricism, 42, 126
Euripides, 86, 147, 169
evil, 76, 79, 81, 96, 111, 122, 128–30,
  138; different notions of, 167–73; no
  generalized formula for, 173–4; and
  Nietzsche, 166–7; pluralization of,
  168; and the sense of shame, 100
evil maxims, 77
existential choice, 158–64
experience, and the self, 23–30

feelings, 25, 136, 138–44; orientative,
  25, 102, 132; reflective, 25
Fischkin, J. S., 4